MW00780236

Healing Relational Trauma
with Attachment-Focused Interventions

HEALING RELATIONAL TRAUMA WITH ATTACHMENT-FOCUSED INTERVENTIONS

Dyadic Developmental Psychotherapy with Children and Families

DANIEL A. HUGHES
KIM S. GOLDING
JULIE HUDSON

W. W. Norton & Company
Independent Publishers Since 1923
New York • London

•

For information about permission to reproduce selections from this book, write to Permissions, W. W. Norton & Company, Inc., 500 Fifth Avenue, New York, NY 10110

For information about special discounts for bulk purchases, please contact W. W. Norton Special Sales at specialsales@wwnorton.com or 800-233-4830

Manufacturing by LSC Harrisonburg
Production manager: Katelyn MacKenzie

Library of Congress Cataloging-in-Publication Data

Names: Hughes, Daniel A., author. | Golding, Kim S., author. | Hudson, Julie (Clinical psychologist), author.
Title: Healing relational trauma with attachment-focused interventions : dyadic developmental psychotherapy with children and families / Daniel A. Hughes, Kim S. Golding, Julie Hudson.
Description: First edition. | New York : W. W. Norton & Company, [2019] | Includes bibliographical references and index.
Identifiers: LCCN 2018006601 | ISBN 9780393712452 (hardcover)
Subjects: | MESH: Reactive Attachment Disorder—therapy | Psychotherapy—methods | Child Abuse—therapy | Parent-Child Relations | Child, Adopted | Child, Foster | Adolescent
Classification: LCC RC480 | NLM WS 350.6 | DDC 616.89/14—dc23 LC record available at https://lccn.loc.gov/2018006601

W. W. Norton & Company, Inc., 500 Fifth Avenue, New York, N.Y. 10110
www.wwnorton.com

W. W. Norton & Company Ltd., 15 Carlisle Street, London W1D 3BS

1 2 3 4 5 6 7 8 9 0

CONTENTS

ACKNOWLEDGMENTS

While the three of us have written this book, it would not have been possible without the support and encouragement of the dyadic developmental psychotherapy (DDP) community. The innovation and creativity that exists has helped DDP to grow and expand in so many ways. We cannot thank everyone by name—it is now such a large community—but please know we appreciate each and every one of you and what you bring to our developing use of DDP.

There are some individual people who have contributed directly to our requests for support in writing this book. All of you have responded quickly and helpfully. Viv Norris contributed her thoughts on combining DDP and Theraplay; Nic Jones on applying DDP with people experiencing learning disability; Edwina Grant on the use of DDP within residential settings; Sian Phillips on her program for schools with such a diligent approach to evaluation; and Alison Keith and Deborah Page, who have contributed much thinking. Thanks to all of those attending Worcester study days in the United Kingdom—our joint thinking about working with children who are violent and working with children experiencing neurodevelopmental challenges has helped us with the writing of these sections. Thank you, Anne-Marie Tipper, for your inspiring work in Kenya and for helping us to include a description of this. Thanks also to Joanne Alper and Rachel Staff of Adoptionplus for exploring the range of DDP within social care and giving us a paragraph or two about exciting new developments.

It has been an immense privilege to work together on this book, and we offer thanks to each other for the mutual encouragement and gentle guidance as we worked on different parts.

As ever, when writing a book, family and friends are not getting quite the intersubjective experience from us that we would like. Connections will be firmly renewed now that it is done, and thanks for putting up with us.

Dan writes: My part in this book has been greatly enhanced by all the learning and sharing that I have done with my three children, Megan, Kri, and Maddie, and my granddaughter, Alice Rose. They continually bring me home to the meanings of attachment and intersubjectivity. Going further back, I am also indebted to my sisters, Kathleen and Mary Pat, and brothers, Jim, Bill, John, and Mike. Further still, my parents, Marie and Bill, and grandmother, Mary.

Kim writes: My part in this book has been supported by my family, Chris, Alex, and Lily, who tolerate my spending part of our lives together writing. Thanks also to Alex for help with figures. My mother has been amazingly tolerant of my lack of attention to her during the last stages of the writing. Her steady support, together with my father when he was alive, has always been the backdrop to my life.

Julie writes: My part in this book has been possible due to Gill Maxwell not only for her daily support but also her inspiration as to how to provide the best possible services for children in social care. Thanks go to our son, Matt, who has taught us what PACE means more than anyone else. Thanks also to Mum , no longer with us, and dad, my rock. There are three individuals I have worked alongside for many years, Alison Keith, Vicky Sutton, and Anna Binnie-Dawson. They have been my safety and continue to show me what intersubjectivity is all about.

Our final thanks go to Deborah Malmud at Norton for believing in this project and tolerating an ever-increasing rise in word count as we discovered how much we had to say.

*Healing Relational Trauma
with Attachment-Focused Interventions*

CHAPTER 1

From Traumatic Relationships to Developmental Relationships

After nourishment, shelter, and companionship, stories are the thing that we need most in the world.

—Philip Pullman

For most of her first 4 years, Sarah had seldom been in the mind and heart of anyone. The absence of such a relationship was her trauma. As a result, her mind and heart had not developed well and were not integrated into a sense of self that was coherent.

Sarah was now a 9-year-old adopted girl who was born in Eastern Europe, abandoned by her mother as an infant, raised in an orphanage until she was 4 years old, and then adopted by a couple from the United States. It was a loving family with an adopted son who was 4 years older than Sarah and doing quite well. But Sarah had much difficulty living in a loving family. In the 5 years since she came to live with them, she was angry, controlling, and increasingly violent, especially toward her adoptive mother, Marie. Her violence led to a broken leg for Marie when Sarah pushed her down the stairs. Many interventions for Sarah and her family were tried without success. For the safety of all concerned, Sarah was placed in a residential program where the principles of intervention were based on an understanding of attachment and developmental trauma.

Her dyadic developmental psychotherapy (DDP) therapist, Kathleen, had been seeing her in therapy over the 4 months since she entered the program. One of Sarah's two attachment aids, Tina, was also present during the therapy sessions. During this session, Sarah complained to Tina about something that she did not like at the cottage and then became angry with Kathleen for trying to start a conversation about it. More often than not, Sarah simply ignored Kathleen when Kathleen tried to engage her. It seemed to Tina that no matter what Sarah did, Kathleen would accept it and then continue the conversation or start a new one with another invitation to become engaged. Sessions similar to this one had occurred again and again in the previous 4 months, with Sarah being very challenging and rejecting and Kathleen being open to Sarah's experience, accepting it and trying to understand a bit more about Sarah's experiences. Kathleen didn't become defensive or move into lecturing or problem solving, always remaining open and engaged with whatever Sarah brought up.

When Sarah refused to join her in a conversation, Kathleen might talk with Tina or even talk to herself about Sarah, always with an attitude of acceptance, mixed with a bit of curiosity about what Sarah might be thinking or empathy about some hard times that she recently had.

Sometimes Kathleen's wish to help Sarah to become more cooperative and engaging made it difficult to accept her defenses. She so wanted to push Sarah into a better life! Then Kathleen would reflect a bit more, recalling the hard times that Sarah must have had during the first 4 years of her life. This invariably helped Kathleen to find compassion for Sarah, which enabled Kathleen to be patient and accept Sarah unconditionally again.

At one point in this session, Tina mentioned that Sarah often complained about life at the cottage, much like her adoptive mother had said that Sarah complained about life at home. Tina added that she thought that Sarah's mother was a good person who cared for Sarah and was committed to her. Sarah ignored this and looked out the window.

Inhibiting a wish to tell Sarah that her mother was in fact someone who did care for her and whom she could trust, Kathleen instead quietly began talking with Tina. She hoped that by not addressing Sarah directly, Sarah would have little to be angry about. Though silent, Sarah often seemed to listen, maybe even think a bit about what Kathleen was saying. That hope kept Kathleen fully present as she spoke with Tina. In a soft and rhythmic manner, Kathleen spoke of Sarah's story:

KATHLEEN: I don't think that Sarah feels safe with mothers, Tina. She might not be sure if she wants a relationship with her mom. When she was a baby, it seems that her first mother didn't take very good care of her. She left her at a police station and never came back. Sarah was sick, thin, very dirty, and sore. She was in a hospital for 2 months and then went to the orphanage. She lived there for almost 3 years—and I don't know if you know this, Tina—there were no mothers in the orphanage! No mother to get to know her, hold and play with her, care for her in a special way. Then when she met her adoptive mother, she really didn't trust her. She was used to taking care of herself so she didn't know what to do when her mother would do things for her and with her. And she'd really get angry when her mother would say no to her. She thought that she said no because she was mean and wanted her to be unhappy! So, I understand, Tina, why Sarah is not too happy in the cottage and wasn't too happy at home. She never had a mother she trusted who could help her to have a life that would show her what happiness was.

A minute or two of silence followed, with Sarah still staring out the window. Then, in a quiet voice, Sarah said, "I miss my mother."

Just as quietly Kathleen said to Tina, "Tell her how you feel, Tina, about her missing her mother."

Tina thought for a moment and then said, "I feel sad for you Sarah, because you're missing your mother and she's not here."

As Tina spoke, Sarah looked at Tina and noticed a few tears in her eyes. Sarah said, "You're crying!"

Then Tina saw that Sarah's face looked vulnerable, and she felt a few more tears.

"Yes, Sarah, I had tears because you're missing your mother and she's not here. And now I have some more tears because I think you've been missing a mother all of your life." At that, Sarah leaned against Tina, who embraced her. Sarah cried and Tina stroked her hair. After a few minutes, Sarah asked Tina when her mother was coming for a visit. Tina replied that she'd be there over the weekend. Sarah smiled and put her head on Tina's shoulder.

Over the previous 4 months, Sarah had gradually begun to notice that she existed in the minds and hearts of Kathleen and Tina. She noticed because Kathleen and Tina repeatedly invited Sarah to join them in synchronized nonverbal–verbal conversations, invitations that sometimes she accepted but more often declined. When Kathleen told Tina the aspect of Sarah's story about not often experiencing a mother, Sarah not only noticed her presence in their minds and hearts but also allowed herself to truly experience them inter-subjectively. Afterward, Tina thought about this conversation and about how part of her had wanted Kathleen to join her in a lecture about how the rules at the cottage were fair and Sarah was being unreasonable. Tina felt grateful that Kathleen had found a way to help her to see and connect with Sarah's vulner-ability and pain underneath the angry deflecting kid she had come to know.

That weekend, Sarah seemed a bit different. She wanted to talk with her mother more. She seemed more relaxed, and Tina sensed a new connection between them. Sarah seemed determined to figure out how to have a mother. She was beginning to question her old story that she was not lovable while becoming aware of a new story that she might be able to have a mother who loved her, who saw something good in her. And slowly, step by step, she was able to do it. She was able to find a way into her mother's mind and heart and discover herself there. Within this relationship, she was able to finally begin to develop her own mind and heart.

Many, many, children are similar to Sarah in beginning their lives experiencing trauma. Some of them have parents who abuse or neglect them. Some of them do not have parents or adults committed to providing them with parental care. These traumas have pervasive, long-lasting effects on the child's developing mind, body, and spirit.

The traumatic relationships that are experienced by the young child are many and varied. They include physical and sexual abuse, but they are not limited to these extreme acts of violation and betrayal. Repetitive expressions of contempt, indifference, rage, and dissatisfaction must also be considered to be traumatic when these expressions are directed toward a child by those whom the child turns to for safety—his or her parents. These expressions are often nonverbal, conveyed by scornful looks, disgusted facial expressions, harsh voice tones, and dismissive gestures. Added to these expressions are words and phrases such as "You're a bad boy!" "Get out of my sight!" "I wish you were dead!" "I never want to look at you again!" and worse. Just as traumatic, if not more so, are relationships where the child is not seen or heard—where the parents are indifferent to their child's presence. These children experience themselves as being invisible, unimportant, of little value. This is the trauma of neglect.

Such traumatic nonverbal and verbal communications teach children to avoid looking into their parents' eyes, to stop listening to their voices, to avoid being touched, and to no longer seek the routine interactions of being cared for and enjoyed. Many traumatized children are then likely to consistently avoid their adoptive parents rather than turn to them for safety. This avoidance comes at the cost of their development because young children need these synchronized nonverbal—and gradually verbal—interactions that are part of healthy caregiving in order to develop neurologically, emotionally, socially, and cognitively. Whereas at birth they wanted to be seen and touched by their parents, they now want to be unseen and untouched by their foster or adoptive parents.

Other traumatized children would rather evoke reactions of rage and disgust than no reactions at all. They would rather be "bad" than be unseen. They have contact with their new parents, but this contact is based on opposition and defiance, anger and deceit. They would rather be abused for their actions toward their parents than be neglected. Both groups of children are developing a sense of self that is very limited ("bad, stupid, lazy, dumb") or fragmented and poorly formed (confused, disorganized, and easily led while lacking any sense of direction of their own).

When children develop patterns of survival that involve them relying on themselves, not others, they do so out of their profound mistrust that others will meet their needs and will do what is best for them. These children assume that the only way they will get what they need from adults is by intimidating them or manipulating them. Some are habitually very "bad," while others are habitually very "good." Some are able to be either "good" or "bad" depending on the circumstances and their judgment about the particular adult's likelihood of responding to one or the other.

Mistrustful children have very narrow focus when they interact with adults—foster parents, teachers, therapists. They focus on what they must do to meet their perceived needs themselves or to induce the adult to meet their needs. They are not interested in discovering more about who they are (their strengths and vulnerabilities) because they have long since concluded that they are bad and unlovable. They are not curious about others and the world around them. Early relational trauma has taught them to focus solely on issues relating to staying safe, so they have little interest in what the adult is interested in and sees as being valuable.

What had Kathleen and Tina done and said that caused Sarah to reflect a bit on her life and begin to be aware of her emptiness and loneliness? What had been said and done over the previous 4 months that caused Sarah to be aware of—and become open to exploring—a type of relationship that she had not experienced as an infant with her birth mother and in the orphanage and which her adoptive parents did not know how to help her to experience? Kathleen and Tina and the others in the program had presented to her, countless times, the components of relationships that would win her trust and facilitate her development.

Children need relationships—as do we all. How they develop is affected in very significant ways by the nature of their relationships.

Dyadic developmental psychotherapy (DDP) enables children who have experienced relational trauma within their original family to benefit from new relational experiences that are crucial for their development. DDP does so by providing relational experiences similar to those provided in healthy parent–child relationships, which were lacking in the early lives of these children. These experiences contain the safety that is crucial for a child's neuropsychological development. They also provide the opportunities for children to learn about themselves and others in a manner that is not distorted by past relational experiences of shame and terror. The relationships present within DDP enable children to learn to identify, regulate, and express their emotional states and also provide them with experiences that teach them how to seek comfort, resolve conflicts, and engage in relationship repair. DDP enables children who have experienced relational trauma to feel safe, often for the first time in their lives—safe to be sad and safe to seek and experience reciprocal joy. In DDP, children learn too that they may develop their unique sense of autonomy while at the same time maintaining a close relationship with someone who will keep them safe and assist them in their development.

CONVERSATIONS

Dyadic developmental psychotherapy was developed to provide therapeutic, healing relationships with children who do not trust their caregivers, teachers, therapists, and wider community. It relies on principles taken from our knowledge of attachment, developmental trauma, and intersubjectivity to inform the development of the therapeutic relationship between the therapist and the child.

The intersubjective experiences that individuals have with infants are truly conversations that are central in human development. They are reciprocal, nonverbal, attuned interactions that occur when our minds, hearts, and bodies are synchronized with each other. Nonverbal attunement is very clear as we interact with infants, but quite similar interactions are equally strong when we are engaged with our friends and partners of all ages. The expressed experiences of one person, influencing and being influenced by the expressed experiences of the other person, are primarily nonverbal and continually fine-tuned in the interactions with each other. Conversations beyond infancy are also verbal, in which words that are congruent with the nonverbal expressions bring additional meanings to the shared experiences. Within a conversation, each person is open to his or her own experience as well as the experience of the other person, and both become engaged with the stories that each brings to the conversation, enhancing both stories through this engagement.

In DDP, the therapist initiates and maintains a conversation with a child. The therapist's openness (toward his own experience and the experience of the child) and engagement (actively influencing and being influenced by the two stories) enables the child to begin to learn how to enter the conversation too. The therapist first shows that it is safe to have a conversation. The therapist's attitude demonstrates to the child that he or she need not fear these conversations. Through the focus on the reciprocal nature of the dialogue, the therapist is showing the child how to have a conversation. This is something that maltreated children are not given much chance of learning during the first years of life. The therapist's ability to hold both her own and the child's experiences in her mind and heart enables her experience to attenuate the trauma-affected experiences of the child, reducing the fear and shame associated with the trauma.

The central experience of the DDP therapist is being aware of and giving expression to his or her mind and heart while at the same time being aware of and accepting the expressions of the minds and hearts of the traumatized children he or she meets. This offers children the experience of a radically engaged and supportive other. These conversations develop a new path beyond the trauma, and on this path *stories* develop. DDP is about creating new stories. Traumatic events strike against our minds and hearts and create a story that is fragmented by gaps and is distorted by strong emotions from which the child shrinks and hides. These stories are rigid, with meanings given to the child by the one abusing him or her. From these jagged stories of shame and terror that arose from relational trauma, DDP is creating stories of connection, strength, and resilience. As human beings, we have no choice but to create stories. Within DDP, we cocreate integrative stories with the child that lead to the development of an integrated *sense of self* and, over time, to a coherent *narrative*.

The theory and research that guides the development of DDP is presented in Chapter 2. Chapters 3, 4, and 5 present the overall framework and experience of DDP. This new way of relating that the child is discovering within the therapeutic room needs to be present within the child's relationship with his parents as well. The parents of the child form an alliance with the DDP therapist and from the safety of that relationship are able to develop a similar relationship with their child, both when they are with their child in his therapy sessions and in the home. This process of working with the child's parents will be discussed in some detail in Chapters 6 and 7.

With children who have experienced early relational trauma, it can be beneficial—if not essential—to facilitate such relationships between the child and his teachers, extended family members, and other significant adults in his life too. The process of developing such relationships within the child's school and community will be discussed in Chapter 8. In Chapter 9, the use of DDP with various subpopulations of children will be considered. Adaptations of DDP for various home settings and out-of-home placements or for individual therapy and supervision will be presented in Chapter 10. Chapter 11 presents our early efforts to develop supporting research for DDP, DDP-informed parenting, and dyadic developmental practice. Finally, in the appendix we mention a few specific examples of Dyadic Developmental Practice.

Our narrative about ourselves and about the world develops the most successfully within attachment relationships that bring us safety and reciprocity, engaging our minds with the minds of others. These relationships—day in and day out—bring us comfort and joy. Our neurobiology is designed for such relationships. We crave them. We thrive within them. We are able to resolve the impact of trauma and discover and actualize our potential within them. These are truly developmental relationships, and without them the child's development will be greatly impaired.

Notes

Throughout the book, the authors use gender pronouns alternately unless referring to a specific person. Also, the authors refer to parents, caregivers, carers, or residential workers as parents unless referring to a specific person.

Many vignettes and case studies of children and parents are presented throughout the book. Unless the authors specifically indicate that reference is being made to a particular case, these vignettes and case studies are composite cases and do not refer to a particular person or persons.

Regarding terminology, *dyadic developmental psychotherapy (DDP)* refers to the stand-alone model of therapy that is presented throughout this book. *DDP-informed parenting* refers to a model of parenting, congruent with DDP, that is utilized by parents with their children whether or not the children are receiving DDP. Finally, *dyadic developmental practice* refers to the community network of services surrounding DDP and DDP-informed parenting that is often necessary to provide support to the child and family.

CHAPTER 2

Guiding Principles from Trauma, Attachment, Intersubjectivity, and Neurobiology

Robert had decided to catch up on his reading and chose a bench in the park on a clear and breezy day, overlooking a playground meant for activity, play, and noise, not reading. When the book that Robert was reading proved to be a bit dull, his attention turned to the playground and to the family who had just arrived. He quickly discovered that they were much more interesting than his book. Within 5 minutes he knew their names. Beth was the mom and Stan was the dad. And what parents they seemed to be! Both were active and observant, both were firm and engaging, both were affectionate and strong. They had a nice rhythm between them, taking turns with leading, being directive, and providing comfort and support. They had four kids, who all seemed to be about the same age! Sally and Jack seemed to be about 7 years old, Donald maybe a bit younger, and Arlene a bit older. They seemed more dissimilar than alike. Robert wondered why Beth and Stan seemed to watch Arlene, who seemed to be the oldest, more closely and to keep her physically closer to them than they did with the other three. It was not long before Robert knew why.

It began slowly and sweetly with Sally assembling a few stones, twigs, and flowers on the edge of the sandbox. She made clear that she hoped to use these to impress Beth. When it was almost finished, Jack pushed Sally into the sand and then kicked the bits of the design all over the ground. Immediately Sally cried, and only a second later little Donald had his arm around her. He comforted her while assuring her that he would help her to build it again. This commotion caused Beth and Stan to spring into action to attend to what Sally and Jack now seemed to require. With their eyes focused elsewhere, Arlene went from quietly playing at their feet to running past them, grabbing Donald by his hair and beginning to drag him across the sand. Beth and Stan immediately pivoted, and their attention went from Sally and Jack to Donald and Arlene. Beth went over quickly to kneel beside Donald. She comforted him while checking him over for any cuts or bruises. Stan ran toward Arlene, who wasted no time before turning and dashing toward the startled man who had been reading on the bench. Robert was speechless when Arlene began screaming at him that Stan was going to beat her and she needed Robert's protection. Stan caught up with Arlene and apologized to Robert for disturbing his leisure. It seemed to Robert that it was Stan who might need to be protected from Arlene's kicking, spitting, and attempts to bite him. Robert wanted to help, but he did not know what he might say or do to make the situation any better. Feeling some embarrassment, Robert tried to become interested in his book. Ten minutes later, Arlene was still yelling at Stan. They were over by the car, and so it was not so noisy. Both Donald and Sally appeared to be doing better with Beth's gentle support. Jack was climbing on the slide, seemingly indifferent to the actions around him but still glancing over quite a bit. Thirty minutes later, they were all in the car as it headed out of the park. Robert still couldn't concentrate on his reading. His mind kept trying to make sense of what had just occurred. What sort of a family was this? What was behind the children's behaviors?

Beth and Stan were foster parents, and they were committed and competent in what they did. While Donald was their biological son, Jack, Sally, and Arlene were foster children. Though they had been caring for all three of their foster children for more than a year, the children really had not changed that much. They presented many challenges in their day-to-day care. Their early traumatic experiences of abuse and neglect continued to affect their functioning in the present.

Why would the incidents of relational traumas that Jack, Sally, and Arlene experienced make it difficult for them to function well in their good home with Beth and Stan? Research suggests that the attachment patterns they developed in response to the abuse continued to influence their patterns of relating long after the abuse had stopped (Troy & Sroufe, 1987). Jack is likely to have developed a pattern of relying on himself while minimizing his need to rely on others (avoidant attachment). This places him at risk for managing stress through minimizing his emotional response to events or being aggressive toward others rather than seeking support from others. Sally is likely to have developed a pattern of relying a great deal on others and not having confidence in herself (ambivalent attachment). She then is likely to greatly need the attention of others. She is at risk of relating in a way that is mutually irritating rather than mutually enjoyable. The relational trauma that Arlene experienced is likely to have been overwhelming to her efforts to develop any pattern of relating to keep herself safe (disorganized attachment). She then is at risk for responding in impulsive and unpredictable ways when under stress. Not having experienced developmental trauma, Donald was able to develop attachment patterns that were the most effective in managing stress (secure attachment). His pattern of being able to rely on both self and other appropriately became a protective factor against the development of difficult behaviors.

DEVELOPMENTAL TRAUMA

The moment that a therapist tries to understand and help a child who has been abused or neglected by his parents, it becomes necessary for the therapist to consider the child's lack of safety through the complex lens of attachment theory and research. When a child is experiencing trauma at the hands of his parents, that child's lack of safety is profound, and the impact on the child's development is pervasive. When young children do not feel safe, they naturally turn toward their parents (their attachment figures) to provide them with safety. When the parents are the cause of the lack of safety, the child is left without any effective means of becoming safe. This trauma, which is intrafamilial and interpersonal, is known as developmental trauma, and it is hard to imagine anything else that would create such a continual experience of not being safe. Children who have experienced developmental trauma are at high risk of not resolving the impact of the trauma even when they are no longer living with their parents who caused the trauma. There are a number of interwoven reasons for this. They do not trust their new parents to keep them safe. They are likely to lack important skills that facilitate their development. They are likely to be acting in ways that reflect the story they developed while experiencing their traumatic relationships rather than being able to develop a new story shaped by their new relationships. Because the primary function of attachment is to generate safety, it is reasonable to consider that attachment interventions would be central in helping these children to begin to resolve their traumatic experiences, heal, and trust their new parents.

Before considering this journey toward safety and healthy development, let us first take a look at the nature of developmental trauma. Over the past 20 years, professionals who have specialized in understanding child abuse and neglect have become increasingly aware of and concerned about the impact of intrafamilial, interpersonal trauma on developing children (Cook et al., 2005). They conclude that the symptoms resulting from such traumas create more profound problems than those associated with post-traumatic stress disorder. They describe these problems as *domains of impairment*, as the effects of impairment in these domains are so pervasive in the developing child. Children who have experienced developmental trauma are considered to be at risk for problems in each of the following seven domains:

- *Attachment*: Insecure patterns or the more serious disorganized pattern. These patterns to varying degrees affect the child's ability to regulate acute or chronic stressful events while also reducing the child's readiness to turn to attachment figures for safety, comfort, and support.
- *Biology*: Difficulties with identification and regulation of core biophysiologic processes. This would include appetite, urination and defecation, body temperature, and recognition of pain.
- *Affect regulation*: Difficulties identifying, regulating, and integrating positive and negative emotional states.
- *Dissociation*: Periodic or frequent lack of awareness and integration of core cognitive and affective experiences in the present moment.
- *Behavior control*: Chaotic behaviors characterized by impulsivity or rigid behaviors characterized by compulsivity.
- *Cognition*: Difficulties with learning, speech and language, sensory integration, as well as reflective and mentalization skills.
- *Self-concept*: Negative and fragmented sense of self.

In recognizing these domains of impairment, it becomes evident that children who have experienced developmental trauma are at risk for failing to develop the complex social, cognitive, emotional, psychological, and even biological skills that are central in dealing with the stresses of the world. As a result, they are likely to experience chronic shame and to avoid addressing the challenges in life that are necessary for attaining their developmental milestones. Their developmental age is likely to be much younger than their chronological age. They also cannot manage stress well because they have great difficulty trusting and turning to adults for guidance, comfort, and support. Relying on themselves they often fail, causing more shame, and often leading to states of rage or dissociation.

We associate home with safety, both as a secure base from which to explore the world and as a safe haven we return to when the stressors of the world feel a bit much. With developmental trauma, the child's core sense of safety, so crucial for every aspect of her development, is violated. Such environments, to quote Daniel Siegel, "directly impair the developing child's affect regulation, shifts in states of mind, and integrative and narrative functions" (2012, p. 329). Yes, being violated by one's own parents does create comprehensive challenges for the young child who is reaching out to experience a complex world. As will be shown throughout this book, dyadic developmental psychotherapy (DDP) serves to assist this child to return to a developmental path that was present at birth or, most likely, at conception. DDP functions to assist this child to regulate his intense emotions long dominated by states of terror and shame and to establish an integrated state of mind and body capable of developing a coherent autobiographical narrative. This process, in large part, occurs through supporting the child in learning to enter into intersubjective conversations with his new parents, trusting them to assist him with stressful events and to guide him in developing a new story and sense of self that makes sense of the differences in his past and present homes. These efforts are complemented by helping the child's new parents to consistently provide his needed care.

A SECURE ATTACHMENT

In the third edition of the *Handbook of Attachment*, the editors strongly state: "In the study of social and emotional development, attachment theory is the most visible and empirically grounded conceptual framework guiding today's research" (Cassidy & Shaver, 2016, p. x). Their conclusion is based on the existence of more than 30,000 studies about the influence of attachment on development from infancy through old age. The highly significant impact of a secure attachment on development may be seen in successful relationships the child has with his parents, with other adults and with peers, as well as in the relationships that adults have with their peers. Secure attachment also facilitates emotional understanding and regulation, social cognition, and the development of conscience, personality, and a positive and integrated self-concept (Thompson, 2016). Reflective functioning and mentalization skills also develop well within a secure attachment (Fonagy, Luyten, Allison, & Campbell, 2016). There is a general consensus that a secure attachment—with regard to the incidence of developmental psychopathology—is a protective factor, whereas insecure patterns, and especially disorganization, are risk factors (DeKlyen & Greenberg, 2016).

Now we need to briefly explore the nature of a secure attachment. An *attachment bond* is one type of an *affectional bond* that we experience throughout our lifetime. There are five characteristics of an affectional bond. First, it is a bond that is not transitory but rather persists over time. Second, it is directed toward a specific person. Third, it is an emotionally significant relationship. Fourth, the individual wishes to maintain proximity or contact with the other person. Fifth, the individual experiences distress at involuntary separations from that person. An *attachment affectional bond* exists when another feature is added to the affectional bond. In an attachment bond, in times of distress, the individual seeks security and comfort within the relationship with the other. A parent experiences an affectional bond with her child, but it is not an attachment bond (or an attachment affectional bond) because the parent does not turn to the child for security and comfort (Cassidy, 2016).

Securely attached children consistently experience safety, and when there is a perceived threat to their safety, they are able to successfully turn to their parents for comfort and security. Experiencing safety routinely, they develop the skills needed to regulate their emotional states and to make sense of their world. They develop a coherent view of self and others (internal working models), and they are more able to develop the complex skills needed to manage the challenges they face and to learn from the opportunities presented to them. Securely attached children do not become dependent adults but rather adults who are able to successfully rely on themselves and to rely on trusted others as the situation calls for it. They are able to manage stress, and they develop a state of resilience in facing any larger challenges ahead.

Attachment is central in human development because it ensures that we are able to regulate our emotions when presented with events that are associated with intense emotional states of terror, shame, despair, and rage. Without such regulatory abilities, we are likely to be overwhelmed not just by the stresses of traumatic events but even by the routine stresses of our lives. Attachment has been considered as primarily a regulatory system enabling our emotions to support, not impede, our development (Schore & Schore, 2014). Attachment is also central in human development because it facilitates the child's ability to develop his inner life so that he is able to make sense of the inter-personal world and of his own inner world of thoughts, feelings, wishes, and intentions. Individuals who are securely attached to others tend to have good reflective functioning along with a greater ability to sen-sitively perceive and understand the minds of others (Fonagy et al., 2016). DDP focuses on regulating the emotional states associated with past relational traumas and current relational stressors and develop-ing new stories that make sense of these past and present events. This leads to a child's development of a more secure attachment to his cur-rent parents and the formation of a more coherent narrative.

INTERSUBJECTIVITY

The central goal of attachment is attaining and maintaining a sense of safety and from there exploring the world. As social mammals, the socio-emotional world of relationships and learning about self and other through relationships is the primary world that young children are exploring. This process of learning is best described as intersubjec-tivity. We develop the meanings of our socio-emotional world through sharing experiences with others.

Intersubjectivity refers to the process where the experience that one person is having while relating with the other person influences the other person's experience at the same time and vice versa. Within intersubjective experiences, the two individuals are having a recipro-cal influence on each other. Because of this reciprocity, the two indi-viduals are continually modifying their experience of both self and other as well as their joint experience of a third person or of an event that they are both experiencing. If a parent is with her infant and is experiencing delight for her infant, the infant is likely to experience himself as delightful and his parent as also being delightful. If another family member of this mother–infant pair is playing with his dog in the garden, as the mother becomes interested in his activity, the infant is likely to be as well. The infant's interest is likely to be influenced by the nature of his mother's interest. When the infant is startled by the loud noise of a truck going down the street, his mother is likely to make explicit her experience of that noise—it merits attention but is nothing to fear—so that her experience will help the infant to reexperience that noise. The other parent sees mom comforting their frightened infant and goes to them expressing relief that there is nothing to be worried about. The three then embrace, and all are likely to experience joint affection, which then creates some happiness for them all. One of the three is likely to then show an interest in something else, and the other two become interested in it and they then explore it together, again the experience of one contributing to the experience of the other and back again.

A reciprocal, synchronized, rhythmic conversation among the two or three family members is occurring, making hundreds of micro-adjustments in the minutes ahead as the flow of interests, affects, and intentions sweeps over and among the family members. As such sequences with this particular family occur again and again, the memories of prior sequences become part of the present experience, building confidence in the strength and continuity of their relationships, which leads to stories that make sense of the conversations and causes them to anticipate that there is more to come. Now the past, present, and future become interwoven in their relationships with each other, and their joint stories become more complex. What they now have with each other is an affectional bond, and because comfort in response to distress is an important part of the relationships, the bonds now involve the infant's attachment to his parents and the partners' attachments with each other.

That sequence, if exposed to microanalysis in a researcher's laboratory, would be a very elaborate, intricate one. And yet there are hundreds of these conversations in a typical day for a family engaged in important, meaningful relationships with each other. These interactions are not a linear process but rather involve intricate feedback loops of reciprocal meanings that are continually being recalibrated. It seems simpler to assume a linear equation where the parent influences her baby through unidirectional actions—reinforcements—which has the intended effect on the baby's functioning. But such an analysis is extremely incomplete, leaving out the vitally important effect that her baby is having on the parent at the same time. If the baby's response to his parent's initiatives toward her baby does not have an effect on the parent, the baby loses a central component of his sense of agency and value. If the baby does not experience self as being able to have a positive effect on—reinforce—his parent, the baby is likely to experience self as not being important to his parent. If this occurs often enough, we might consider the infant as being emotionally neglected. Reciprocity in the parent–infant relationship is crucial for the infant's developing sense of self and for the parent's developing sense of self-as-parent. Reciprocity, too, is a central aspect of all meaningful conversations and relationships, whether with friends, colleagues, partners, or neighbors, throughout life. It is first learned in the intersubjective conversations that parents and babies have. It is no wonder that children who have been maltreated by their parents have great difficulty engaging with others in a reciprocal manner in future relationships as well.

One of the leading authorities on infant intersubjectivity is Colwyn Trevarthen from the University of Edinburgh. He has stated to many of his students over the years that we do not understand our baby by observing our baby. We understand our baby by being actively engaged with our baby in moment-to-moment, intersubjective conversations of shared, attuned meanings. Such conversations all occur without the baby using words! Trevarthen summarized his years of study as follows: "[This book] presents many kinds of evidence to support the view that we are evolved to know, think, communicate, create new things and care for one another in movement—through a sense of being in rhythmic time with motives and in tune with feelings to share the energy and harmony of meaning and of relating" (Malloch & Trevarthen, 2009, p. 8). Yes, the complex behaviors of our family and friends, reflecting their more complex affective states, interests, and intentions, continually influence our own complex experiences—and theirs as well.

Trevarthen (2016) indicates that when the infant enters synchronized rhythms of nonverbal expressions with a parent, the infant is learning to share meanings with the parent, which leads to a variety of states involving shared interests, affective states, tasks, and eventually words and more elaborate conversations. The infant's intersubjective experiences are primarily affective, and these have been called states of "attunement" by Daniel Stern (2000). This intersubjective sharing is deepened when the parent and child are matched affectively through intensity, rhythm, beat, contours, duration, and shape. These "vitality affects" are central in these nonverbal communications and are at the core of understanding and feeling understood when relating with an infant. Core socio-emotional communications of the sense of self continue to be experienced intersubjectively at all ages within this synchronized nonverbal manner, through facial and vocal expressions, along with gestures and touch.

These shared experiences are rhythmic, nonverbal, and synchronized, moment to moment, with split-second adjustments to the movements of each other. The emerging, organizing, integrating self of the infant is discovering its energy and form within these shared "dancing" moments with the organized, but still organizing, self of the parent. They are safely together, and with that safety they are cocreating a joint narrative. This joint narrative, in turn, permeates the self of each and continues, when they are apart, to contribute to the ongoing development of the self. These experiences are in the here-and-now. They have to be if they are primarily nonverbal and synchronized.

The securely attached child is vitally aware of his parent, not in the anxious, vigilant manner of the maltreated child who is continually determining whether he is safe or not, but in the open and engaged manner of the child who is deeply curious about the world that is both interesting and delightful. These ongoing intersubjective conversations lead the child to feeling delightful (as the parent experiences and communicates delight), lovable (as the parent experiences and communicates love), interesting (as the parent experiences and communicates interest), and so on. Along with these conversations, there are times when the baby and his parent are simply being together, feeling connected, not really exploring the new. These times of being relaxed and connected together complement and often consolidate the learning that occurs within the reciprocal conversations that they are having about self, other, and the world. And the securely attached child also experiences delight, interest, and amazement while engaging with objects and events in the world because her parent has those experiences too. Together, often as they alternate in taking the lead in their conversations, the infant and parent are cocreating stories of self, other, and engagements with the world while coregulating the emotions associated with those experiences. This same process is the central process of DDP.

Let's consider again the foster family mentioned at the onset of this chapter. Donald had a secure attachment with his parents, Beth and Stan. From his position of safety, he learned about himself, them, and the world through intersubjective conversations and relaxed connections that he experienced with them, beginning when he was born. He discovered that he was clever and compassionate, resourceful and delightful. He might make mistakes, but he could learn from them, and he was still unconditionally loved—and lovable. He became like his parents, becoming reflective, empathetic, and learning to regulate his emotions. He lived and developed stories that formed his sense of himself and his parents within their caring experiences of him. Donald's development was greatly influenced by his parents and by the intersubjective conversations they had with him.

Sally, Jack, and Arlene were not so fortunate. Their intersubjective conversations with their parents were few, and their resultant stories were negative (unlovable, boring, unimportant, bad, selfish, lazy). These experiences we call neglect and abuse. They did not experience themselves as being safe when with their parents, so they became vigilant and had to rely on themselves and develop strategies that might create safety—aggression, avoidance, manipulation, opposition. Not relying on their parents, they were guarded against their parents' influence and were not open to intersubjective conversations with them or with future carers.

Dyadic developmental psychotherapy functions to provide such intersubjective conversations in the therapy session and in the child's day-to-day care. The DDP therapist and carer need to discover positive qualities in the child under the vigilant and defiant behaviors that the child displays and then give expression to these discoveries intersubjectively.

What might Beth and Stan do to help Sally, Jack, and Arlene, possibly with some direct or indirect help from a DDP therapist? For Sally, they could provide comfort to the degree that she accepts it. If she struggles accepting it, they could wonder with her about not having experienced much comfort in her life and how she makes sense of that. Once they had confidence that Jack and Arlene would allow them to relate with playfulness, acceptance, curiosity, and empathy (PACE), Beth and Stan might sit with them separately, engage them with an intersubjective conversation, and be curious with them about how they make sense of their actions toward Sally and Donald. Beth and Stan can express empathy if any themes emerge such as Jack and Arlene feeling ignored, having their sense of being unloved activated, or being reminded of what they never received themselves. Jack and Arlene might then need to focus on repairing the parent–child relationships that were affected by their actions and Beth and Stan's responses. Jack and Arlene need to experience—most likely again and again—that their behavior is not going to break their relationship with Beth and Stan, who still experience Jack and Arlene as being important to them and worthy of care.

Let's look at an example where a child has had a lack of positive intersubjective experiences and therefore did not discover that she is of value.

A 16-year-old foster girl, Callie, had just entered her seventh placement. After having been sexually abused by her father, she entered foster care when she was 8 years old. Her challenging behaviors led to failed foster placements, leading her to a group facility, a psychiatric hospital, another group home, another failed foster placement, and now a placement with a foster mom, Jean. She attended DDP sessions with Jean because that had been the one condition whereby Jean would agree to the placement. Callie was not very motivated to engage in DDP, and her primary responses to questions consisted in "I don't know," "I don't care," "That's stupid," "Whatever," or "Boring." The DDP therapist continued to express interest in her daily life, in spite of Callie's disinterest in the therapist's interest. When Callie replied that she did not know what she did after school, her therapist expressed disbelief and, without anger, expressed animated confusion over the fact that she would not tell her. Callie finally said that she had played soccer. Another five questions followed, and when the therapist finally learned that Callie had scored the winning goal for her school's soccer team, she exclaimed, "Wonderful!" Callie seemed to be uncomfortable with the therapist's enthusiasm over what she had done, so she made fun of her. This led to further confusion on her therapist's part and further questions as to what she did after the game. After a bit, the therapist learned that Callie had helped her 4-year-old foster brother to learn how to play a game, and she again exclaimed, "Wonderful!" Callie then rolled her eyes. A short time later, she learned that Callie had helped Jean do the dishes after dinner, and she exclaimed, "Wonderful!" The fourth "Wonderful!" followed Callie's stating that she had read a bedtime story to her foster brother. Then Callie smiled. Her therapist had been expressing genuine positive experiences of Callie over various things that she did, and she gradually became less anxious and began to accept her therapist's experience of her. A few weeks later, Jean told the DDP therapist that Callie seemed to now be enjoying Jean's positive experiences of her, and a short time after that, Callie seemed to begin to seek such expressions.

The expression "Wonderful!" was not a rational evaluation of Callie and her worth, but rather it was a shared experience of delight in her and her actions. Intersubjective experience is not a judgment; it is simply a shared experience. When Callie began to accept Jean's positive shared experiences of her as well, both Jean and her therapist began to anticipate that Callie was developing a story of herself that included being "wonderful." Her sense of self was beginning to become more positive and integrated. Why was this so important? Because Callie had too few such experiences during her early years of life. Her resultant sense of self contained a pervasive sense of inadequacy and shame. There seemed to be nothing special about her, nothing "wonderful." It took a while for her to feel safe enough with her therapist and Jean to become open to their positive experiences of her. Such experiences were a threat to her, and she was reluctant to believe that they might be real. As she gradually trusted them, she became open to their experience of her and to her own new experiences of Jean and her therapist. This made it easier for them to continue to discover her unique qualities that for much of her life had never been experienced by the important people in her life.

If we therapists step back and observe a child, we see an individual. The individuals that we see in our therapeutic offices or in foster homes are at risk of having difficulties managing stressful events; regulating their emotions; making sense of daily events; communicating what they think, feel, or want; and manifesting social behaviors such as cooperation, sharing, empathy, and taking turns. We summarize these behaviors and refer to them as the "self" of the child. If we as therapists become engaged in reciprocal conversations with the unique child, initiating and responding to expressions of interests, emotional states, ideas, memories, wishes, expectations, and perceptions, we are likely to experience this child's relational history that is permeating the "self" that we had observed. We are able to infer the child's past relationships when we experience how he mistrusts our motives, fears our affection, and anticipates our rejection. His past is also evident when he defends against our efforts to influence him, experiences shame when we wonder about his history and behaviors, and withdraws into distracting and dissociative states when our relationship with him feels like it is too challenging to manage. And it is in that reciprocal conversation, where the child is first experiencing mistrust, shame, and fear, that we are able to experience a way forward that may help the child to experience trust, pride, and safety with us. It is this process where we relate with the child in an open and engaged manner that the child is able to begin to experience safety in our relationship and become open to intersubjective conversations with us. These experiences will lead to the discovery of a more coherent and integrated sense of self that is embedded in safety and pride. This, too, is the process of DDP. As mentioned earlier, Trevarthen states that we understand a baby by being engaged with the baby. In DDP, we therapists understand the children we treat and care for by entering into reciprocal conversations with them and then discovering intersubjectively the qualities that they have. .

Here briefly is the story of another child in which the focus is on his abundance of negative intersubjective experiences. Bill is a 9-year-old boy who has a few small chores that his foster parents would like him to do after school each day. Their expectations often lead him to become angry, and then withdrawn, sometimes leaving him upset for the whole time before dinner. As the therapist wondered with him about his distress over having to do the chores, Bill realized that he often thought it was unfair that he had to do the chores. As this experience was accepted, it led Bill to begin to think that his parents wanted him to be unhappy or they would let him play the whole time after school. As Bill continued to wonder with the therapist about the event, he discovered that when he feels unhappy, it reminds him of his first 6 years when he lived with his birth parents, when it seemed that he was unhappy all of the time. That realization left him sad that he really has had a hard life, not having had the happiness that he thought many other children had growing up. That was what was really unfair! He was able then to tell his foster father that often he did feel sad because it seemed to him that he was not happy very often. His foster father's empathy led to a deeper recognition of how hard Bill's life had been, causing him to reduce Bill's chores a bit, which led Bill to be able to complete the few remaining chores easily and to begin to experience a greater degree of happiness in his daily life. In Bill's new story, he was able to recognize the extent of the unhappiness of his past and its influence on the frustrations of the present. As Bill became vulnerable in his reflecting about his difficult life, the therapist focused on support and comfort for the child rather than further explorations. His foster father's empathy for his past unhappiness caused Bill to discover more clearly the degree of happiness embedded in his current life.

A child needs new attachment relationships in order to resolve and integrate traumatic experiences that result from violations of trust in attachment relationships, the absence of safety, and stories based on shame and fear. Within these new relationships, the child needs inter-subjective conversations that develop into new stories that are embed-ded in love, compassion, care, and commitment—because of qualities within him. These intersubjective experiences reflect who he is.

INTERPERSONAL NEUROBIOLOGY

As various complex technologies have developed over the past 20 years, neuroscientists have been able to take important steps in better understanding the structure and functioning of the brain. And what they are discovering confirms the findings of attachment, intersubjec-tivity, and trauma with respect to the vital importance of safety and attachment-based relationships for our ongoing development. The brain is considered to be inherently interpersonal. It is designed for relationships, it functions best within safe relationships, and rela-tionships are crucial for its various regions to be able to function in an integrative manner. The many studies that have demonstrated the interpersonal nature of the human brain have led to an area of spe-cialty known as interpersonal neurobiology (IPNB). The writings of Daniel Siegel (2012), Allan Schore (2012), and others have led the way in helping us to understand this exciting new area of scientific knowl-edge and its applications in many areas of study meant to improve the human condition.

The consensus among those who study the functioning of the brain is that the brain works best when the individual is experienc-ing safety. The early warning system in the brain—a region in the subcortex known as the amygdala, located in both the left and right hemispheres—functions almost entirely to maintain safety. This region of the brain determines within one quarter of a second (without the aid of the cortex, which takes longer and might waste precious moments) whether there is a threat to safety or not. If there is a threat, that region of the brain signals the lower brain stem to engage in fight, flight, or freeze on the basis of what reaction will best protect the individual.

When threatened, the individual is not concerned with learning about the world or developing the self. He only is concerned about survival. When stress is chronic and there is little experience of safety, the young child is likely to adopt a habitual defensive state where he is vigilant toward signs of threat, not able to see signs of safety, and greatly limited in his ability to learn about himself and others.

If the amygdala does not experience an immediate source of threat, then it activates the cortex in order for the person to acquire a better understanding of the event itself. With input from the cortex, the amygdala may sense that while the event is not a threat to the very survival of the person, it is a threat to the person's sense of self. In that case, the amygdala insulates the self by activating a defensive position as opposed to becoming fully engaged with the other person or event. Now the person may not respond to the threat with the full fight–flight–freeze reaction but rather with a more subtle defensive response to reduce embarrassment, a sense of rejection, or shame.

In our discussion of intersubjectivity, we explored how the earliest development of the sense of self emerges through the presence of synchronized, nonverbal conversations. This is supported by our increasing knowledge of the socio-emotional areas of the brain that are involved in these conversations and in facial expressions, voice prosody, and touch/ gestural movements. These are critical in the child's developing attachment, affect regulation abilities, and sense of self (Schore & Schore, 2014). According to Schore and Schore, the experienced clinician needs to "become expert in nonverbal intersubjective processes and implicit relational knowledge that enhance therapeutic effectiveness" (2014, p. 191). Therapeutic change is seen as occurring within these affective, intersubjective, reciprocal conversations between therapist and client rather than through rational insights. This is likely to be even more the case in working with children, especially traumatized children, who tend to have affect regulation difficulties.

When the young child is safe, he has success in his early efforts to explore the world of self and others. His brain begins to utilize and integrate the cortex with the subcortex (top and bottom), as well as the front with the back, and the right with the left. When an infant who is in distress experiences comfort from his attachment figure, this experience of comfort generates the development of nerve fibers connecting the lower region of the anterior cingulate cortex with the amygdala. This is crucial for the development of necessary cognitive, emotional, sensorimotor integration. Similar neurologic developments occur when the infant is experiencing attuned experiences of joy as well as basic moments of shared interests, intentions, or light, reciprocal affective states. The nonverbal expressions of the infant and parent become synchronized, being continually fine-tuned in order to match each other's affective experience and focus. When the infant is experiencing safety, the infant's priority is to experience these reciprocal, intersubjective states of mind and body with a sensitive and responsive caregiver. When the infant is not feeling safe, he still seeks these intersubjective states in order to experience comfort and to feel safe again. This process is crucial for the development of secure attachments as well as the integration of interpersonal and intrapersonal processes.

The knowledge obtained by our new understandings of the brain have significant applications for psychotherapy (Cozolino, 2017; Solomon & Siegel, 2017), including psychotherapy involving children and their parents in DDP (Baylin & Hughes, 2016).

Children who have experienced developmental trauma are likely to habitually mistrust their parents and develop habits of self-reliance and the avoidance of vulnerability and comfort. Even when these children feel safe physically, an integrative aspect of their cortex, the default mode network (DMN), consistently prepares them for psychological threats to safety, creating chronic defensiveness (Baylin & Hughes, 2016).

Caring for a child who mistrusts the parent because of developmental trauma is very difficult neurologically. When a child consistently and actively rejects or passively fails to respond to parental care, the parent is in danger of experiencing a neurobiological state of blocked care (Hughes & Baylin, 2012). In blocked care, four key neurobiological systems that are active in caring for a child (approach, reward, getting to know, and seeing meaning and value in routine activities) tend to become inactive. A parent experiencing blocked care is likely to be able to continue to "do the job" of giving care, but the parent's heart is often not involved.

Another body of neurobiological research that has great value to the interventions and goals of DDP is the polyvagal theory of Stephen Porges (2011, 2017). This theory involves the neurobiological systems that extend throughout the body, not being restricted to the brain. Porges focuses on the autonomic nervous system (ANS), which involves the sympathetic and parasympathetic branches. The autonomic nervous system determines how the person functions when the individual is experiencing either threat (fight, flight, or freeze as well as a more primitive vegetative state) or safety. When safe, the individual is able to activate the ventral vagal circuit of the parasympathetic branch. This activates various areas of the subcortex that Porges refers to as the social engagement system. This system is crucial for social mammals to develop the skills that are needed to survive and thrive within the social community. When this system is active, the individual is in an open and engaged—as opposed to defensive—state of mind.

When open and engaged, the individual is open to relating to another in the manner needed to learn best from the other person, to influence and be influenced by the other. When safe, the individual is able to detect subtleties in the human voice and expressions in the human eye and face much better than when not feeling safe. When safe, the individual is able to recognize nonverbal cues and engage in reciprocal conversations more capably than when feeling defensive. The social engagement system involving the ventral vagal circuit provides a neurobiological understanding for the presence of intersubjectivity and the need for safety if intersubjective learning is to create a positive sense of self and a coherent narrative. When we are not feeling safe, we are not likely to notice subtle meanings conveyed in nonverbal expressions. We are also at risk to give meanings to expressions on the basis of previous experiences. For example, traumatized children may perceive a facial expression of being bored or mildly frustrated as a sign of rage and danger.

If one person, with this open and engaged state of mind, interacts with another person in a defensive state, the two states strive to become synchronized. Because of the priority given to safety, when one person is defensive, this is likely to evoke a defensive response in the other. Traumatized children habitually engage others defensively and therefore evoke defensiveness in the parents and therapists with whom they interact. If the parent and therapist are able to inhibit this neurobiological tendency to become defensive and instead remain open and engaged while interacting with the defensive child, the child is likely to gradually become open and engaged, at least for a time. The ability to recognize the tendency to become defensive when meeting a defensive child, inhibit it, and remain open and engaged is crucial for successful caregiving and therapy for the traumatized child.

The polyvagal theory and the open and engaged state of mind are also important for other reasons that are congruent with the interventions practiced in DDP. Dr. Porges says that the open and engaged state of mind is facilitated when an individual experiences acceptance rather than evaluation. In DDP, acceptance—total acceptance of the inner life of the child—is seen as central to the therapeutic stance that is necessary to create safety and intersubjective learning. Also, voice prosody characterized by rhythm and modulated tones, as opposed to a rational argument or lecture, is considered to be crucial in developing an open and engaged state rather than a defensive one. The DDP therapist speaks with the traumatized child in a very modulated, rhythmic, conversational manner, much like the way that a storyteller conveys a story. This form of prosody in the DDP therapist's voice facilitates safety while holding the child's interest in and engagement with what is being said. In the example given at the beginning of the chapter, if Beth and Stan were to be successful in engaging Jack and Arlene in a manner that would help these children to learn from the events that occurred at the playground, Beth and Stan would have to be open and engaged while they spoke with the children. This would increase the likelihood that these children will not be defensive and enable them to listen without shame. They might then be able to gradually make sense of their behaviors differently, understanding that they reflect their early traumas, not that they are bad.

CONCLUSION

Dyadic developmental psychotherapy is greatly influenced by the findings of attachment, intersubjectivity, and interpersonal neurobiology to better understand developmental trauma. With this knowledge base, we propose ways to intervene to resolve this severe relational trauma and facilitate normal development. These ways include a focus on development of affect regulation and reflective functioning along with discovery of ways to have conversations and to develop stories with trusted others, leading to an integrated sense of self and a coherent narrative.

We hope to demonstrate in the following chapters how these theories and related research are brought to life through the many processes and procedures of DDP. These processes reduce fear and shame, integrate cognitive and emotional states, develop coherent stories, and strengthen attachment relationships through experiences of comfort and joy.

CHAPTER 3

PACE: The Foundation of Safe and Healthy Relationships

When parents talk to their children with playfulness, acceptance, curiosity and empathy, the children experience the parents' deep interest in and understanding of them. This helps the children to feel secure and unconditionally loved. Dan put these four relational elements together as PACE when developing Dyadic Developmental Psychotherapy (DDP). PACE is the central therapeutic stance and relational attitude of DDP. It is an effective manner of relating to all children that facilitates their safety and learning (Hughes, 2011; Golding & Hughes, 2012). It is not only utilized by the therapist but is also taught to parents, teachers, and other adults who are in the child's life. PACE is at the heart of parenting, and it is the heartbeat in therapy. An attitude of PACE allows the children to feel unconditionally loved and accepted, helping them dare to feel "good enough" after all.

PACE is central in all aspects of DDP, DDP-informed parenting, and dyadic developmental practice; therefore, it is described first. Subsequent chapters will demonstrate how PACE is of great value for therapists (Chapter 4), parents (Chapters 6 and 7), and social workers, teachers, and other adults (Chapter 8) who are engaged with children that have experienced developmental trauma and are now struggling to trust the adults who are reaching out to them in all areas of their lives.

PACE is where trust begins, allowing mistrust to exit. Mistrust is a tricky character, however. It continues to reappear. Only when PACE accepts mistrust too will it hand over the stage to trust. PACE is therefore a way of being toward the child in all her parts. As the child experiences being deeply accepted by the adults, she can come to accept herself. This is the beginning of learning that she is a good person and that parents can be trusted after all.

WHERE IT ALL BEGINS:
COMMUNICATING WITH INFANTS

PACE is first found in the synchronized conversations that we have with our babies.

Jess is 3 months old. It is early morning and she is stirring. She opens her eyes and looks around. She experiences contentment as her gaze is caught by the pattern of light the Sun is making on her blanket. Jess becomes aware of discomfort too; her tummy is empty and her bottom feels uncomfortable. She begins to whimper. There is silence around her; the absence of someone that makes her feel better. Jess cries harder. Mom arrives, responding to the fear she can hear in her small daughter's call. She bends down and picks Jess up. Gently she holds Jess against her, rocking slightly as she soothes Jess with her voice. Jess snuggles in, and contentment returns.

Let's listen in to their conversation:

> MOM: Hello Jess, I am here. Look at you, all upset. Did you think I wasn't coming? Here I am. Look at those tears; so upset when mommy wasn't here. Come on let's get that diaper changed. Here we are, onto the mat. I bet you are feeling all uncomfortable; let's get this off. Ooh I can see a lovely round tummy (blows a raspberry on Jess's tummy). That's funny, isn't it? (repeats). You like that. Whoops, are you in the mood to wriggle? Just let me get you clean and dry. There, that will feel more comfortable. Here you are. Let's see how strong these legs are this morning. Look at you, clever girl. That's it, up and down. Now, how is that tummy this morning, hungry I bet?

This is PACE at its most natural. Jess's mother is completely focused on her young baby and what is going on internally for the baby. She is curious about Jess's emotional experience, guessing that Jess is frightened, uncomfortable, playful, and hungry. She accepts each state and meets it with an empathetic response. She is playful and nurturing, helping Jess to manage the experience of finding herself alone, rediscovering her mother, and having her diaper changed before she is fed. Jess feels safe and secure; the horror of being alone quickly receding as her call is answered. Her mother helps her to feel that all is right in her small world. Her mother's nonverbal and verbal responses help Jess to feel understood and regulated. Jess does not yet understand the words, but she is discovering her story as her experience is made sense of and her needs are met.

Parents of small children instinctively use a PACE attitude toward their babies. As long as they have had reasonable care themselves, they know how to emotionally connect with their children; being curious, accepting, and empathetic toward their children's internal experience and being playful at the right moments. PACE is central to secure attachment. PACE is therefore central within DDP, to help children who have not had secure attachment experiences—children who have learned mistrust instead of trust in parents. PACE for children who have experienced developmental trauma is crucial because they have had so few experiences of the reciprocal conversations that were continually present for secure babies and toddlers. Adults need to persist with PACE, being with the child so that she can learn another way of being herself: a way of being that is connected instead of disconnected; trusting instead of mistrusting. In PACE, the child can discover the unconditional love and acceptance she needed but which was absent earlier in her life.

DECONSTRUCTING PACE

PACE is a whole attitude, a way of being that provides the other with an emotionally connected experience within the interaction. It is an attitude we can hold toward ourselves, with each other, and one we can offer to children. This provides children with a different experience of relationships. In this section, we will deconstruct PACE, reflecting on each element in turn. In focusing on the parts, however, we need to ensure that we embrace the whole.

Playfulness

PACE is relational; playfulness within PACE is relational too. It comes and goes with the moment, but playfulness is always there as a possibility in the background. The playful in relationships is important because it allows us to find joy; moments when we can be light and filled with fun. In playfulness, we discover the strength and uniqueness of the child and celebrate this in a way that is not evaluative. Playfulness gives everyone a break from the trauma and its effects. It provides a vision of a larger context to a relationship—one that is not always problem saturated. When we can hold onto this vision, it builds hope in the present and for the future. No matter how hard a particular event or time is, if we can find some lightness to our experience through playfulness, we will have a sense that things are not hopeless.

If we think about the difference between being open and engaged or defensive, playful represents the open and engaged state. Play and humor are protective; the part of the brain that is activated in fun is different from the part of the brain that is activated in shame.

Children who have experienced developmental trauma find closeness and intimacy difficult. They fear feeling close and therefore avoid these states. Playful moments can provide them with an opportunity to realize that not all relationships are the same. Playfulness can give children positive emotion in small doses; a way of putting a toe into the water of relationship. It is affection-light and therefore not as threatening as deeper, more intimate moments. Children who are frightened of nurture and affection might experiment with closeness in play. It therefore provides the child with a different experience of a relationship, one in which she can safely experience being thought about and attended to through the joy and fascination of relational playfulness.

Children who cannot regulate emotion will find emotions alarming and in turn the emotions grow bigger: anger becomes rage, fear becomes terror, sadness becomes despair, and shame intensifies. It seems better to avoid emotional experience if this is how it feels. The positive emotions are also difficult to regulate: excitement, joy and love. When developmentally traumatized children experience these, they become anxious. Children will turn their backs on emotional experience that feels so out of control. Playfulness allows some positive emotion that these children can cope with. It is a way of promoting connection and security. This helps the child to discover that emotions are safe and that adults can help her with them, a coregulation that can begin the process of learning self-regulation. Playfulness can help the child to experience being happy, having moments of enjoyment, and to discover that it is safe to experience this with the parent—not manic happiness meant to hide from distress behind a mask of false positive affect, but true relational joy.

Playfulness is engaging but should not be used to avoid or minimize conflict or distress. It is not helpful to use humor as a distraction from talking about experience. Often this happens because the experience is real for the child but uncomfortable for the adults. This avoidance is not helpful for the child and is likely to lead to the experience of shame. The children need to experience acceptance for the whole of them, including the angrier or vulnerable parts. It is also important not to use playfulness to get a message across. This is quite common in some cultures; for example, the British will often disguise sarcasm behind a veneer of playful, a subtle way to let the child know something we do not want to talk about openly. The developmentally traumatized child is unlikely to get the message, but will experience the lack of emotional connection within this interaction. This is likely to strengthen mistrust and again increase feelings of shame.

Sometimes playfulness can be misjudged; the child experiences us as making fun of her. This will happen from time to time. It is important in these moments that the adult notices and repairs the relationship, taking responsibility for this error, then all will be well again.

Playful, then, is a fun, relational stance that demonstrates the child is liked and the adult wants to spend time with her. Shared joy and fun become less frightening and increase the emotional connection with the child while trust strengthens and mistrust weakens.

Acceptance

Acceptance is easy to convey to babies; it is a "no matter what" stance that allows the baby to experience unconditional love. As the child matures, this becomes tricky. We need to combine acceptance of the child with disapproval for some of the child's behaviors. We love you, but we don't like your behavior is a distinction that the developmentally traumatized child cannot make. Disapproval and correction of behavior is experienced as self not being good enough, and shame and mistrust are strengthened. If we want to help the child to understand this distinction, then we need to be very clear about our acceptance of her internal experience. We explicitly express that the child's inner life is accepted unconditionally and without evaluation. Your inner world of thoughts, feelings, wishes, fears, beliefs, and desires are neither right nor wrong, they just are. Behavior may need to be considered, with appropriate limits, to ensure that everyone is safe, but this is done without evaluation of the child's inner life. The child experiences her inner life, whether expressed verbally or nonverbally, as being safe with the therapist and the parent. The adults are not trying to change this experience but accept that it is what it is, and then demonstrate curiosity about it. This curiosity often leads from the current experience to an understanding of its roots in past experiences of relational trauma. By accepting the current experience, we are able to assist the child to understand how the current experience relates to prior traumatic experiences, to understand how those traumas still have an impact on the child today.

For example, the child might resist having a relationship with us. Understandably, we might want to work even harder to establish this relationship. This however increases the child's resistance. Instead accept, without evaluation, that this is what the child wants. Help the child to see that this makes sense to us given her past experience of relationships. We wonder about this, but we do not try to change the child's mind. If we evaluate the child's wish not to have a relationship; we are communicating a lack of acceptance. We try to convince the child not to be frightened; we try to talk her into the relationship she does not want. The child becomes defensive and mistrust strengthens. Instead, through establishing a reciprocal conversation, discover the story in the desire not to have a relationship; narrate this using a storytelling tone. Let acceptance be conveyed verbally, but also nonverbally. We are relaxed, and interested; our tone is light and conversational. We do not reject what the child is telling us, neither are we shocked by the experience she is revealing. As the child experiences our acceptance, she is likely to be more receptive to us. Trust and social engagement increase, and defensiveness decreases. The child can take the relationship one step at a time, without pressure to do what she is not yet ready to do. The therapist and parent embrace the child's mistrust with the same acceptance as any tentative trust the child is displaying. The child experiences that she is acceptable to us, and trust strengthens. The child develops confidence that when she needs to move back into mistrust for a while, this will be okay. With no motive to change the child and what she is experiencing, the child is freed to begin to change, as little by little her fear of relationships decreases.

Curiosity

Dyadic developmental psychotherapy and practice is about discovering stories with the children and their parents: narratives of experience. We all come to know the child better as her story unfolds. Curiosity is the search for the story. It helps us to find an alternative story, not the problem-saturated story that is full of shame, fear, and despair. A story instead of hope and renewal, as the child experiences herself as understood and accepted. Curiosity is an attitude of not knowing as the therapist or parent expresses an active, nonjudgmental interest in the experience of the child. This awakens the child's curiosity, and the story is created between them.

We will have our own story for the other, filled with our own assumptions, hopes, and expectations. Discovering another's story means not imposing this story upon him. Only then can we truly discover the other's experience. As this is received nonjudgmentally, the child gets an experience of being known and accepted. Sometimes the child misperceives our motives and experiences judgment when none is intended. Sometimes our desire for things to be different slips into the narrative anyway. The adult is alert to these moments so that he can quickly repair the relationship and return to the previous accepting stance.

Children are natural storytellers. Even before they can talk, they want to share their experience with others through their nonverbal conversations. The cocreation of a story is easy with a healthy child. Jess, whom we met at the beginning of this chapter, is absorbing stories as an infant, and as she matures she increasingly joins in. Jess and her parents will cocreate Jess's experience. Her curiosity is lively and animated. Even in dysregulation, she turns easily to the parents who wrap her story around her as they coregulate her experience. Jess gradually comes to regulate and reflect with ease.

How sad then to see this curiosity stifled in the developmentally traumatized child. With no one expressing interest in her internal experience early in life, she matures without being confident and safe enough to explore it now. Alternatively, others may have seen her inner life, but only through a lens of shame and rejection. She was shown that her thoughts, feelings, and wishes were wrong in some way; maybe that they were bad, selfish, or immature. No wonder she has stopped being curious. No wonder she avoids reciprocal conversations and avoids developing stories. No wonder she does not know what she feels, thinks, believes, or wants. We need to take the lead here, with our safe conversations and our wondering curiosity. Curiosity is not a fact-finding mission. We do not simply want to know what has happened, making assumptions about the meaning of this for the child. Instead, we want to make sense of this experience, understanding its current meaning and opening the possibility of cocreating new meanings. This becomes an act of discovery between us as the child becomes curious about this experience also. Neither good care nor good therapy is able to change the facts of the child's past. But good care and good therapy are able to assist the child in developing new meanings of these facts.

Empathy

If we had a universal pill to help us to feel better, then empathy would be one of its ingredients. Empathy helps us to communicate our acceptance and understanding while helping to regulate the child's experience. The child might become distressed; overwhelmed with remembering; fearful that she is becoming exposed in her badness for all to see. Whatever emotional response the child experiences as the story is being discovered, the therapist needs to coregulate this. Empathy provides an affective component that can resonate with the child's experience, coregulating where this experience is unsettling. Empathy also provides a reflective component, increasing understanding of the events. Only with both components can the dialogue continue with the child remaining open and engaged with us. As the therapist experiences empathy for the child, she actively communicates this both verbally and nonverbally. The child experiences the therapist as being with her in the exploration and does not feel alone in her experience. The therapist works hard to make sense of the child's experience, without becoming dysregulated by it. In this way, she can be actively present with the child, open to whatever experience is going to emerge next. The therapist remains empathetically present, neither minimizing nor trying to change what is emerging. The therapist is not afraid of the child's experience and does not try to reassure the child. The therapist is simply with the child in the experience; fully present affectively and reflectively. If the child chooses to move away from the experience, then this choice is accepted also with empathy and perhaps with some curiosity, but never with judgment. With this stance of acceptance and empathy, the child experiences safety and can find new meaning in what is being discovered.

Playfulness, acceptance, curiosity, and empathy can together help a child manage what would otherwise be a difficult experience. It is an attitude that is very natural for healthy adults to use with young children. Here is an example based on Kim Golding's recent experience while visiting a nature reserve in New Zealand with a friend and her 4-year-old granddaughter (with thanks to the family for allowing Kim to share this).

We had arrived at the kiwi house, which had to be in darkness to allow viewing of the kiwis.

> **SAMMY:** I don't want to go in there. Let's miss this one.
> **GRANDMOTHER:** Kim has come a long way to see the kiwis, let's go in.
> **SAMMY:** No, let's miss this one.
> **KIM:** Are you worried because it's dark? Kiwis like the dark, but we don't, do we? It's hard going into this one.

Sammy walks into the enclosure.

> **KIM:** Hey, look, here is a kiwi, can you see it eating?
> **SAMMY:** [Not wanting to stop] Let's go.
> **KIM:** Yes, it is very dark isn't it? You want to move through quickly, to get into the light again. Hey, Sammy, I just noticed your sneakers have lights on them, wow!

Sammy looks pleased and takes a few steps so that the lights are triggered.

> **KIM:** Hey, do you know what? We are alright. Your sneakers are going to show us the way through the dark!

Sammy looks pleased and walks through the enclosure without further worry.

This is just a simple example of a healthy and secure child being helped to manage a difficult experience. She was open to the adults around her, able to let them coregulate her emotion. A small moment in the day, with a brief story about being worried about the dark.

Developmentally traumatized children can experience curiosity and empathy as alarming. They are not used to being known and fear what might be discovered. Empathy makes them feel more vulnerable. They prefer to feel "strong" by detaching from the vulnerable emotions. The therapist needs to remain confident in the process, but be prepared to go slowly. Light empathy can gradually deepen and brief curiosity can be extended over time as the child becomes more comfortable with this. If the child reacts strongly to the empathetic responses from the therapist, it is important that the therapist reflect on this. It may be a sign that he needs to slow down. The child is allowing herself to become known; without acceptance of the need to go more slowly, this knowing will go underground again. Empathy conveys the acceptance for what is being discovered between them, as well as the awareness that these discoveries may create distress—which the child will not experience alone.

RECONSTRUCTING PACE IN THERAPY: A WAY OF BEING

Having considered the different elements of PACE, we now want to spend some time thinking about how the therapist can combine these into a whole. PACE is a way of being with others that allows emotional connection to develop. It is a way of engaging the other in the relationship in a way that feels natural and nonthreatening. In using PACE, we are demonstrating our deep interest in getting to know the other, understanding her strengths but also her vulnerabilities and accepting these equally. We are curious but nonjudgmental, exploring the current experience but also reflecting on the past when that appears relevant. We experience empathy in response to her distress and provide her with support and comfort. In this way, we discover the stories that are at the heart of the other and know her more completely as a result.

Notice that in relating with PACE, there is no motivation to change the other person; PACE is not a technique designed to make the other think or feel differently. It is a stance of radical acceptance. As I get to know you, I will accept you in all your parts. If I find I am uncomfortable with some of your parts, I will search for new understanding and empathy. In this way, I will accept those parts of you too, even at times when I cannot accept behaviors related to them. I will embrace and celebrate your trust; but I will equally embrace and empathize with your mistrust. This does mean putting a, sometimes understandable, tendency to fix to one side. We may hope for change to emerge out of the new experience of relationship that we are offering, but it is not an immediate goal.

Think of PACE as a circle (Figure 3.1). There is no beginning point; it is used as a whole. Acceptance is always present, curiosity and empathy interweave to carry the momentum of the story forward, and

Figure 3.1 PACE as a circular process. (Modified from figure M2.S1.3 in *Foundations for Attachment Training Resource* by Kim S. Golding, 2017, p. 107, with permission from Jessica Kingsley Publishers.)

playfulness comes in and out as appropriate. This playfulness conveys optimism that the child's trauma can be managed; it will not always dominate family life. This builds hope that change is possible with time and provides a positive response to the strengths that the therapist can see within the family. The *P* of PACE complements *ACE*; allowing breaks from what feels like the harder work in sessions. This gives everyone some light relief.

Sometimes we begin with a light acceptance and empathy, acknowledging where we perceive the child to be and expressing empathy for her challenges and distress. Our curiosity will then let us understand this more deeply, and we can express acceptance and empathy more deeply (Figure 3.2). Again, playfulness is there at moments to provide a connection that is fun and joyful, to lighten the experience of the relationship and allow the child to trust and feel safe, and thus to be able to join us in our exploration and discovery of her. The narrative is discovered together as the child experiences the relationship as regulating.

Figure 3.2 Deepening PACE. (Modified from figure M2.S1.4 in *Foundations for Attachment Training Resource* by Kim S. Golding, 2017, p. 107, with permission from Jessica Kingsley Publishers.)

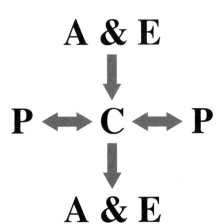

Figure 3.3 Beginning with playfulness.

Then again we might begin with playfulness, allowing us to connect around themes that are less threatening. As we have this playful engagement, a different theme might emerge, perhaps around something more difficult or significant in some way. The therapist connects with this theme in the same way as he did around the lighter theme, with deep interest and a storytelling style. *ACE* joins with the *P* to help the other feel safe in the exploration (Figure 3.3).

A developmentally traumatized child might respond to the "PACE-ful" therapist in a range of ways. This type of engagement is likely to feel strange, and maybe uncomfortable. Having someone want to know you can be alarming when a child perceives herself as no good; perhaps the child does not want to be discovered. However, it can also be strangely nice to find someone who accepts you no matter what. The child finds trust easier when her experience meets with acceptance. She finds that her life itself is easier when she does not feel so alone.

The therapist accepts the child in whatever response she displays. He introduces the child to the relationship slowly, responsively, and mindfully. He goes at a pace set by the child but is not afraid to lead the child further when appropriate. He strives to stay intersubjectively connected, able to know when he is going too slow or too fast, adjusting as he needs to. If he gets it wrong, he does not get anxious but strives to adjust to what the child needs, repairing the relationship along the way. He moves seamlessly between lighter, more playful themes and the harder, perhaps more significant ones, moving between these depending on what the child needs at the time. The child perceives no difference in what the therapist wants from her. PACE is experienced as an interest in being known and discovered in whatever topic is guiding the chat, with acceptance helping this to feel safe.

The storytelling stance is a constant, engaging the child with the therapist's interest in her. The attitude of PACE is communicated clearly through the nonverbal aspect of this storytelling. Storytelling lends itself to being playful, and acceptance is conveyed with the relaxed, meandering tone, communicating to the child that whatever she says or experiences is okay. Curiosity is experienced as nonjudgmental, because the questioning conveys a wondering rather than a "tell me why" tone. Wondering does not expect a response from the child and is therefore less anxiety-provoking than when a child is questioned directly. The therapist conveys empathy lightly or deeply depending on the emotion he gives to his voice, guided by his judgment of what the child is able to tolerate.

PACE, then, is a way of being when therapist and parents are with the child, building emotional connection without expectations of the child. The child discovers safety in connection and begins, slowly and tentatively, to experience trust in the adults. As she does this, she is learning and discovering new things about herself and the adults she is relating to: new learning that can eventually, and over time, reverse the mistrust that was a product of early experience.

Here is an example of PACE with a developmentally traumatized adolescent, Jaz, during a therapy session. She is supported by her key worker from the residential home where she is living.

THERAPIST: You are looking worried today. Is something bothering you?

The therapist pauses, allowing Jaz time to think about this and answer if she wants to. Jaz stares intently at her shoes and does not answer.

THERAPIST: I hear Joe is leaving. I guess that might have made you feel a bit wobbly?

JAZ: What? Are you a mind reader or something? You're a witch, you are.

THERAPIST: It feels like I'm a witch, does it? Is that because I am making guesses about what you might be feeling?

JAZ: You know what I am thinking. It's kind of freaky.

THERAPIST: That feels strange, does it, when I guess right? I bet your key workers do that too, sometimes, don't they?

JAZ: Yes, they're freaky too!

THERAPIST: I am thinking how strange that is for you, when people close to you seem to know what you are thinking and feeling. Does it worry you? When people know you like this, it's strange isn't it?

JAZ: Yes, too right!

THERAPIST: Strange, nice or strange, scary?

JAZ: A bit scary really. I don't want people to know what I am thinking.

THERAPIST: [Laughing] Yes, there are some thoughts we all want to keep to ourselves aren't there?

JAZ: Too right. I don't want him to know what I think [indicates key worker]. Loser!

KEY WORKER: [Playfully] Yep, keep your thoughts to yourself young lady. I'm not sure I want to know them!

THERAPIST: I wonder how come it is so strange for you, experiencing us being able to kind of tune in to you and get a sense of what you are feeling, and what you are thinking.

JAZ: [Shrugs] You're all just witches; a bunch of freaks.

THERAPIST: Hey Jaz, I've just thought of something. I am wondering what it was like for you when you were little. Perhaps your mom didn't know how to tune in to you. Maybe that's why it is strange now. Children get used to it, when they are little; their parents making sense of how they feel and what they think. Maybe that didn't happen for you?

JAZ: [Looking sad] I don't think my mom thought about anyone but herself. [With more anger] She was a total loser!

THERAPIST: That makes me feel sad, thinking of you as a real little girl, full of feelings and thoughts, and no one helping you to make sense of it. No wonder it feels a bit scary when we do it now. You don't know that people can do that, because you didn't experience it when you were little.

KEY WORKER: I never thought how hard this must be for you. We want to understand how you are feeling, but for you that just feels weird.

JAZ: [Looking thoughtful] Yes, I guess. [Shakes herself] You're still a bunch of freaks you know!

THERAPIST: Ah, freaks because we are getting to know and like you and are having some success with both?

JAZ: Yeah.

THERAPIST: Then I hope that you're mostly okay with our being freaks.

JAZ: I guess.

PACE FOR ALL

PACE will be optimized if it is built into the many relationships that surround the child and family. Therapist to parent, parents to each other and to their children, PACE will enhance and strengthen all relationships.

From the first meeting with the therapist, parents will be experiencing the attitude of PACE. It is this experience, explored more fully in Chapter 6, even more than education or reading about PACE that will help parents to adopt PACE as a way of being within their families.

If school staff can experience and be educated in the attitude of PACE, they will be able to bring this into the classroom. This will add to the experience of safety being provided for the children.

In addition, children and their families sit within teams of people: social care, education, and health. When these teams are trauma informed, attachment aware, and able to embrace PACE as an attitude, the child will truly be encountering a new world. Connection and safety will be all around. This will allow the child to develop and mature in healthy, therapeutic environments, maximizing the possibility that hurts from trauma can heal.

PACE starts at the bottom with the immediate relationships that the child is encountering with parents and teachers. PACE is also passed down from the top: manager to employee, supervisor to supervisee. When those surrounding you express PACE as they relate with you, it becomes much easier to experience PACE toward those you are surrounding. A manager "PACE-fully" supports a social worker; the social worker is then able to be "PACE-ful" to the foster carer; and the foster carer finds she can respond to her child with PACE, staying open and engaged when she would normally become defensive. PACE becomes a way of being within the communities surrounding the child, and safety builds for all.

PACE FOR SELF

In holding an attitude of PACE for others, it is important that we can also be "PACE-ful" toward ourselves: as therapists, as parents, as educators, as social workers. In being open to and aware of our own inner experience, we are more likely to be able to stay open and engaged to the inner experience of others. An attitude of PACE protects against defensive responding and helps us to find our way back when we do become defensive. Applying PACE to ourselves also helps us to forgive ourselves when we make mistakes, become defensive, or show misplaced irritation.

Playfulness is the lighter side of discovering our own inner experience. Looking inward does not need to be deep and serious; it can also be light and playful. In the playful, we can increase our feelings of confidence and experience more hope for the future.

Acceptance provides us with our own sense of psychological safety. Just as with the child, we accept our own inner experience without judgment. When we make mistakes, PACE enables us to accept them, learn from them, repair our relationship with the other, and not dwell in shame. If we find ourselves slipping into shame because we hold particular thoughts and feelings, we can seek out support from others. When we experience empathy for ourselves over our own hard times and challenges, we are able to address these and journey forward toward the life that we want. Acceptance and empathy toward ourselves can be further increased with our curiosity. As we curiously explore, we come to know ourselves more deeply without judgment and with compassion. The outcome of our curiosity and acceptance is to further deepen an empathetic attitude toward ourselves.

PACE for self will help us to maintain this way of being with others, even when their actions make it hard for us to remain open and engaged with them. We need to be compassionate toward ourselves, know that this is hard, and that we will falter. We have the capacity to recover, repair, and continue to offer the open and engaged relationships that we know will benefit us all in the long term.

CONCLUSION

Parenting children can be hard; parenting traumatized children is harder still. It is easy to get caught up in a cycle of defensive responding, whether therapist, practitioner, or parent. This strengthens the mistrust that the child has brought to the relationship. PACE is a way of being that can help us out of this cycle. With PACE for ourselves, each other, and for the children, we can all stay open and engaged, helping the child to discover a new way of being in the process. PACE is central in therapy, parenting, education, and in all the relationships surrounding ourselves and the children in our care. We will now turn our attention more deeply to the nature of the therapy, parenting, and specific settings where the child with developmental trauma needs to become engaged if she is to heal and thrive.

CHAPTER 4

The Experience of Dyadic Developmental Psychotherapy

Dyadic developmental psychotherapy (DDP) was developed for the treatment of children and young people who have experienced developmental trauma. Frequently, children who have been abused and neglected are not able to either resolve the traumatic relational events that they have experienced or develop secure attachment relationships with new caregivers. They are isolated and have limited abilities to enter into the healing and restorative conversations needed to develop new relational stories that can enrich and support them. They are locked in the fragmented sense of self and others that is permeated with fear and shame. The developmental abilities that they need for an integrated sense of self and a coherent narrative are not in place. The intent of DDP is to facilitate the development of these core skills.

Sometimes parents and professionals wonder what makes DDP effective in helping children to resolve past relational traumas. When we describe what makes DDP somewhat different from other therapies, we might receive puzzled looks. "That's it?"

"Aren't all therapies like that?" "You just talk with kids?" DDP is effective because it begins by not assuming that these children are safe, not assuming that they are able to have conversations, develop stories, possess a sense of self, and experience an ongoing coherent identity that we call a narrative. We do not assume that these skills are present, rather we assume that most likely they are not or only to a limited extent. Yet, these are the fundamentals needed for a healthy and full social and emotional life. Developmental trauma robbed them of those skills. DDP hopes to restore those skills or even assist children in developing them for the first time. Understanding how to develop those skills with the 3-, 5-, 10-, or 15-year-old with developmental trauma is to understand the experience of DDP.

The experience of DDP is modeled on the relational activities of the infant and parent that are central to the infant's integrated emotional, social, and cognitive development and that lead to his emerging autobiographical narrative. To get things started, the infant—and parent—need to experience a sense of *safety*. Without safety, there is little energy to discover each other within the relationship. With safety, initial patterns of interactions begin to emerge between parent and infant that are the foundation of all subsequent interactions. These are the synchronized nonverbal *conversations* that occur between them. These conversations gradually come to include words, which enable them to expand from the here-and-now into the past and the future. These conversations include blocks of meaning that evolve into *stories* that they tell each other. When the parent's nonverbal initiatives and responses become in synch with what the infant is telling him or her nonverbally over time and with repeated experiences, these conversations provide the structure and experience that allows the infant to begin to develop stories that hold the meanings of the experiences that they are having together. Through shared interests and joint activities, the stories form the infant's emerging *sense of self* that reflects the organization of the physical, emotional, social, and cognitive skills that she is developing. Patterns of priorities and experiences develop, and these become the young child's evolving *autobiographical narrative*. These abilities and activities are characteristic of relationships at all ages and are crucial for an individual's continuing psychological development.

Children who have experienced developmental trauma have great difficulty engaging in these relational activities. Focusing on either defensive self-protection or attacking the other, they avoid reciprocal conversations, regardless of the topic. Their only concern is establishing safety, and not being able to attain that, they are lost in a never-ending series of defensive behaviors that preclude healthy development. They judge all relationships as to whether or not the other person is a threat to their safety. Lacking relational success, they invariably see others as dangerous. Without the predictability of an integrated self, their ability to form a coherent narrative is restricted. This lack of coherence is the core feature of disorganized attachment patterns. It is for these traumatized children that DDP was developed.

CENTRAL COMPONENTS OF DDP

There are a number of features of DDP that support traumatized children in developing the relational skills they need to develop greater security, resolve the experiences of developmental trauma, and facilitate new relationships. The central components of DDP that enable this process to be successful will be presented first, then the process of DDP—moving from feeling safe to forming a coherent narrative—will be described.

PACE

Playfulness, acceptance, curiosity, and empathy (PACE) is described quite fully in Chapter 3 and will appear in other chapters as well. It is central to every stage of the experience of DDP. When the therapist is habitually in the attitude of PACE, it is much easier for her to initiate and maintain the intersubjective experience for both child and parent. PACE focuses on experience, which gives meaning to behavior. With PACE, the experiences and behaviors of both parent and child are important. The therapist accepts all experiences (even when limiting behavior), is curious about them, and often becomes engaged affectively with playfulness or empathy to the experience of the other.

PACE creates the here-and-now experience that needs to exist for DDP to be effective. The DDP therapist engages in conversations with the child and parent with complete acceptance and a deep curiosity about the meanings of events to parent or child. She understands and helps the developing stories to become more coherent and has a sense of empathetic compassion for the very hard times that the child has had and most likely continues to have. The DDP therapist conveys acceptance of each and every experience that the child expresses. Curiosity and empathy often work in alternating, cyclical patterns. The therapist wonders about a child's experience and then expresses empathy for aspects of it that appear to be stressful for the child. The deeper experience of the event then often leads to more curiosity, which in turn activates empathy again. Playfulness may or may not be central to the experience depending on the emotion being explored. Even when it is not central, playfulness will still be in the background, conveying a sense of lightness and confidence that the therapeutic process will reduce the impact of the trauma while creating hope for the future.

PACE enables the therapist to not only discover the strengths of the child but also to uncover her vulnerabilities that have been hidden by shame. It assists the therapist in deepening the quality of the conversation so that it contains new meanings and ways forward while reducing the need for self-protection. PACE helps the therapist to avoid making assumptions about what the child is thinking or feeling, or giving lectures, or moving too quickly to problem solving. It gives priority to safely discovering and sharing experiences and, from there, enabling the child to develop a coherent narrative.

Affective–Reflective Dialogue

The DDP therapist ensures that there are both affective and reflective aspects to the conversation. The affective part involves both the emotions associated with the events being discussed and the affective experiences and expressions of both the child and therapist as they talk together about those events. When the fear associated with a traumatic event is likely to be experienced by the child as he talks about it with the therapist, his experience of fear in the present is expressed affectively, and the therapist is attuned to it, matching the child affectively and co-regulating his fearful emotions. The coregulation of the child's affect by the therapist enables him to remain safe while exploring very stressful events.

When the emotions associated with the traumatic events are being coregulated, the child is much more able to successfully engage in the reflective parts of the conversation. This enables him to experience a traumatic event again through the therapist's mind, which does not contain the traumatic meanings given by the perpetrator. This developing ability to safely reflect allows the child to discover new meanings of the trauma. These meanings, containing little of the shame and terror of the previous meanings held by the child alone, will then be integrated into a more coherent narrative of self and other.

Follow–Lead–Follow

Both individuals contribute, alternating between initiating and responding, in the affective–reflective dialogue. The therapist follows any discussion led by the child, being interested in it, exploring it, adding to it. Within the rhythm of the conversation, the therapist also leads the child into areas of his life that he does not bring up. This involves any area that might be of some interest to the child, not simply the traumatic or stressful events. Then the therapist follows the child's response to that initiative, always taking this response as a guide to where the conversation goes next. When stressful events are embedded within the flow of the conversation about any and all aspects of the child's life, he will more easily explore the harder aspects of his life. These include stressful, shame-inducing events in day-to-day life with his parents as well as the original traumas underlying them. The unspoken message is that this conversation provides safe exploration with someone who understands you, cares for you, respects you, and who will not go faster than you are ready to go. After each conversation, the various traumatic events will not be nearly so terrifying, nor so shameful.

Often the therapist quite *actively takes the lead* in the conversation when she knows that the child does not have much experience with positive intersubjective conversations and may simply not know what to say. The therapist makes it easier by initiating a conversation about an event, person, or thing that the child is interested in rather than asking open-ended questions. The therapist prepares for meeting with the child by asking his parents about all aspects of his daily life. Then with the child, she explores the context of an event that he participated in and then begins exploring the ways in which he might have experienced the event. The therapist first wonders about the thoughts and feelings that might have been associated with the event. From there, the therapist wonders how the experience affected him. The therapist is following the affective and reflective expressions of the child, going more deeply and comprehensively into the events of his life, in order to help him to construct a story about them. All the while the unfolding of the event being explored is affecting the therapist too. The therapist and child are experiencing that past event together in the present—intersubjectively.

The therapist leads with curiosity that is entirely nonjudgmental about the child's thoughts, feelings, and wishes, all aspects of his inner life. Curiosity also involves an emotional component. The therapist frequently expresses curiosity about the child's life with nonverbal expressions that convey a full range of emotional meaning. Sometimes the voice tone, facial expressions, and gestures convey a nonintrusive, meandering interest in aspects of his life. Sometimes they convey a sense of urgency to understand. At other times, curiosity is embedded in empathy, when they are exploring something hard. When the non-verbal expressions suggest that it is something important, the child often concentrates more intensely on what the therapist is about to say. Another time, the therapist might hold the child's interest with an unexpected look and exclamation about something that he just thought of, leading to surprise and deeper engagement in the conversation. The therapist might bang his hand on the arm of the couch while exclaiming, "That's it! Now it makes sense!" In order for the therapist to initiate and maintain conversations with a quiet and defensive child, she needs to be a bit of a storyteller!

Interactive Repair

The DDP therapist is committed to repairing the relationship with the child (or parent) whenever there is a break, regardless of the source of the break. Sometimes the child becomes angry, defensive, or withdraws from the therapist because the therapist introduces a topic (no matter how sensitively and tentatively) that causes him to experience a negative emotional state. Similarly, a parent may experience the therapist's question or comment as being judgmental, critical, and as blaming her for the child's difficulties. This creates a lack of safety and trust toward the therapist and necessitates that the therapist repairs the break. The therapist makes the repair by focusing on the break using PACE.

When the therapist talks with the child with one intention in mind and the child's response indicates that it was not experienced as intended, the therapist notes the unintended impact and seeks to make a repair. This either changes the intention itself or the way in which it was conveyed. The child knows then that his response to the therapist matters. The child's wishes are not ignored. He is listened to and respected, and he is able to genuinely influence the therapist. The therapist's most basic intention is to cooperate with the child and to include the child's intentions in the conversation.

Sometimes too, the therapist initiates or responds to the child or parent in a nontherapeutic manner. At times, the therapist is not in synch with the child's inner life. At other times, the therapist may relate impatiently, be inattentive, be evaluative about the inner life of the child, or adopt an expert stance that fails to convey an interest in and respect for the experience of the child or parent. The therapist might be preoccupied by worries in her own life or be tired and irritable. All of these circumstances require that the therapist recognizes that she has stopped being intersubjectively connected and attuned and that she needs to actively acknowledge and make a repair to the therapeutic relationship before they can once more move forward together.

"Talking For" and "Talking About"

The therapist may assist the child in finding the words for his experiences by *"talking for" the child*. The therapist is aware of the child's nonverbal expressions and identifies them as being communications about which they might have a conversation. These nonverbal expressions are named, without judgment, showing him that the therapist is interested in his thoughts, feelings, and wishes. Sometimes the child is not aware of having thoughts or feelings being expressed nonverbally until the therapist gives words to them. Or he may be aware of thoughts and feelings but not feel safe enough to speak about what he is experiencing. Examples of comments by a therapist:

- "I wonder if you're thinking, 'I don't know if I want Susan to talk about this.'"
- "I think that right now you might want to say, 'I'm kind of worried about what will happen if I tell my mom what I thought then.'"
- "Right now, you might be running out of energy for this and want to say, 'Enough remembering what happened! It just makes me sad thinking about it, so why do it!'"

Sometimes she might *speak about the child* to the parent when the child is unwilling or unable to enter into a conversation with her. She might speak about the child in a way that the child would know that he is welcome to join the conversation, but is free not to as well. She might say to the parent "Right now your child might rather not engage in a conversation . . . and that's fine" to prevent the parent from becoming impatient with her child or worried that he is not working hard enough. She might wonder about the child's thoughts, without judging them in any way, as an invitation for him to tell the therapist something that he might be thinking about. Feeling safe while listening to the conversation between the therapist and parent, the child might then feel safe enough to express his experiences too. Even if he remains silent, he is likely to be listening and through his listening considering new aspects of himself.

The therapist thinking out loud is a variation of "talking about" the child in which he is safely and quietly receptive to what the therapist is saying. The therapist's voice is rhythmic and modulated, inviting the child to listen without conveying a sense of trying to influence him. It tends to be a safer experience than is silence, where the child is likely to imagine that the therapist is bored or annoyed with the child while also considering his future to be hopeless.

One example of thinking out loud involved a DDP therapist with an 11-year-old boy and his mother. His parents were divorced, and the boy seldom saw his father. He had mentioned to the therapist in the previous session that his father would be coming to town for a visit with him during the upcoming week, and he was anxious about it. The therapist forgot to bring that up during the initial part of this session. The boy was much quieter than usual. The therapist said, looking out the window, speaking to herself:

> THERAPIST: Jim is not talking very much today. I wonder why? Maybe he just wants me to get to know the silent parts of himself, which is fine. Maybe he wants to tell me something but he is not sure how to say it. Maybe he's just not in the mood to talk much today, which is also okay. No matter what his reasons, I'm fine, though I would feel badly if he's not talking because he's a bit annoyed with me for some reason and he's not sure about telling me. I wonder what he might be annoyed with me about, if he is. Oh . . . I just remembered, he told me last week about his dad visiting with him this week and I forgot to ask him how it went. Oh, my. Yes, he might be annoyed with me—for good reasons—since that visit was important to him, and he might think that I didn't care how it went. I feel sorry that I forgot. I wonder if he'll give me another chance? I guess the best thing to do is to ask him now how the visit went.

The therapist asked Jim, and Jim told her. He mentioned that he was somewhat disappointed with the visit because his father forgot to bring him a gift that he'd said he would give him the next time that he saw him.

Through these specific ways of supporting the child's ongoing participation in the therapy, the therapist and the child are able to engage in the relational sequence mentioned earlier, from safety and conversations to his autobiographical narrative. Of course, it all begins with safety.

THE PROCESS OF DDP

The process of DDP is modelled on the development of a secure attachment. Through the reciprocal interactions of the therapeutic relationship, the integration of the child's sense of self is facilitated. This process begins with safety.

Safety

We do not assume that children who experienced relational trauma but now live in safe homes with loving and committed parents will feel safe. Yet, they need to begin to feel safe if they are to begin to place the trauma behind them. Safety is the first experience that we want the children—whom we have come to know and care about—to have.

Developmental trauma is a relational trauma that involves the child's attachment relationships. The primary function of attachment is to provide safety for the child through a relationship with someone who is committed to his care. Developmental trauma violates the child's trust in the attachment figure. This also makes it unlikely that he will trust others. The simple passage of time will not develop the readiness to trust that is needed for a safe relationship. A therapy developed to address developmental trauma therefore needs to be continually aware of the child's need for safety within the relationship.

The open and engaged state that is central in the polyvagal theory of Stephen Porges is also central in creating and maintaining safety within the session. The therapist begins by not becoming defensive but rather remaining open and engaged when the child relates in the self-protective manner that he has developed in response to relational trauma. Lacking reciprocity in his manner of relating, the child is likely to often be oppositional, withdrawn, angry, argumentative, or evasive. Such actions often evoke a defensive response from others in the child's life that consists in anger, fear, giving up, or feelings of inadequacy. The therapist will need to be aware of her own tendency to respond in that way, accept it, inhibit it, and maintain the open and engaged state. She is likely to be able to do that if her own attachment patterns are secure, if she is able to engage the child with PACE, and if she is able to hold the child and his history in her mind with understanding and compassion. She needs as well to be aware of any particular challenges to her ability to remain open and engaged and to address them with reflection, supervision, and possibly therapy herself.

When the child's current parents are willing and able to provide safety for the child, they are present in the therapy sessions to provide comfort and support while any stressful themes are being explored. Safety for the parents is also important. If the parents do not feel safe, their child is not likely to feel safe either. If the parents feel blamed for the child's struggles, experience shame for their mistakes, or no longer experience empathy for their traumatized child, they will feel defensive and be less likely to support the child's safety in the session. The therapist needs to respect and accept the inner life of the parents while addressing any behaviors that might not be helping the child. At these times, the therapist may increase sessions with the parents alone.

The therapist is mindful of the importance of her nonverbal expressions in creating and maintaining the child's sense of safety. Her facial expressions are relaxed and engaging, her voice prosody is melodic and rhythmic, and her posture and gestures are open and invite the possibility of making a connection. These nonverbal expressions are not fixed and rigid but rather are responsive to any expressions of the child that suggest fear or mistrust. The therapist's nonverbal expressions invite an open and engaged relationship with the child but do not try to force it. These nonverbal communications from therapist to child are also authentic—being based on the therapist's genuine motivation to connect and to understand. Traumatized children and adolescents will be quick to notice anything that is forced, phony, or formulaic.

The therapist notices any cues that the child is not feeling safe. These include lack of eye contact, a harsh or agitated voice prosody, fidgeting, distracting, passive compliance, and day dreaming. A lack of safety for the child may have resulted from the therapist leading the discussion into themes that the child habitually avoids, in which case the therapist always sets aside the theme if it is compromising the child's sense of safety. The theme is not explored further until safety has been reestablished. If the child is having difficulty regulating stressful emotions, the therapist coregulates the affective expression of the emotion to assist the child in not becoming dysregulated. Sometimes the emotional intimacy that comes from having a conversation with the therapist and parent creates anxiety for the child. The therapist responds to the child then with PACE.

The DDP therapist is always aware of the degree to which the child is safe in his daily life. If the degree of safety in the child's current life is not strong, then the themes explored in therapy will be chosen to support his daily life (current shame, relationship conflicts and repair). The therapist avoids initiating exploration of past traumatic events until the child's home life is more settled so as not to further jeopardize current safety.

Only when child, parent, and therapist feel safe is DDP able to proceed.

Synchronized Nonverbal–Verbal Conversations

We do not assume that children who have experienced developmental trauma have the ability to engage in reciprocal conversations that are in synch both nonverbally and verbally. Not feeling safe—yes. But not being able to have a conversation? Are we sure? Yes, if we are referring to the reciprocal conversations that we first had as babies, then with our best friends, our partner, our children, and our parents again— where we place our minds together and wander about our memories, thoughts, feelings, dreams, with give and take, sharing and discovering, laughing and learning. The experience of DDP involves having conversations with children who struggle to have them, often through both lack of ability and lack of interest. Often when children do not engage in conversations, we tend to forget the need for reciprocity and resort to lectures, giving information, asking questions, or teaching specific skills. The experience of DDP involves finding ways to create reciprocal conversations with children who have not previously had such experiences.

The findings of infant intersubjectivity, described in Chapter 2, are our guide for developing interactions that enable the traumatized child to engage in synchronized nonverbal–verbal conversations with us. These findings clearly demonstrate how the parent and infant are engaged in extensive, reciprocal conversations about their affective, attentional, and intentional states long before the infant is able to use or understand words.

The DDP therapist is continually aware that these synchronized conversations represent the foundation of the child's therapeutic experience. From the instant that the therapist enters the waiting room, her eyes, face, voice, and gestures need to convey safety and also that she is glad to see the child, is interested in him, likes him, and is ready to give priority to his thoughts, feelings, and intentions. Without conscious awareness, the child will sense whether her view of him confirms or differs from his view of himself. If she seems distant, frustrated, or preoccupied, he will sense that he is boring, frustrating, or of little interest to her. That would confirm his sense of self, which most likely is full of shame and a sense of inadequacy.

If she does show that she is happy to see him and is interested in him, this most likely will be confusing. It will be hard for the child to easily dismiss his therapist's positive experience when she communicates it authentically through her nonverbal expressions. Because his negative self-concept is so all-pervasive, if she adopts a professional, detached, or neutral stance, he is likely to simply assume that she is inhibiting a negative experience of him. The therapist's active expression of her positive experience of the child will create confusion for him—a confusion that shakes his sense of certainty about his negative experience of himself. This leads to seeds of doubt about the meaning of the traumatic origins of his self-loathing and a beginning sense of curiosity over who else he might be.

When a therapist is assuming an intersubjective stance in which her thoughts, feelings, and intentions are affected by and are meant to have an influence on the inner life of the child, then the reciprocal conversations between the child and therapist are extremely important. The therapist's nonverbal–verbal affective expressions enable the child to know what impact his story is having on the therapist. At the same time, these expressions enable the therapist to coregulate those emotions of the child that are associated with the story being explored. The therapist's reflective—though still primarily nonverbal—expressions enable the therapist to join the child in understanding the story of his trauma and cocreating new meanings of the story.

As was mentioned in Chapter 2, intersubjective conversations have three major components. The first component is attunement, the synchronizing of affective states. When the therapist matches the affective expressions of the child's emotion with a congruent affective expression, this helps the child to regulate his emotion. The child is likely to experience the therapist's attuned response to his emotional state as compassion and understanding. Thus, if the child is angry and expressing it with intensity in his voice and a very stern facial expression, and the therapist matches this intensity *without being angry herself,* the child is likely to feel understood and at the same time become more regulated.

For example, 12-year-old Keith was being seen by a DDP therapist who introduced the topic of Keith's father into the dialogue. His father had abused and then abandoned Keith.

> KEITH: [Exclaiming] Don't you say anything about my father! You're just going to trash him like everyone else does, and I don't want to hear it!
>
> THERAPIST: [With a voice matching Keith's in rhythm and intensity] You think that I'm going to try to trash your father! Of course, you wouldn't want to talk about him if that's what I wanted to do—bring up everything wrong that he ever did!
>
> KEITH: [Voice now still intense, but also conveying more discouragement than anger] I know he screwed up! I get that! But, I don't like to be reminded of it all the time. I don't like to keep thinking about it and feeling like crap.
>
> THERAPIST: [Voice less intense and becoming quiet and gentle as she speaks] Yeah, I get that! Whatever he might have done wrong is likely to have caused you a lot of pain. Why feel it again? You've had so many hard times because of that stuff. So many hard times.
>
> KEITH: Yeah, I just wished it could have all worked out better.
>
> THERAPIST: [Matching Keith's sad and subdued expression] How much better things would have been.

The second component involves sharing awareness with the other. When the therapist conveys her experience of the person, object, or event that the child is focusing on, this enables the child to experience the therapist's perspective and integrate this into a new experience of it. For example, a child experienced abuse as meaning that he is bad. The therapist conveys her experience—nonverbally and verbally— which is that the parent betrayed the child's trust. The child is now open to reexperiencing the memory of the abuse with new possible meanings. The child is more likely to focus his awareness on difficult themes when the therapist maintains a rhythmic, storytelling voice, clearly conveying empathy in her tone. The child is also likely to join the therapist in attending to a theme that the therapist initiates if they take turns in deciding what they will have a conversation about and whether the child goes first.

The third component involves having complementary intentions about the current joint activity. We call this *cooperation*, and it enables the child to be more readily influenced by the mind of the therapist. In order for the conversation to contain reciprocal, complementary intentions, the therapist will have to be sure that she holds an intention that the child is likely to accept. If the therapist wants to change the child, she is likely to meet resistance. If, however, the therapist simply has the intention to get to know the child, cooperation and engagement is much more likely. As the therapist comes to discover the child, her developing knowledge is then likely to influence the child's developing knowledge of himself. The abused child often experiences habitual loneliness while also feeling anxious about being known. He is more willing to become known, and less alone, when confident that his therapist will not judge him and is truly interested in all of him, not just his traumas.

As the therapist blends the nonverbal and verbal aspects of the conversation, frequently it will be the nonverbal component that holds the child's attention, evokes his trust in the therapist, and conveys much of the affective meaning of the conversation. The components of PACE are communicated most strongly nonverbally. The therapist's voice tone and facial expressions convey whether the therapist is accepting or evaluating the child while exploring an event in his life. Because of these same nonverbal expressions, the therapist's curiosity is likely to be seen as simply being a desire to understand the child's experience.

At the start of a therapy session unless the child immediately gives expression to strong emotions or an expressed need to explore a particular stressful theme, the therapist leads the initial conversation into light, interesting, enjoyable topics that are likely to engage the child. The therapist must not fake an interest in these topics but rather must be genuinely interested in the child's perspective and experience of whatever is being discussed. This early process enables a synchronized connection to emerge between the child and therapist that creates momentum for further connections between them. The child is likely to feel safe, comfortable, and engaged with the therapist. Without pausing or breaking the momentum or conversational tone, the therapist then introduces a more stressful theme, and often the child remains engaged in the dialogue, which now involves this more difficult topic. It is important that the therapist maintains the same relaxed, open and engaged vocal quality in her voice during this transition to the new theme rather than becoming serious and tense.

Both individuals contribute, alternating between initiating and responding, in the affective–reflective conversation. The therapist follows any discussion led by the child, being interested in it, exploring it, adding to it. Within the rhythm of the conversation, the therapist also leads the child into areas of his life that the child does not bring up. This involves any area of the child's life, not simply the traumatic or stressful events. Sometimes the child does not speak of positive events, often because they are not congruent with his sense of shame—they do not "fit" his sense of who he is and what he deserves. The therapist follows the child's response to her initiatives, always taking this response as a guide to where the conversation goes next. When stressful events are embedded within the flow of the conversation about any and all aspects of the child's life, the child is likely to naturally explore the harder aspects of his life, including stressful, shame-inducing events in day-to-day life with his parents as well as the original traumas underlying them. The unspoken message is: "This conversation provides safe exploration with someone who understands you, cares for you, respects you, and who will not go faster than you are ready to go." After such a conversation, the trauma will not be nearly so terrifying, nor so shameful.

Now for an example of a DDP session with a teenager who was not interested in having a synchronized conversation with his therapist.

Stephen, age 16, had been in foster care for 11 years and was known for his defensive and abrasive manner of relating. He had a knack for setting a tone that caused others to feel inadequate and to become tense, annoyed, or to feel like giving up. He wasted no time trying to evoke one or more of those feelings with Tim, the DDP therapist, after Tim greeted him with a relaxed, open, and engaged welcome when Stephen and his social worker came to his office.

"Like you really give a damn how I'm doing!"

Matching the rhythm and intensity of Stephen's voice while staying open and engaged, Tim replied, "And if I don't care at all about you and how you're doing, you're not going to want to be here at all, and you wouldn't trust me if I told you what day of the week it was!"

"You got that right so let's end this quick!"

"But what if I do care? Then I would want to get to know you."

"Well I don't want to know you! I don't need you."

"It seems to me that you've been on your own your whole life in big ways, and it might do you some good if someone got to know you and maybe helped you to figure out what you want—what you think is best for you."

"I've been on my own my whole damn life—and I'm going to keep it that way!" What was noticeable now was Stephen's voice. It remained challenging, but it was also conversational—in sync. He talked *and* listened, and he had integrated Tim's words into his response. Tim's matched affective responses fostered a conversation with Stephen even though Stephen was still defensive.

"I get why you might want to! You've survived so far by taking care of yourself, relying on yourself. I'm not saying that you should stop doing that. I'm just wondering why you also can't let someone in sometimes. Get to know you a bit—what's the harm in that?"

"If I did I certainly wouldn't pick an old fart like you."

"That makes some sense. I wonder too if it would make sense to pick someone who won't use you, or take from you, or try to change you? Someone who accepts you as you are and tries to help you to figure out what you want in life, who is the person you want to be." Tim's responses now were less intense than were Stephen's. Tim was gently leading him into a more reflective state of mind, seeing if Stephen might become open to more vulnerable experiences.

"What could you help me with! You know nothing about my life." Stephen is actually a bit less defensive, being more open to Tim's experience.

"I know that under your anger and mistrust you probably have times where you have doubts and want to give up. I don't know the pain that you went through, but I do know about hard times and I know about ways to make hard times—no matter what they are—not become too much for us. Help me to understand the parts that I don't know." Tim is inviting more vulnerability.

"My parents sucked! Nothing you say is going to change that!" Stephen's defensive stance comes forward again.

"What are the hardest parts about being the son of parents who sucked?"

"That they didn't care about me" (said in a detached but less defensive way).

"Ah . . . so you had to find a way to be strong all the time. While inside you might have wanted to scream and cry."

"I don't cry!" (The therapist moved forward too far into vulnerable states; the word *cry* evoked a defensive response from Stephen.)

"Then tell me how you learned not to cry. And how you made the sadness go away."

"I stayed strong by not thinking about anything."

"I'm glad that you did that. You couldn't rely on anyone so you had to stay strong by yourself. It would have been so much harder if you had thought about things by yourself. I wonder, if you were able to trust someone, you might figure out how you can have a good life, doing things with people you like, who are important to you, in spite of having parents who sucked."

"Like that's going to happen" (said with some sadness, not anger).

"Maybe it will, maybe we can figure out a way."

"Maybe."

By now the conversation was becoming synchronized—with matched affect—around Stephen's vulnerable experiences. He was more open and engaged and less defensive. The conversation also had a meandering flow to it that held their attention. Tim accepted whatever Stephen said and was often curious about it. When there was an opening, Tim expressed empathy for his hard times. Tim invited Stephen into playfulness, to lighten up the discussion a bit and to suggest that he was not just interested in talking about problems. Tim wanted to know him—all of him—and he wanted to chat about routine things in life and just create a connection with him. Trusting the rhythm of the affective–reflective dialogue, Tim would let the content emerge as it might, inviting those reluctant bits to enter when they seemed ready.

The open and engaged attitude is central in maintaining the momentum of reciprocal conversations. But there also need to be pauses when the child and therapist are simply feeling relaxed and connected. These pauses may be initiated by the child, who simply becomes less engaged in the conversation. In this case, the therapist accepts that the child's attention is moving away from the conversation. The child might simply be relaxing between themes in the conversation or going inward, reflecting a bit on what was just explored or something else entirely. There is a natural ebb and flow, engagement and disengagement in all conversations. Feeling relaxed and connected, the child may simply be consolidating the transforming explorations that just occurred—or the child might simply feel like "hanging out" for a bit.

Creating Stories

If a child who experienced relational trauma does not feel safe and has difficulty engaging in conversations, might we assume that she will have great difficulty with creating stories that make sense of the events of her life? Yes. Relational trauma has brought to her pervasive experiences of shame and fear that have greatly limited her ability to connect words to her inner life as well as to see—or rely on—what is offered in new relationships. DDP is a place where stories are created with this child that involve discovering her own mind and heart and sharing it with the newly discovered mind and heart of someone else.

Developmental trauma—relational trauma involving our attachment figures —does not stop traumatizing the child when the original traumatic events are stopped. The stories that the child developed to make sense of the traumas—I'm bad, lazy, unlovable or my parents are mean, cruel, not worthy of trust—are still present in the child's mind and are giving meaning to current events and behaviors. Each act of the child—angry outbursts, lying, defiance, not sharing—confirms the original stories that were developed by the child secondary to the trauma. Each act of the new parents—saying "no," not being available, expecting certain behaviors—confirms the original stories. His symptoms and defenses, his parents' routine discipline, frustrations, and expectations—all confirm the stories developed by the child after the original relational trauma. No wonder it is hard to convince him that he did not deserve to be abused and neglected when the frustrations of daily living and his challenging behaviors caused by the trauma confirm in his mind (a mind organized around shame and mistrust) that he did deserve to be abused and neglected.

Upon the foundation of having conversations with children, the DDP therapist then begins to build stories that question the trauma-based stories of the child's past. During the experience of the traumatic event, the child absorbed meanings from the mind of the abuser that diminished his sense of self-worth while leaving him with a fractured, poorly integrated sense of self. The child is likely to have created a story of the event that had embedded in it deep personal shame, a sense of hopelessness, and a mistrust of others. The details of his current life find a place within the trauma-organized story. When the foster parent shows affection for her foster child, who is convinced that he is unlovable, the child will change the meaning of the affection to conform to his trauma-based story. The foster child will believe that the affection is a sign of various other intentions such as his foster parent doing her job, manipulating the child to be good, or tricking the child into trusting her so that she is better able to hurt him in the future. This child needs a new story that has a place where affection is a sign that the foster parent likes and enjoys him because he is actually lovable. After creating doubts about the validity of the trauma-based story, there will be room in the child's mind for considering a new story.

As the DDP therapist first engages the child in therapy, her focus is on establishing the child's sense of safety and assisting him in feeling safe while he develops the readiness and ability to become engaged in synchronized conversations. As child and therapist become engaged in these reciprocal dialogues, this experience itself facilitates the child's general social and emotional development, being similar to the experience of the synchronized intersubjective conversations between parent and infant. Within the momentum of these conversations, the therapist highlights or introduces blocks of meaning as they explore recent events in the child's life.

For example, as they chat about the family having gone on a picnic, the therapist might explore the activities that they did and imagine that they might have been excited, felt happy, and experienced some surprises and laughter. The therapist might also imagine that some family members enjoyed one thing and others enjoyed a different thing. There might be a question about what they had to eat and whether or not it was the child's favorite food. If not, what is? Was everyone tired at the end of the day? Plans for future picnics? Want to do anything differently the next time? At the end of the session, the therapist might reflect on the picnic and place it in the context of other things that the family liked to do together.

The child most likely does not have much experience of reflecting on events of his life with regard to thoughts, feelings, and wishes that are associated with those events. He has less experience sharing with others what those events mean to him. Through engaging in conversations like this one about the picnic, the child is developing his interest and ability in having conversations with his family about routine events of his life. This in turn will make those events more noteworthy, and his relationships with the others who shared those events with him will take on special meanings.

In the above story of the picnic, the therapist may have simply brought out the thoughts and feelings of the various family members associated with the events. That in itself would have significant value for a child who was not used to intersubjective conversations about the events of his life. However, the therapist might also choose to explore the experiences further for deeper or more complex meanings. For example, in first developing the story, they might have talked about how when dad was cooking the hamburgers, mom had given dad's dessert to the kids because she said that he ate too many sweets and they were doing him a favor. When he found out, he chased mom around the campground, but he slipped and fell in some mud. The therapist might choose to wonder about what that sequence might mean. Why wasn't dad angry with them for eating his dessert? Why did mom let them eat dessert before eating their hamburgers? Was mom serious about dad needing to eat less sweets? Why did it matter to her? Did she worry about dad's health? Do they really love each other? Why do they? Do they ever really get angry at each other? What is that like? Do the kids worry that they might stop loving each other? Do they tease each other much? Is it ever scary? Do they laugh a lot? What does it mean that they laugh a lot? Do they feel closer to each other when laughing or when hugging? What's it like living in a family where people enjoy being with each other and having fun together so much? Does he hug or tease mom or dad more? Why? The therapist might wonder about many things associated with one event. Each possibility might lead to another 10 things to wonder about. Each act of wondering might help the child to develop the ability to create new intersubjective stories, with increasingly more complex meanings, to reflect the events happening in his new family.

Or, the therapist might choose to use the recent event (the picnic) to contrast the child's life now with the life in which he developed his old story about himself and his first family in which he experienced developmental trauma. Did he ever go on picnics in his first home? Did he do other things that were a lot of fun? What would his first father have done if his mother had given his father's dessert to him to eat? Did he recall being very happy in his first home? Did he get many hugs? Did he think that it was his fault—that there was something wrong with him or that he might be bad? Here the therapist is helping the child to reflect on the story he might have had while living with his first parents, who traumatized him or failed to protect him from trauma.

In developing these stories with the child, the therapist is being curious without judgment about what the child thought or felt. She is encouraging the child to be curious, to reflect, and to start to think of what story he might have developed to make sense of his life that contained relational trauma—a story that would have accounted for his fears, anger, loneliness, shame, as well as his behaviors and those of his parents.

As the child reflected on that story, the therapist might wonder about other possible meanings to account for what happened and for the very hard experiences that he had. Together, the therapist and child are cocreating a new story to account for those past events. Maybe a 4-year-old boy had not been bad when he was locked in a closet. Maybe he was not selfish and did not deserve to be slapped for crying when he wanted a toy that his brother had. Such reflections might well evoke vulnerable feelings of fear, sadness, or shame that the therapist would need to be sensitive to in order to coregulate whatever distress the child might be experiencing while recalling those events. In this way, the child is able to safely wonder about the past and cocreate new meanings to account for the traumatic events that he experienced. Here the therapist is not trying to talk the child out of his old story. The therapist simply wonders about it, leaving room for doubts about its validity and openings for new meanings and new stories.

As the old story becomes more open to new meanings, there is likely to be greater openness for the child to develop a new story to account for the events of his new home. If he had not been stupid then, maybe now when his current parents seem proud of something that he does, maybe he is able to experience his strengths more fully. If he had not been unlovable then, maybe when his adoptive parents tell him that they love him, they are telling the truth. Maybe he is lovable. The child does not learn that he has these strengths by being verbally told that he has them. Rather, he learns that he has them through the intersubjective experiences that his parents have of him, experiences that gradually become formed into a story.

As the therapist is focusing on having a reciprocal conversation with a child, she is aware of the forward movement of the dialogue as it pulls various events and relationships into a pattern that is the opening of a story. This is the horizontal movement of the conversation. As she then focuses on developing the story, she is engaged more in a vertical movement in the conversation in which she goes more deeply into the meanings of the events as well as the thoughts, feelings, and wishes associated with the events.

Ben is a 10-year-old foster boy who is in his third session of DDP with his foster father, Louis. Early in the session, the therapist spoke to Ben about the reasons that he came into foster care when he was 4 years old. The therapist spoke of a day when a neighbor stopped by when Ben was home with his father. While his father prepared some coffee, Ben was excited over the interest that the neighbor showed in him. When his father returned to the living room, Ben accidentally spilled the coffee on his father. His father yelled, swore at Ben, and slapped him across the face. He then dragged Ben down the hall and locked him in the closet. When the neighbor criticized his father, his father told him to leave. The neighbor went home and called the police. When they came to the house, the police saw the bruise on Ben's face. His father would not cooperate with them, and they took Ben to the office of a social worker. Later that afternoon when Ben's parents still would not cooperate, Ben entered foster care. Over the next 3 years, Ben lived in three foster homes, but his parents did not cooperate with efforts to have him returned to their care. For the most recent 3 years, Ben has been in long-term foster care with Louis and Angela, and there has been very little contact with his parents.

The DDP therapist told the story gently and with empathy, conveying as well the stress that Ben must have felt when his father hit, swore at, and locked him in the closet. Ben sat quietly, clearly somewhat sad while hearing this story that he most certainly had some explicit memories about. When the therapist asked if it made sense why he came into foster care, Ben replied that it did. When asked how it made sense, Ben said simply, "I was bad."

Often when an abusive event is recalled in therapy, the child becomes anxious as the event is being explored. The therapist constantly monitored Ben's nonverbal expressions as he was listening to her relate the event to be certain that he was able to regulate any emerging anxiety or shame. She also focused on her own nonverbal expressions as she related the event. Her gentle and empathetic expressions provided Ben with support in dealing with the stressful themes, and this helped to ensure his safety. Ben's sense of safety, in turn, enabled him to be aware of and communicate his experience of shame associated with that event. Why shame? Because the meaning of that event—and most likely many similar events prior to it—came from the perpetrator of the event. The meaning was expressed by the perpetrator's intense nonverbal expressions of rage, and possibly disgust or contempt, along with any swear words or destructive names and threats. In situations where a child is being traumatized by his own parents, the impact of the trauma is especially profound because the terror experienced is joined with shame. The child is led to shame through the parent's story about his child's behavior and his response. In healthy parent–child relationships, the child discovers meanings of love, joy, pride, and confidence through intersubjective stories that the child and his parents create together. In such relationships, even when there is conflict, the child often experiences understanding and empathy, and trusts that the parent's motives are well meaning. In situations of maltreatment, the child discovers meanings that he is bad, unlovable, stupid, or selfish through the story imposed on the event by the parent.

How might the DDP therapist help Ben? Not through reason about child abuse and arguments that he was not bad. The therapist's reason cannot match the power of the story forced on the child by the maltreating parent. A child learns a new story about self and events that he is exposed to primarily through intersubjective conversations with adults. Ben needed the therapist's intersubjective conversation about the event involving his spilling the coffee and being hit, sworn at, and locked in the closet. So, the therapist told a new story about the event, this time conveying *her experience* of that event so that Ben could then have an intersubjective experience of it with a person other than his father. She conveyed her experience primarily nonverbally, expressing her confusion, shock, sadness, and distress over what had happened. A sample of what she said over the next 10 minutes follows:

THERAPIST: Oh, Ben! You were having such a good time playing with the neighbor! Such a good time! You were only 4 and quite a bouncy and active boy—and you bumped the table and the coffee spilled on your dad, and you might have said "Dad! I'm sorry! I'm sorry! I didn't mean to!" and your dad slapped you across the face! Oh no! He slapped you across the face! Oh no! This is your dad! Your dad! You must have gotten so scared! You didn't feel safe with your dad! You were so scared! And then, he screamed, and took your arm, and pulled you, dragged you, down the hall! You must have been so scared, maybe crying or maybe too scared to cry! And pushed you into the closet, and slammed the door! And it was so dark in the closet! So dark! Oh, Ben, how hard that must have been! And then you thought that it was your fault! You were *bad*! And that might have made it worse!

By the end of this story Ben was crying, and he allowed his foster father to put his arm around him.

When the DDP therapist expressed her subjective experience of that event to him within an intersubjective story, Ben now had her experience along with that of his father. He had thought that his father's experience was an objective reality, not a subjective experience. Now that there were two experiences of the same event, Ben was given the mental space to begin to question his father's experience. The therapist did not say that his father was a bad person, but she did convey confusion over why his father might have done what he did to Ben and her belief that what his father's actions did hurt Ben. But the session was not yet finished. There was another person present whose experience of that event might create further doubts about the meaning of the event expressed by Ben's father.

The therapist turned to Louis and asked him how he made sense of what had happened. Louis gave his experience in a manner that was similar to what she expressed. His voice also conveyed confusion over what Ben's father had done, sadness that he had been hurt so badly and also that Ben thought that it was his fault. He did not use arguments nor say that Ben's father was a bad person. After expressing empathy, Louis said how he would have responded to that event and how he would respond in the future when Ben does something wrong. Now Louis had tears and he hugged Ben tightly. Later that evening, Ben's foster mother, Angela, conveyed her subjective experience, also experienced by Ben intersubjectively.

Ben now had four intersubjective experiences of that abusive event: those of his father, his therapist, Louis, and Angela. What was "real"? Ben now had the opportunity to develop his own coherent story of that event, being influenced by four other stories, not restricted to that of the perpetrator. Over time, Ben was able to develop new meanings of other abusive events that he had experienced with his parents. And he was able to develop new meanings about his foster parents' discipline, about his own "misbehaviors," and about his foster parents' signs of love and care for him. These new meanings contained a story for Ben about his relationship with his foster parents that was not embedded in shame and mistrust.

The DDP therapist cocreates new stories of the past and present as they emerge from conversations that are of special relevance to the child. The content of these stories is taken from both the child's history as well as the child's felt sense of what is important to him in the present. The child's current experiences and meanings are the door-openers to the stories that are guiding the child's daily actions.

Through synchronized conversations, there is an increased ability and opportunity for the child to develop stories about the current events in his life. As he is more comfortable with this new storytelling skill, he is able to wonder about deeper meanings and begin to be curious about the possibilities presented to him now. He is also likely to be more able to contrast the stories that are being cocreated in the present with the therapist and adoptive parents and the past stories that had largely been created for him by those who had traumatized him.

An Integrative Sense of Self

The child who has experienced developmental trauma is the child whose sense of self is fragmented and disorganized. Because of terror, shame, and the lack of opportunity, that child lacked sufficient relationships that would generate safety and the intersubjective conversations and stories needed for the integration of a sense of self. The initial reciprocal nonverbal and verbal conversations proved to be shameful and to create terror, causing the child to avoid those experiences and not develop the relational skills needed to engage in future conversations. Early stories involving shame of self and mistrust of others shut down the child's early interest in learning about himself and the world and his development of stories when the opportunity came that would involve pride, comfort, joy, exploration, and discovery.

Once the child consistently begins to feel safe and is able to engage in synchronized conversations, he is safe to explore the interpersonal world. This leads to the development of new stories about the meanings of past traumatic events and about the current behaviors of both himself and his caregivers. As all of these stories find places in his mind, he begins the process of developing a new, more integrated sense of self. Developing the ability and readiness to enter into conversations and organize stories is the hardest part of DDP. That's where the action is! He is learning to use his mind differently—allowing it to interact with other minds—and he is learning to trust the process of exploring the meanings of his own behaviors and the behaviors of others. As the process occurs again and again, involving all sorts of events, trust gradually develops. He is trusting the initiatives and responses of his parents and therapist. And he is also trusting that he will be able to construct a self that is capable of experiencing both comfort and joy.

The child is discovering that "who he is" is not a given, objective reality defined by those who traumatized him in the past. "Who he is" is a work in progress, an evolving sense of himself that is emerging from the ongoing intersubjective experiences that he has with his new parents and therapist. The most fundamental new realization about himself is that "who he is" is inherently of such worth and interest to them that he actually resides in the minds of his caregivers and therapist. What he thinks, feels, and wants is of value to his parents, and they hold this awareness of him and his inner life in mind while making decisions about what is best for him and the family. As he resides safely in their mind, they are discovering qualities that reflect their emerging sense of who he is and who he is capable of being. "He" is lovable, interesting, enjoyable, clever, delightful. "He" is also vulnerable, scared, lonely, angry, and confused. As he lives with them and shares experiences with them, he is discovering that all of these characteristics are accepted by them as they come to know and care for him. He is developing a sense of self that is becoming whole and integrative, reflecting that he is loved and cared for unconditionally, even if some of his behaviors are evaluated and limited.

As the child participates in DDP, he is discovering a sense of self that includes his challenging behaviors, his cautious avoidance, and his flights into dissociation. Being accepted unconditionally, all of his experiences are able to enter into his developing sense of self. He no longer needs to defend against and deny in shame aspects of self that are now welcome into his sense of self. Because no experiences need to be rejected and denied, he is able to develop a self that is able to contain past, present, and future experiences. This new integrative self in turn demonstrates the resilience and the open and engaged stance needed to develop new stories from the events that the child is encountering.

This sense of self is emerging from the intersubjective experiences that the child is having with his parents and DDP therapist. Because of the nature of intersubjectivity—an essential component of these synchronized conversations and emerging stories—the child *knows* that his therapist and parents are responding to qualities of who he is. Their responses are not the results of obligations or acts of charity. They are both discovering and responding to qualities in him. These same qualities cause them to initiate interactions with him and to seek his responses. He is having an impact on them just as they are having an impact on him. As these patterns of conversations and emerging stories continue, the integrating dynamic is his new sense of self.

Of course, as the child makes progress in developing this new sense of self, he will encounter stressful events and difficult days where nothing seems to be going well. He will be at risk for doubts about his ability to really be able to have a much better life than he experienced in his traumatic life in the past. He will be vulnerable to experiencing shame again that causes him to think that lasting change is hopeless. The process where the child is able to accept his vulnerabilities and challenges, his doubts and his behaviors that reflect habits developed in the past, will enable the child to go through those hard times and resume his path of progress and development. This process where he slips and is able to stand again will be greatly enhanced when his new parents are standing with him, experiencing all of him with PACE.

A Coherent Autobiographical Narrative

Over time, the developing conversations, stories, and an integrated sense of self enable the child to create a coherent autobiographical narrative. No longer is she ashamed or afraid of remembering events from her past. No longer are there gaps in her memory associated with the relational traumas that she experienced. Her memory of those events may well evoke anger, sadness, or fear, but not rage, despair, or terror. They do not lead to emotional dysregulation or to a complex web of defenses and "symptoms" needed to maintain some sense of precarious safety.

The narrative that the child developed in response to trauma was rigid, having been formed at first when the child was open and engaged with her original parents. In response to their betrayal of her trust, she tried desperately to protect her delicate sense of self by doing what she could to avoid synchronized conversations with them. The resultant sense of self and developing narrative emerged from repetitive efforts to survive defensively. Gaps emerged in her perceptions, behavioral possibilities, memories, and abilities, especially those associated with self-worth and trust.

A coherent narrative is able to form not by denying and avoiding thoughts about the traumatic events and relationships of her past but rather by having those events open to her comprehensive awareness of herself without shame or terror. She is able to make sense of the differing stories that she learned during her years of trauma and her years of good care. She is able to understand the causes, experiences, and consequences of mistrusting others as she did in the past as well as the causes, experiences, and consequences of her trusting her new parents and other safe people in her life. Being open and engaged with past memories and current events and relationships, she is increasingly able to form a more consistent and comprehensive narrative. Her narrative is both coherent and flexible, evolving and guiding her development into the future.

FULLY DISCOVERING AND ACCEPTING JAMES, AN ADOPTED ADOLESCENT

James was placed with his adoptive parents, Lucy and Jon, shortly before his 12th birthday. During his first 11 years, he had experienced developmental trauma in many ways and with many caregivers. With his mother and two of her partners, he had experienced ongoing neglect and periodic physical abuse during his first 5 years. He lived in his first foster home for the next 2 years and, because his foster carers said that there were no problems, the social worker's contact with James was very limited. Then his school made a referral saying that he was often dirty and hungry and seemed to be especially frightened whenever he was corrected. This led to an investigation, which found that James was not receiving the care that he needed. When interviewed, two older foster kids living in that home also described very marginal care and punitive discipline.

During the next 4 years, James lived in three more foster placements. He was often challenging, being either oppositional or withdrawn and difficult to connect with. There were periods where he seemed happy and engaging, but these did not last long. The first two of these placements seemed to provide good care, but James did not show consistent progress in his functioning, and his carers found his anger too difficult for them to manage. In his final foster placement of 18 months, he received excellent care and at times he seemed to respond to his foster carers' energy, structure, and interest in him. When efforts intensified to find him an adoptive home, he withdrew and seemed indifferent. Why should he finally figure out how to get close to parents when he was going to be moving again?

James was black. Only the third of his four foster placements was with a black family. The other three were white families, as was the family that was planning to adopt him. His social worker, Ruth, made many efforts to find a suitable black family where James could live, but she was unable to find one. She wished that greater efforts were made to reach out to the black community for suitable placements. He needed a stable home, and she hoped that it would be possible for him to find that with Jon and Lucy in spite of their race.

Jon and Lucy

Jon and Lucy were in their early forties. They had been married for 15 years. They had a 13-year-old daughter, Tara, and they began thinking about adoption a few years earlier when they were told that they were unlikely to have another biological child. Jon was the human resources manager for a midsize company, and Lucy taught literature and coached cross-country at the local high school. Lucy was closer to her family of origin than Jon was with his. Jon described himself as having lived in a "typical two-child family in a typical midwestern city." He and his brother did not see each other often, nor did either see their parents more than a few times a year. There were no major conflicts; they just were not that close. Jon did not think that he had a difficult childhood, though he often felt lonely and wished that they had been closer. He remembered envying his best friend's easier relationship with his parents—an openness that didn't seem possible with his parents. Lucy was much closer to her parents and her three siblings. She recalled a lot of conflicts growing up but a lot of laughter too.

Life had its ups and downs for both Jon and Lucy during their early years of adulthood. Jon was not very motivated in college and drank more than he should have. He had to take a semester off because of his poor grades, and his parents were disappointed and somewhat punitive in their response. He lived with them and worked as a waiter and struggled with doubts, shame, and a sense that he had let them down. When he went back to college, he got close to a few of his professors, who encouraged him and helped him to feel that he could achieve, and he seemed to find his way. Lucy's struggles also involved tension with her parents, and her father in particular, as she struggled to choose a career. They had pushed her to study to become a physician, and they were disappointed when she chose literature. When she struggled earning a living after she graduated, they seemed to take an "I told you so" attitude. She remained closer to her siblings during those early years. As her siblings also began to leave home and her parents retired from their stressful careers, Lucy noticed a change in her parents.

They seemed more reflective and made overt efforts to show her how proud they were of her, her achievements, and her love of literature. On one visit home when she was 25, her parents talked openly about their sadness that they had got it wrong for her: In their anxiety for her to be financially secure, they had ignored who she was and what it was that lit her up. They apologized for not having supported her dreams enough.

Lucy saw herself as having been and continuing to be a strong, self-reliant person. While there had been a good deal of emotional connections within her family, she did not recall many times when she would cry and turn to her parents for comfort.

Lucy and Jon had worked hard at getting to know each other and to develop a strong, loving, reciprocal relationship. When they disagreed, Lucy wanted to talk it out and resolve it immediately, while Jon wanted to avoid it. Lucy often experienced Jon's withdrawal as indifference, while Jon experienced Lucy's challenges as rejecting and somewhat alarming. It took a number of years before they were able to recognize each other's ways of coping with stress and find a middle way that was more comfortable for each. Both struggled in the past, and still at times now, with being vulnerable and seeking comfort from each other.

Adoption: The First Two Years

The first year after adopting James was rocky. They had been warned that he would have trouble adjusting to living with them because of his history, but they had not realized that it would be quite this hard. Two committed and caring adults met one strong, guarded, and self-reliant 11-year-old boy. As they struggled getting to know each other, working out issues of trust and meaning, Lucy would jump right in and push against James's defiance. She would then pull herself back and try to make sense of it before her second effort. Jon would pull back and try to make sense of it first before then trying to see if there was a way around the conflict. James would do a bit of both before exploding or running down the street. But by the end of the day, most days, they seemed to find a way to take a breath, get a connection, and just let it go and relax together. But each time, Lucy and Jon worried that all of them really were not letting it all go. Things, unspoken things, might be piling up, and the closeness that they were hoping to have with James was not developing. James wanted distance, not a connection with them.

And then toward the end of the first year, the tension within James seemed to explode. Tara was the focal point of his rage. She was the birth child. She was white. She could do no wrong. She was the good child, and he was the bad one. Lucy's efforts to reassure him were met with laughter and contempt. Tara withdrew and became irritable and then sad. Lucy and Jon felt protective of Tara, believing that James was not being fair. They tried to understand, but they kept thinking: he had been with them for a year. Why had he not settled into the family by now? Why was he so cruel to Tara when she was so nice and patient with him? Why couldn't he see that they were not prejudiced? They might correct him more than they corrected Tara, but not because he was black. He just misbehaved so much more.

Toward the middle of the second year of the placement, with the help of a referral from their social worker, they sought therapy from Ed, a therapist who specialized in working with adoptive families and who was certified in DDP. They gave the above history with a sense of worry and discouragement, though they also expressed a strong commitment to making the adoption successful. They were willing to approach James differently if that were necessary for him to be able to trust them more and be able to accept their guidance, direction, and affection. They demonstrated a deep understanding about why it would be so hard for him to trust them after his 11 years of little safety and continuity in his life, which included his first 5 years of abuse, neglect, and multiple losses. In the third session with Lucy and Jon, Ed spoke with them about PACE and its value in developing trust and deepening their relationship with James. By the fourth session, they had explored the need to raise him on the basis of his developmental—not chronological—age and to work to provide him with the degree of structure and supervision that he needed in his life, rather than focusing on finding more effective specific consequences for his behaviors. Ed stressed with them how crucial it was for them all to develop a deeper understanding of James's inner world and to actively show their empathy for his mistrust of them and his conviction that he was not good enough for them. Ed stressed that not being prejudiced toward him was not nearly enough for James if he were ever to be convinced that they understood and unconditionally accepted and loved him. They would have to show him that they realized that being black was a reality for him that was likely to permeate all of his experiences living in a white family in a white community. They needed to understand more about his experiences of being a black boy raised in a white family.

In the fifth session, Jon and Lucy expressed uncertainties about trusting Ed. Jon heard something that Ed had said as suggesting that they were not providing James with sufficient clear authority—and that Ed was implying that James being raised by two white, compassionate, middle-class parents might not be what he needed. Ed apologized for having expressed his thoughts in a way that gave this impression, and he spent some time backing up and focusing on what he had done that made Jon and Lucy feel this. He knew that this level of exploration and understanding was essential if he wanted them to truly feel safe with him and to be able in the future to share their uncertainties about their work together when James joined their meetings.

Ed was clear in letting Jon and Lucy know his confidence that they were strong enough to provide James with the direction and containment that he needed. He also stated that he was trying to find a better way of connecting with Jon and Lucy around the idea that we all have family stories from our experiences of being parented. These stories are likely to develop to shape our strengths and vulnerabilities when we become parents. Knowing our own triggers is likely to help us to stop falling into unhelpful patterns that parenting a traumatized child will probably otherwise elicit. Ed shared some of his wonderings about their stories including his sense that—in part because of how they were raised—both of them might be more uncomfortable with conflict than James was. Jon might become anxious during conflict and work to avoid it. If so, his anxiety would likely be evident to James and cause him to be both anxious himself and also more defiant in response to Jon's anxiety. He thought that Lucy might have trouble with conflict because she was so intent on having a close relationship with James and felt threatened when he seemed to be rejecting her. At any sign of a problem between them, she seemed to become frustrated and then more active in trying to make the conflict disappear. This might cause James to feel that some aspects of who he was were not good enough for her, that he was a disappointment to her, and that she could not tolerate any difference between them. Ed was able to reflect toward the end of this session how the "conflict" between him and them seemed to have led to a deeper understanding of what the three of them thought and felt and, if they had resisted expressing their differences, this understanding would not have emerged. A similar process might occur with James if they were able to accept the conflicts as they occurred and make sense of what they meant.

As they explored together ideas about James's mistrust and fears of letting himself rely on others due to his history of abuse and neglect, Ed worked hard to convey just how much he saw their love and good intentions for both of their children. As Jon and Lucy started to feel safer with Ed, they were able to share more deeply how parenting their terrified, feisty son affected them both—in different and similar ways. They also felt safer to explore the complex issues surrounding the fact that James was black and they were not. This was also likely to be contributing to James's struggles to trust them and to feel that they could understand and know him. Jon and Lucy began to understand more fully that telling James that they loved him and that his being black did not affect their love for him in any way was unlikely to reassure him. It might even make him feel that they were minimizing just how crucial an issue this was for him to be able to explore and express his feelings about.

As they talked together trying to imagine something of James's experience, Jon and Lucy identified that in connecting so strongly with their deeply held sense that skin color and race made no impact on how they felt about people in general and about James in particular, they had been ignoring James's thoughts, fears, and wishes. They had wanted to demonstrate that they were not prey to the racism so evident in American culture, but in so doing they might have been showing James that they could not see his experiences.

As they developed this idea further, they discovered that maybe they had wanted to minimize just how big an issue this was likely to be for James. Not just because they did not see it but also because they were terrified that they were not good enough for James and that nothing they could do would ever take away the profound sense of difference and dislocation they imagined James might be experiencing. They discovered their own hidden feelings that maybe others—teachers, friends, family—were judging them and finding them wanting.

Ed focused throughout these early parent sessions on the value of being able to accept James's thoughts, feelings, and wishes that might be associated with conflicts and address any behaviors that might not be considered okay. What did those behaviors mean? PACE was crucial in understanding the meaning of James's behavior, and with this understanding, ideas of connecting with and supporting their son would emerge that would make difficult behaviors less intense.

Ed also thought that their understanding of what the behaviors meant could lead to the behaviors becoming less frequent. They also focused on the importance of finding ways to connect with James after a conflict—how to continually repair their relationship with him so that conflict and breaks in the relationship could happen and then be repaired. Ed shared his deeply held beliefs about conflicts being an ordinary part of any intimate relationship but a part that most of us struggle with. If parents can manage to reduce defensiveness at these times and work together to figure things out, ruptures and repairs can actually strengthen relationships rather than harm them. Jon and Lucy realized that the challenges they faced around conflicts in their relationship with James were similar to those they faced in their relationship too.

The eighth session was the first session with James and his adoptive parents together. James seemed tense at first, maybe a bit vigilant about the purpose of the meeting and what might be expected of him. Ed's casual comment about the game that was showing on his iPad brought a smile and an early, brief conversation, followed by a longer one about the trip that James and his parents had recently taken to the shore. James was hesitant to initiate anything and his responses were brief, but with Ed taking the lead, James seemed to settle into the rhythm of the conversation adding quite a bit about what he had learned about whales.

Without changing the rhythm of his vocal expressions, Ed turned his attention to a recent event at home.

"You guys seemed to have had a great time whale watching! I'd love to see the photos that you took of the whale breeching next session. And I guess the next day was a bit harder when you were hoping to go to a movie with the kid down the street and your dad wanted your help in the garden. What made that so hard for you, James?"

"I wanted to spend some time with Kevin, and he wouldn't let me!" James's tone immediately became more intense.

Ed too spoke more intensely, while maintaining the same vocal rhythms as he had used while speaking about the family trip. "Ah, and it sounds like you really wanted to spend the afternoon with Kevin! I wonder why your dad said "no"?

James continued, becoming louder still, "It always has to be what he wants! He doesn't care what I want!"

Ed, conveying in his voice only a desire to understand, not to give any suggestions: "That would be hard, James, if your dad doesn't care about what you want. Does it seem like that a lot?"

"He doesn't care about me! He only wants to keep the house clean and to fix things up, and he wants me to always help him!"

Jon began to protest.

Ed interrupted him, turned to James, matched the intensity of his voice and exclaimed, "Oh, James, you think that your dad only cares about your helping him, not about you! If that's what it seems to you, that would make it very hard!"

"That's always how it happens! And when I get mad about it, then they say I need therapy! And I know what's coming next! They're going to call Ruth and tell her to move me! That's what happened in those other homes."

James was bringing his story of rejection and then abandonment into the conversation. Another family was disappointed in him. Any disagreement would represent to him a conflict that meant he was not good enough for them. Ed would take this opportunity to turn the conversation toward developing a possible new story.

Ed stayed with him in his intensity. "And it seems to be happening again! It's hard for you to believe that they want my help to make the family work better. That they want to understand you better! That they want me to help you to understand you better! It's hard to believe that because that's *not* what happened when you saw a therapist those other times!"

James, expecting reassurance or an argument, did not seem to know what to say. So, Ed continued, softening his voice and expressing a desire to understand—not to judge—what he was experiencing. "What do you think they're thinking and feeling about you now James? What do you think?"

"I don't care! If they don't want me, I don't want them!"

"If they don't want you, James? Why wouldn't they want you?"

"Because I'm not good enough for them! What do you think?"

"I think that would be very hard if you thought that you weren't good enough for them! Does it seem that you're not good enough for them whenever you're not getting along?"

"I'm not the good boy they wanted! I'm not the boy they wanted!"

"Have they told you that, James? Have they said that?"

"No, but I know! I know that they think that, they're just afraid to say it!"

"Oh, James, I'm sorry that you think that! And I'm sorry if they think that but don't say it! Could I tell them that and see what they say! I'd like to know what they'll say if I tell them that!"

James nodded and Ed turned to Jon and Lucy, making it clear that he was speaking for James, "Mom and Dad! I do think that you don't want me anymore! I do think that you feel that. I think that you wanted a good boy and I'm not a good boy. I'm not the boy you want and you're going to tell me that you want me to live somewhere else. That you don't want me to be your son anymore."

In the first two sentences, Ed spoke with the same intensity that he had used with James. Then his voice gradually became quieter, and by the end there was vulnerability in his voice. Ed was not only using the words that he thought would reflect James's story, but he also was using the nonverbal expressions congruent with the words. Such communications often evoke an affective–reflective response within the child comparable to what he would have experienced if he had expressed the words himself. When the parent then responds to the child, this response is experienced as part of a synchronized conversation between parent and child that enables the child to truly feel that he is understood.

Jon replied, using some of the words that they had used when Ed was giving him examples of PACE during their prior sessions. "Oh, James, no wonder you get upset with me and Lucy! No wonder. When we have an argument, you think that we don't want you! That we think that you're not the boy that we want and that we don't want to still be your parents! No wonder it's been hard for you at times with us. You don't trust us! You don't trust that we still want you! That you are our son and will always be our son."

Still speaking for James, Ed said, "You expect me to believe that you don't care if I'm good or not!"

"James, we do want you to do what you call 'good' and what we'd say is good for you and us and the family. We do want that! But you might do something else sometimes. Maybe that's what you call 'bad.' Well, James, we love you, you're our son."

Lucy joined in, "James we love you when you're 'good' and we love you when you're 'bad.' We love all of you—good and bad. And we hope that you'll love all of us sometime—what we do that you think is 'good' and what we do that you think is 'bad.'"

James spoke quietly and deliberately: "But you'd love me more if I were white!"

Jon and Lucy began to protest, but Ed quickly interrupted them. He could see how vulnerable James was. He was expressing a core aspect of his mistrust, of his shame, and his doubt that things could ever be different. Maybe he could stop being "bad," but he could not stop being black.

Ed matched James's affective expression: "That took such courage to tell your parents that. That is such a hard truth—you are black, they are white. How can anything ever be different?"

James became more subdued: "It's just how it is. They're taking care of me. But I'm different from them. I am always going to be black and they want to pretend that I won't be. Or it won't matter. Maybe not to them, but it will always matter to me."

Ed then said, "And I'm a white therapist, James! You're sitting here with three white people. Does my being white make it more difficult?"

"No, it's just more of the same. That's my life."

Ed did not pursue that issue then but realized that he needed to be mindful of it in future sessions. Now he needed to stay with James's relationship with his parents. Quietly he continued the dialogue: "Yes, James, you will always be black. And it will always matter to you. I am glad that you told your parents that. They need to know."

"I'm not sure that they're listening."

"Let's find out, James. Would you tell them again?"

"I'm black and you can't pretend that I'm not."

Lucy spoke first, "You are black, James, you are. And . . . I . . . am sorry . . . I did try to pretend that you're not, and I can see now how that hurt you. I tried to look at you and see my son, not my black son. But you are my black son. And I did not see you."

Jon followed, "I didn't either, James. I'm really sorry. I thought that was what you needed, that your color did not matter to me. Oh, no, James, you must feel so different from us, and so alone! We didn't see how much being black means to you, and why wouldn't it?"

Ed spoke then: "I think that they heard you James. Your dad said that you must feel so alone. Partly because you're different from them—you're black. Partly because your parents did not understand why this matters so much;

that you know that they know that they have a black son, and that matters! Do you think they might get that a little bit, James?"

James replied, "I don't know. I don't think white people can understand what it's like to be black. Even though I lived with them for over a year, I don't think they understand much."

Jon then responded, "I'm sorry, James. I don't think we've tried hard enough. We'd like to try now and try hard. Will you help us?"

James said, "I don't know."

Ed commented: "What a hard, hard talk you three are having! You're all experiencing a lot of pain now. Thanks, James, for your honesty, every step of the way. And thanks, Jon and Lucy, for listening and for not trying to talk James out of his experience. If he decides to help you, it's because you listen and that he begins to trust you that you really do want to get to know him, all of him."

Often, adoptive parents—and therapists—think that it is best if they are "color-blind" when the child is of a different race. They often assume that themes of trauma, attachment, and loss are universal and these are the important issues. They assume that if their love for the child is unconditional, then racial differences are not important. But race is important. A black child raised by white parents is a reality that is noticed, experienced, and creates a sense of "other" that needs to be acknowledged and integrated into the realities involved in creating a family.

By the end of the second year, James did seem to want to help his parents become the parents he needed them to be. They stumbled, he stumbled, Tara stumbled. Once she said that James had it easier than she did because he was black and she was white. That did not get much sympathy from the other three in the family. Jon and Lucy worried that James might be furious with her about that. Rather, he seemed to be glad, as if her comments proved his point that his being black made him different from her. She did not experience him as her brother. He could live with that truth easier than with her pretending it were not so.

Adoption: The Third Year

Over the course of the next year when James turned 14, with Ed's help, and especially his empathy for how hard it was, they all seemed to get better at making things better for their family. A number of times

James got closer to his parents and then pushed against them to create some distance. It is difficult to love, trust, and rely on your parents when you have previously been violated by your first parents. Love and vulnerability caused James to be anxious. Could he trust being in a family again? Would he be able to give them the love that they wanted? Did he want to? Did he want their love? James seemed to be trying to live now without a story to guide him. He was thinking that his original story formed by abuse and rejection need not be the complete story of who he was and would be. But his day-to-day experiences were confusing, his behaviors were often unpredictable, and he could not make sense of who he really was.

Lucy and Jon often seemed to relax when James got closer and then react with strong disappointment when it did not last. They knew that they should hold back and remain steady, trying not to anticipate the good or the bad, but it was hard to do that. They so much wanted to have a close relationship with James. Ed had many sessions with them without James, relating with them using PACE in a way similar to how he was hoping that they could continue to relate with James. They had a hard time trying to accept that his being black and their being white did matter so much to him. Step by step, they were able to accept that it did matter to him, and then it started to matter to them too, again, step by step. Their son was black, and they were not.

Ed also focused on keeping their relationship with each other strong. They needed their reciprocal care, sharing, and energy if they were to continue to parent James consistently in the way that he needed. They really needed to learn to allow themselves to be comforted by the other, something that they did not have that much practice doing when they were growing up.

During one particularly difficult period of time, Lucy had gotten angry with James and yelled that he should act more like his sister. The pain that Lucy saw in James's eyes—a moment before she saw rage too, helped her to understand him and his behavior more than anything else that they had gone through. James yelled that she was not his sister and that they were not his parents so he could act any way that he wanted to act. Over a number of sessions, Ed focused with Lucy and Jon on how to repair their relationship with James and help him to express his conviction that they loved Tara more than they would ever love him. That was the last time that Lucy expressed her anger toward James in a way that was so hurtful and shaming.

During one session after another challenging few weeks at home, James spoke with anger and certainty to his parents: "You'll never understand me. You'll never know what it's like to be black!"

Jon, who seemed to jump in quicker now than he did in earlier sessions, and to jump in with a lot of energy too, said, "I never will understand what it is like to be black, James. Please help me to understand as much as I am able." And this time James did.

"People look at you all the time like you're going to do something you're not supposed to do. People talk to you like they're doing you a favor. People who work in stores watch you all the time because they think you're going to steal something. No matter what's going on, people show you that you're different from them. You're not as good as they are."

Jon and Lucy sat quietly. James accepted his mother's hand, something that he often refused when he was upset.

James spoke again, this time more quietly: "Being black is being different from almost everyone I see. More than that, being black is not being good enough. Being black is being different and not good enough, even in my own family. Even with you."

This time, Lucy responded immediately, but not with words. She pulled James to her and she cried. He did not pull away, but he seemed to freeze at first. Then he embraced her back and cried with her. After a bit, she wiped her tears and his tears. She put her hands on his cheeks, stared into his eyes and said quietly, with a smile, "I love you with all my heart and mind because you are my black son. I am so, so sorry that my being white makes it hard for you to feel that. Hard to know that you matter to me so much." James stared into Lucy's eyes. Then he hugged her again, and even got closer when Jon hugged them both.

One lovely session did not produce a resolution of James's developmental trauma or a secure attachment with his adoptive family. Many other themes came up, and came up again. These included James's grief over the loss of his birth parents and the shame that he felt about it. Somehow it had to have been his fault. Also, how James felt more anxiety about receiving comfort for his fears than the fears themselves. After a conflict, his sense of shame caused him to freeze and have great difficulty engaging in relationship repair. School and peer relationships remained challenging for him. He often thought that it was unfair that there was so much work involved with his assignments; he became aware of a sense of loss of his childhood, as he had such little opportunity to be a child during the first 11 years of his life. He had a hard time trusting his peers, being very sensitive to the experience of loss and rejection when a friendship would wane. And always, always, he was a young black teen living in a white family, attending a mostly white school, and living in a mostly white community.

Adoption: The Years Following

James's adolescence was hard for him and his family. It was harder still because Tara too was having difficulties. She had her own challenges of adolescence along with struggles with James and the tension in their home. Also, her parents often were unsure as to how to guide and limit Tara. They regretted the distress that James's adoption caused her, and sometimes they might not have been clear about what was expected of her out of their wish to only support her and not have conflicts with her. They realized eventually that their attitude of PACE was equally important in their relationship with Tara as it was for James. They set limits with PACE. Also, with PACE, they helped Tara to be able to talk to them about her ambivalence toward James. She cried and expressed guilt when she told them that sometimes she wished that they had not adopted him. As they really listened to her, she was able to express her fear that the prejudice that James faced for being black was much more difficult than her regular adolescent struggles of being liked, fitting in, and finding her place in school. She also worried that at the end of the day, James would only reject her because of the differences between them and try to find his birth family when he turned 18. When Ed heard this, he expressed his admiration for how the four of them were able to talk about these big worries and doubts together—as a family.

Gradually, James came to trust Lucy and Jon—trust their motives, their commitment, and their decisions for him. And their love for him. James wanted the freedoms that many of his peers wanted, and he struggled when his parents denied permission. But he did not struggle too hard. He seemed to know that he wasn't ready for some of those freedoms. Plus, he seemed to be less interested in independence than his peers were. He was still enjoying the closeness that he was learning to feel with his family, and he seemed to be reluctant to grow up too fast. Often, as he moved through adolescence, he seemed content to do family activities.

After James graduated from high school, he went to a university close to home, and he visited home often. He was studying to be an architect, a choice that seemed perfectly suited to his interests and abilities. It was not an easy time at the university. During the first semester, he had what almost seemed like panic attacks, being consumed by fears that Lucy and Jon had been in a car accident. During the second year, he struggled with drinking too much, missing some classes, and getting some poor grades as a result. But each year being easier than the last, he did graduate, and he became an architect. Then he entered a committed relationship, and later still he became a father. Many steps were a struggle. More steps than not took James forward in his journey to discover who he was, to develop a coherent narrative.

CONCLUSION

The experience of DDP is both the same and different for each child, family, and therapist that engages in it. What is universal in DDP is the experience of safety, conversations, stories, an integrated sense of self, and a coherent narrative. And that too is what is unique about DDP every time it assists a child who has experienced relational trauma to develop a coherent narrative within a new home.

CHAPTER 5

The Nuts and Bolts of Dyadic Developmental Psychotherapy

Dyadic developmental psychotherapy (DDP) tends to be more complex than other therapies need to be because traumatized children often have complex developmental needs and challenges, and their parents or caregivers are expected to have an active part in their therapy. Traumatized children and their families may have other agencies actively involved with them, and there may need to be a network of providers to better coordinate services that are integrated and without contradictory goals.

OVERVIEW OF THERAPY

Having presented the core experience of DDP in the previous chapter, we now provide an overview of how the therapy progresses from initial referral to its ending.

Referrals

It is not always necessary to consider networks, as DDP is a therapy for all children and families, not only when children experience developmental trauma. A referral by birth parents for their anxious 12-year-old son with no educational concerns simply involves meeting the family. Referrals for a child with a child-protection plan, or living in a residential children's home, or in her fifth foster home with a care plan involving adoption warrants a different approach, one that involves careful consideration with parents, other professionals, and networks. DDP interventions are individually tailored, which contributes to their effectiveness. Interventions can include therapy, network consultation, parental consultation, and parent training groups.

It is helpful to take time to get to know referrers, asking what they hope for and what interventions have been tried. If they hope that children with developmental traumas can be effectively helped by short-term individual therapy, it is important to take time to inform referrers about the approach and the reasons behind the different aspects of the model. The therapist needs to make a good clinical case to help referrers understand the approach so they can make an informed decision.

Decision Making about a Referral

An initial telephone call or meeting with referrers is helpful to discuss their hopes and expectations for the work. This enables clarification about the aims of intervention and whether a combination of consultation, parent training, and therapy is recommended. Take into account complex circumstances, such as care plans, court recommendations, and social care adoption support assessments. Determine who represents the child, who has statutory responsibilities, who has authority to make decisions on behalf of the child, and who provides the funding for the intervention.

An Initial Introductory Meeting

The DDP therapist may suggest an initial meeting with the parents (and referring professional if there is one) in order to ensure that they understand the nature of DDP. This may not be needed for the parents and therapist when a straightforward referral is made by the parents and the questions of both parents and therapist are able to be addressed on the telephone. If there are more complex issues involving developmental trauma and other services, a preparatory meeting might be of value before the intervention begins with the parents.. During this meeting, it would be important to tell the parents what will be expected of them throughout the course of therapy. This includes the following:

- Parents are seen as a crucial part of this therapeutic approach and are asked to take a central and active role in the therapy.
- Parents are seen without their child, possibly for many sessions, before the child joins for therapy.

- The parents' own childhood experiences and attachment histories are explored, one reason being that parents may have their own experiences that are triggered by some aspect of caring for their child.
- Therapy focuses on the relationship between the parents and the child.
- If there are two parents, both are involved in therapy and consultations whenever possible.
- Parental sessions continue alongside therapy.
- The therapist has contact with parents before each parent–child therapy session (either face to face or by telephone) and sometimes after a therapy session.
- Parental consultation and support often continues when therapy finishes.
- The approach can involve stand-alone parenting interventions without the child being seen for therapy.
- Other professionals are also regularly included in thinking about the work, with parents involved in network or "team around the child" consultations.

The therapist may also want to inform the parents of the attachment trauma principles that provide the format for DDP. These principles will have implications for parenting that may differ from current parenting practices that the parents use. A brief description of the typical therapy session might be helpful to better ensure that the parents may make an informed decision about beginning the intervention.

This preparatory meeting may be of value for the therapist too. This is the time to ask the parents for copies of previous reports and assessments about the child's functioning. If the parents describe complex learning or developmental problems that have not been assessed, the therapist might request that those assessments be done before or at the early stage of the therapy. If other professionals are actively involved with the child, the therapist and parents might explore whether it would be of value to have network meetings to ensure that all services are integrated and all needs of the child are being addressed. If the parents are having their own struggles, either because of the challenges of raising the traumatized child or for separate issues, the therapist will explore whether these have been or need to be addressed. Finally, the therapist might explore with the parents whether the child has been informed about the likelihood of therapy, and if so, what the child has been told. The therapist might suggest ways to tell the child about the sessions, stressing the value of the child and parents meeting with someone to help the family as a whole with their challenges or to help the parents and child to work together in addressing some of the child's challenges.

Initial Sessions with Parents Alone

If the parents and therapist decide to initiate a course of therapy, the initial therapy sessions will serve the therapist as an informal assessment of the particular challenges and strengths of this family—both child and parents—that will be useful as a guide for the ongoing sessions. The therapist first meets with the parents alone for one or more sessions both to obtain a summary of the child and family histories and to explore the child's actions that the parents are concerned about as well as their efforts to date in addressing those challenges. This exploration will include their own parenting challenges. It helps the therapist to determine what support they may need and what strengths they have to call upon. The therapist will address whether the parents are experiencing blocked care as well as their attachment history and its influence on their parenting. As part of this initial phase of working with the parents alone, the therapist may include a session or two with the parents and child together to develop initial impressions of both the child and the parent–child relationship.

After that, the therapist will often meet alone again with the parents for one or more sessions to provide his clinical impressions of the child and family and more specific recommendations for how the therapy will proceed. Depending on the family and services suggested, the therapist will provide the parents with either a formal or informal summary of his clinical impressions and his recommendations for the course of therapy. Recommendations regarding the value of any ongoing contact or network meetings with other professionals will be discussed as well as any issues regarding confidentiality. During these initial sessions with the parents alone, the therapist is developing his thoughts as to whether joint sessions are needed and, if so, when they can begin. These thoughts involve whether the parents:

- Make sense of what it means to work with an attachment-focused model of therapy and understand the nature of the therapeutic sessions that will occur when the child is also present (e.g., that sessions don't start with the parents recounting the troubling behaviors of the child since they last met with the therapist).

- Are comfortable with exploring their attachment histories, being prepared to look at their own experiences that are being triggered by some aspect of caring for their child.

- Are committed to be involved in therapy with their child for sufficient time.

- Understand that the therapist will show interest in and be curious about all behaviors and feelings of the child. This may include behaviors that the parents find difficult, such as aggression, stealing, or lying. This will be hard to accept if the parents are not confident about the reasons behind the therapist showing a nonjudgmental and nonevaluative stance toward their child's wishes, feelings, motives, and desires underneath these behaviors. If parents don't understand that this acceptance increases safety for the child and thereby an open and engaged stance, parents can feel they are being undermined or not understood by the therapist or that she is siding with their child against them.

- Have established a trusting enough relationship with the therapist for them to accept her guidance during therapy and act on agreed cues from the therapist to shift their stance to one that is more therapeutic or to let the therapist take the lead.

- Can stay emotionally regulated enough to notice when the therapist needs to guide or coach them rather than be preoccupied with their own responses.

- Can manage the relationship with the child such that they can regulate their own emotional state, not becoming emotionally overwhelmed within the session but remaining open to sharing their evoked responses when this is helpful. This balance is difficult and requires much support from and trust in the therapist.

- Recognize the need to both acknowledge mistakes and repair relationships as part of enabling the child to experience the attachment sequence. Repair also needs to take place between the adults when they make mistakes.

- Can seek and accept help from the therapist rather than continuing with misplaced, self-reliant and avoidant strategies to get through the day or the therapy session.

- Have a beginning understanding of playfulness, acceptance, curiosity, and empathy (PACE) and be willing to develop their skills in relating to their child with PACE.

It is really difficult for parents to know what is in a therapist's mind when communication using PACE is discussed theoretically among them. The parents make sense of their experience of PACE through their relationship with the therapist. This doesn't mean, however, that they can translate this experience into their own "PACE-ful" communication with their child, who is unlikely to be supportive of their attempts. It helps prepare the parents for how to respond to their child during therapy if the therapist role-plays possible scenarios with them. These might include an adopted daughter telling her parents that they love their birth son more than her, that she doesn't care about them, or relating more about early abusive experiences. Role-plays might also involve the therapist showing nonjudgmental curiosity toward their daughter including acceptance of the wishes, feelings, and perceptions underneath challenging behavior, such as her stealing money from them. DDP involves establishing emotional connections before setting limits, and through role-play parents can explore the feelings such interactions evoke, in safety outside of therapy sessions, such as their anger at the therapist because they really want her to join them in rebuking their daughter. As with most people, parents will initially experience role-plays as awkward and something to be endured. Over time, the helpfulness can outweigh their embarrassment.

A frequent question from parents is why are you working with us to this extent? Why are you not seeing my child, at least sometimes, as he is the one with the problems? It is a significant change from some approaches for the parents to hear the therapist say that they are the ones who are going to make the most difference; they have the most impact on the child's recovery; that the therapist focuses on the relationship between them and their child. The therapist acknowledges how hard and confusing this can be to make sense of. She explores and accepts the parents' experience, such as their perception that, regardless of what she says, the therapist must feel they are to blame for their child's difficulties if she insists on seeing them without the child. This perception may be particularly strong when based in a general mental health context, in which many therapists work individually with children, always involving the parents in some way but not seeing them as the main agents of change.

Sometimes the time never arrives when the parents are able to support therapy as in the DDP model despite the parents' and the therapist's best efforts. If this possibility is included in the early referral discussions, it becomes a shared decision between everyone concerned. Options may include the following:

- The therapist offers a more narrowly focused therapy with the parents and the child that the parents can be included in safely. Focused narrative work is one example.
- Two therapists become involved: One therapist uses the DDP model and sees the child individually at the same time as the parental consultation is provided by the second therapist, perhaps for 45 minutes. Then a joint session can take place with both therapists, the parents, and the child for 30 or 45 minutes. The parents are coached and helped by the therapist who sees them for consultation. This can provide enough safety as the therapist does not also need to focus on the child. The child's safety is increased as he has his own therapist present. Over time, it can be possible to increase the time that parents and child are together. This is not easy to do well. Good planning and sensitivity are required, and therapists need to know each other's work well. Some DDP therapists prefer to routinely work in pairs and are skilled at working in this way from the start of the work.
- Sometimes another member of the network can provide individual work with the child, such as a family support worker or the child's social worker or youth justice worker. If these sessions are planned as part of a comprehensive, relationship-focused intervention, shared meetings including the therapist and parents can happen regularly.

Starting Therapy with the Parent and the Child

Even when the joint sessions begin, the therapist will still meet (or speak by telephone) with the parents alone prior to the onset of a joint session. This is not something that only happens at the start of therapy or when there is an increase in concern or difficulty. This is an important part of the approach and happens before each therapy session. If a parent has experienced frustration, sadness, and irritation since the last session, these can be expressed and explored with the therapist to ensure that the parent is regulated and able to focus on the child once the session starts. The therapist also asks about enjoyable and successful events as well as troubling events of the week that might be talked about to begin the session. After this, plans can be made as to which behaviors and events might be brought into the session. There might be more distant events that the therapist believes the child is now ready to explore. These pre-session plans are not rigid and may be modified or set aside entirely if something emerges early in the session that the therapist believes needs to be attended to. The therapist does not want to begin the session with the parent and child together by asking, "How has it been since our last session?" If a parent starts the session by highlighting the troubles and disagreements during the week or is critical, the child will quickly move into defensive responses and a mistrustful, withdrawn, or oppositional stance. Much repair will then be required before therapeutic work recognized as DDP can start. The parent and therapist need to be ready to start a session using the DDP core principles including PACE the moment the session with the child starts. Most often, the therapist will initiate with one or more of the successful and enjoyable recent events to enable the conversation to begin without defensiveness and only introduce the more troubling events or themes after the momentum of the conversation has been established.

Sometimes it is necessary to change the balance and rhythm between parental consultations and therapy to enable the therapist to see parents more often. This can happen for a number of reasons, one example being that the parents are attuned, sensitive, and can use PACE well when they are regulated and the stress is low but lose their capacity for empathy and acceptance in therapy when stress increases. This could be due to child factors, such as being excluded from school or the level of violence increasing. It could be due to adult factors, such as a close family member needing care. More time might then be needed with parents to support them and help them learn, remember, and practice self-regulation and self-care. The network might also need time to increase support, such as family support workers being at the home during key times of increased stress, such as after school.

Here is an example as to how the process of therapy can work in practice when the parents need to be seen for more sessions:

Lesley is exhausted and is irritated by her partner, who works later and later—she thinks to avoid having to be back for Finn's bedtime. Finn is their long-term foster son. Lesley seems engaged during pre-therapy telephone calls. In therapy, however, she seems distant and needs more cues, more times when the therapist "talks for" her to help Lesley respond with PACE to Finn. Lesley shows her disappointment in Finn's need for help with his homework. She criticizes his foster dad in sessions. Finn becomes less and less engaged. The therapist sees how easy it will be for herself to step in, to become the one who engages Finn; to quicken the pace, to show high interest and curiosity; working harder and harder to model to Lesley how she hopes she can be—how she knows she can be.

Her next parental consultation with both parents isn't booked for another 4 weeks. This is too long. She makes a decision now so that she can talk this over with Finn. She can be clear with him when he will see her next. She knows she can't add in extra appointments to see both parents without Finn because her schedule is full. She therefore has to alter the balance of sessions.

She says to them both, "Remember I said at the start that sometimes I may see more of you, Lesley, with Finn's foster dad and not see you, Finn, for a while. This is one of those times. Finn, I'm going to see you in 3 weeks' time, and for the next 2 weeks I'm going to see your foster mom and dad at the times when you and I usually meet. I want to have a chat with them about a few things."

Children generally know when their parents are struggling. It creates safety for them to see their therapist noticing and doing something about it with the adults taking responsibility. They have often been the ones looking out for the adults in the past.

Finn's anxiety may rise, but this anxiety is there anyway. He feels the tension in his home. Not doing his homework distracts his foster mom from her sadness for a while. His therapist sends him a card, just to let him know she is thinking about him and hasn't forgotten him.

The therapist meets with Lesley and Jim, her partner, twice in those 3 weeks. Lesley tells her therapist she believes Jim is having a relationship with someone else. Jim says "if only he had the energy." He tells Lesley it was her choice to foster; he has his job. After a while, he talks about feeling he has no place with Finn. He works late because he can't stand the hurt he feels when Finn never wants him to read a story—only his foster mom. It's always Lesley. Lesley tells Jim he has no idea how exhausted this is making her. They agreed to do this fostering together even though she is the named carer. He just has to be firm with Finn in the evenings and accept no nonsense.

This narrative thread, so often experienced by foster or adoptive parents, was explored over the next two meetings. Lesley came to believe that Jim was not having a relationship with someone else. They both came to the next therapy session with Finn where they continued their story in a different way. Both parents joined in the narrative threads started by the therapist about how hard it was for Finn to learn how to be close to two parents at once. He had only ever had one parent, his birth mother, and the men he knew were mean to him. Finn didn't know how to be a son with a dad. Jim tells Finn he loves him and is always there. With the therapist's guidance, "talking for" Jim a little at the start, Jim tells Finn he likes seeing the way he and Lesley were getting close, after all the tough times Finn had with his other mom. Maybe he and Finn could both take the dog for a walk over the weekend and pick blackberries so they can make a pie together. Mom loves blackberry and apple pie.

This example demonstrates the fluid and flexible nature of DDP in which the therapist and parents are open to increasing parental work when either the parents or the therapist feel this is required to maintain the attuned, intersubjective stance needed during therapy involving the child. This flow, this balance, with the parent–child relationship at the center, is the foundation of effective therapy.

Endings

As with all therapy, working with endings starts as soon as therapy begins. In DDP, the therapist usually indicates that 9 months of joint sessions with the parent and child is often necessary, though more time may be requited. There are other options such as long-term parental consultation with perhaps 6 to 12 sessions of therapy provided alongside, when needed, as the child grows up.

When a long-term intervention model is used, as in the adoption support model described in Chapter 10 , therapy with the parent and child can be included, when needed, with consultation for parents and the network occurring long-term. This model has also been used effectively for long-term foster care. This provides a different perspective to ending therapy, which can be seen in terms of "We have done enough together for now; we can get together again when needed." One example of this with long-term kinship foster care follows:

An 8-year-old withdrawn boy is seen for therapy with his grandparents for 18 sessions. The family court decides that his grandparents will have his care. This goes well. Therapy ends with a clear plan agreed to by the network, with the child fully involved, that the therapy will resume 6 months before he starts secondary school. It is anticipated that this change will be extremely hard for him. Therapy takes place as planned for 12 sessions, and the transition goes well. His grandparents are seen every 4 months in between and afterward. Their grandson has always insisted he will return to live with his mother when he is 16. Further therapy is arranged when he is 15 to help him think through his plans. This also takes place, all with the same therapist who continued to be involved.

Therapy includes sessions with his mother and grandmother. He decides to stay with his grandmother and is supported in ways to keep in contact with his mother while protecting himself from her drug-misusing lifestyle. This includes planned visits (which he lets his grandmother, social worker, and therapist help him with) when he is 16 to see his mother in the hospital after she is admitted close to death following an overdose.

When working toward a final end, which is more likely than the scenario above, the cessation of sessions can be considered for many reasons and depends on the initial goals. There are some general relationship guidelines therapists use to indicate when it might be time to clearly plan an end to therapy with the parent and child. These include the following:

- The parents comfortably and confidently use PACE at home and engage in interactive repair.
- The child is able to manage conflicts with repair without habitual shame and dysregulation.
- The parents know when and how to seek help for themselves.
- The child talks openly and without shame about both pleasurable and stressful events in his day.
- The child seeks help and comfort from his primary attachment figure.
- All family members enjoy reciprocal interactions.
- The parents can anticipate possible setbacks, due to transitions or changes, with any return to past unhelpful ways of coping by the child seen as something to be expected and not a cause for despair.
- The child has a coherent narrative about his life that he feels familiar with and can tell his story when it is in his best interests to do so.

Many DDP therapists, as they cocreate narratives during therapy, write these down with the child and parent. There are many ways to collate and write these (Golding, 2014b). It can be a part of endings to give these to the child. These are always seen as interactive narratives and never static; there to be added to. Parents often say in later years that they see these stories in their child's bedrooms having been returned to by the child. Parents can then notice and talk with their child, wondering what might have been on his or her mind.

During endings, the importance of the relationship between the child, parents, and therapist and between the child and therapist is acknowledged by the therapist. Regardless of the amount of preparation, as with any therapy ending in any model, sometimes children will protest loudly that they will not let it happen ("I won't let you leave me. You can't, I won't allow it."); others escalate behavior to show sessions can't possibly end. Others just stop coming for the first time, to avoid having to go through any kind of goodbye. This may be the first time the child has been part of a planned, thought-about ending. It will bring up all the other endings that have not gone so well. Also, the child can become highly anxious about life without the therapist meeting with him and his parents. This often bears no relationship to whether the child seems to want to come to sessions. The parents also often become anxious as to whether they can manage. If they are still coming for consultations, these worries can be directly addressed.

This is where careful consideration comes in about the best type of ending for the child and parents. A gradual ending can reduce anxiety, moving from weekly to fortnightly to monthly. Another ending can be to stop sessions with a review a few months ahead. There are many combinations, and the main consideration is for the therapist to ensure the child experiences a good ending. Good endings don't avoid the associated anxiety, loss, and, sometimes, relief. Helping the child experience whatever may arise is a shared task for the therapist and parents. If DDP has been successful, then the child will be able to manage the ending more easily than in other therapies because the child has a more secure relationship with his parents to whom he is able to turn for comfort about the loss of the regular contact with the therapist.

Just as therapy is provided within an attachment trauma perspective, so are endings. Consideration will be given to how to validate the child's relationship with the therapist as an attachment relationship for a child who probably has little direct experience that goodbyes can mean staying in touch. It is not unusual to count up the "losses with no contact" for a child and reach 40 to 50 people by the age of 12. In this context, it can be helpful as part of therapy ending to involve some way of letting the child know the therapist does keep him or her in mind. This is done with the parents' involvement, never as a special relationship. Sending birthday or Christmas cards comes with problems, such as when does the therapist stop? What if the therapist forgets one year? These times are so fraught with links to unsent cards by other lost people. Sending occasional ad hoc cards via the parents can be a different, more helpful way.

Kerry has been Gina's therapist over two foster placements for two years when Gina was twelve to fourteen years old. Gina knows her social worker keeps Kerry in touch about where she is and how she is doing. When Gina finished her GSCEs, Kerry sent Gina a card.

Gina is soon to be 18. Gina asks her social worker to ask Kerry to come to her 18th birthday party. After taking this to supervision, Kerry accepts the invite and goes for a short while. Gina seems both surprised and delighted to see Kerry there. She takes her around to her friends, introducing Kerry proudly as her therapist. Nothing more, no qualification or explanation was needed. Kerry was an important part of Gina's life that was full of foster carers and social workers. The ones she keeps in mind as narrative threads she values were all invited to her party. As she leaves Gina's party, Kerry remembers all the reasons she worried about going—that this was not the right way for a therapist to behave. She now knows she made the right decision to go.

LEO: THE BOY WHO TALKS WITH A CROW

The example described in this section follows a real-life intervention that Kim Golding carried out with a young child and his adoptive parents. The family has kindly given permission for Kim to share this, and all names and identifying details have been changed. This example demonstrates that there are many "nuts and bolts" during the course of DDP, depending on the unique needs of each child and family. What is consistent throughout, however, is that DDP begins with the parents and the strong premise that it is they who will provide the child who has developmental trauma with the most life-changing joint experiences upon which to build new stories and a coherent narrative.

A young, thin boy with a tousle of dark hair approaches me. He is friendly, with a lively curiosity and a bubbly, infectious charm. He chats away as if he has always known me. It is hard not to be captivated by him. Tall for his 4 years, just now he seems a lot older. I see no sign of the angry, aggressive child I have been hearing about for the past year. Neither do I see the scared child I know is within. He knows what my name is, who I am, and that I have been working with his mom and dad, helping them to take care of him. In truth, he has not come to see me today but for an assessment with my trainee clinical psychologist. Leo, however, has targeted me for his charm, he knows who he needs to be safe with, understanding that I am the boss here, an unerring instinct that only comes from early frightening experience of relationships.

Early Experience

Leo was born following a pregnancy that will have been stressful for him, experience already imprinting on the early development of his nervous system. His birth mother probably did not care for herself well. She is recorded as being underweight during the pregnancy. It is likely that she lived in a climate of violence and fear. Labor was prolonged, and delivery difficult, but mother and child were discharged the following morning. The health visitor notes describe his mother as not coping from the earliest of visits. Behind these early notes there is an image of Leo left to cry in a climate of stress and recriminations. His birth father is a shadowy, angry figure in the background. Extended family appear supportive but are probably complicit in this frightening early environment. Soon there are bigger concerns as Leo is found with injuries to his body. Enough is enough, and Leo is removed when he is 5 weeks old.

Leo's first foster placement is with an elderly couple, soon to retire. They mean well, but the environment is unstimulating. When he is 10 months old, Leo moves again. These foster carers are kind and committed. They care for Leo well and work hard to give him a successful transition to adoption. As is usual practice while decisions are being made, Leo has weekly contact with his birth family until he is a year old. It is hard to imagine the confusion and fear of a small child who finds himself cared for by so many people, some strange and unfamiliar but safe, without pain, and then the sudden reoccurrence of the familiar smells and sounds, accompanied by the visceral fear that is associated with the other people. Finally, all of these people gone, and a new family, new sights, new sounds, new smells, and always the worry: When will the pain and loss come again?

Moving to Adoption

At 17 months of age, Leo moves to live with his adoptive parents, April and Don. Like Leo, they are white and British. They have a birth son, Michael, and are completing their family through adoption. Leo, well into toddlerhood, is already a lively, active child. There is none of the so-called honeymoon period: Leo arrives as a demanding, determined, self-sufficient child, initially small in stature, but already mature for his age, at least in outward appearance.

Over the next couple of years, Leo increasingly presents as a highly controlling child. He is oppositional, he refuses to sit in his pushchair, threatens to undo his seat belt, and generally opposes the many day-to-day things that a toddler needs to do within the family routines. He can also be very stubborn: He has refused to eat for 3 to 4 days at a time. If he does not want to do something he will rage: He goes rigid, shakes, and is very difficult to calm. He becomes angry when his feelings are named but sometimes will tolerate being held until he can calm. Leo demonstrates these same behaviors at the nursery where he attends while mom works. Sleep appears to be a refuge for Leo: He sleeps well and excessively. His bed feels like a place of safety, he keeps precious things there, and he rarely gets up in the morning to seek out his parents.

There is little sign of Leo being able to use parents as a secure base. If hurt, he actively pushes them away. The outside world is, however, a source of greater anxiety. He appears confident, but Leo's hypervigilance is evident: He scans and notices every detail within moments of entering a room. He takes control through his charm, his demands, and sometimes his oppositional and aggressive behaviors. He brings the anxiety home with him, directed as anger toward mom. Because of ghosts from the past, he cannot seek her for comfort despite his need. He fears the pain she might inflict and so he attacks the source of confusion.

There are some glimmers of progress within the first years. He begins to approach mom and dad, at least with minor hurts, and he has allowed himself to be vulnerable after a rage, sobbing and allowing mom to comfort him. These small signs of progress can get lost in the challenge of helping this little boy, and his parents are increasingly exhausted and worried about the future.

Intervention Phase 1

The family is referred when Leo is 3 years old. As is typical for our service, we initially offer consultation for parents and the network surrounding the family. We help them to understand Leo as a child who is highly insecure, centered around fears of abandonment and rejection: He is hypervigilant to the smallest perceived sign of disapproval from others. He moves into shame very quickly, leading to intense rage. He tries to manage all his fears through a range of controlling behaviors, which includes making sure that others attend to him through highly demanding behaviors. In this way, he coerces others to attend to him so that he does not have to rely on their presence when needed. At his most vulnerable, however, he switches to more self-reliant behaviors, rejecting help and support and inhibiting signs of distress. Leo is showing the classic behaviors associated with a disorganized-controlling attachment pattern of relating.

We move into a year of working with parents, helping them to adopt a DDP-informed parenting approach, which is supported by April's attendance at a Nurturing Attachments group (Golding, 2014a). April and Don provide a highly predictable, attentive, and nurturing environment for Leo: They provide high levels of regulatory support at a sensory and emotional level, supported by a PACE attitude. They repair ruptures in the relationship so that Leo experiences love as unconditional. They provide reflections to Leo about his experience, reflections that he finds hard to tolerate. These have to be in small doses, helping him to learn to tolerate his inner world being made sense of. Some tentative security begins to grow at home, but it is fragile, and Leo remains a highly controlling child prone to aggressive outbursts. The world outside of home remains very stressful for Leo as a long struggle to find a suitable schooling environment begins.

Intervention Phase 2

When Leo is 4 years old, we decide to add some direct work to the continuing parenting support. We begin with an observational assessment based on the Marschak interaction method (MIM). This is a structured observational assessment of the parent–child relationship that has been developed and used by the Theraplay organization (Booth & Jernberg, 2009). This assessment demonstrates April and Don's growing skill in managing Leo's insecurity. They provide a safe, nurturing, and containing environment that is well structured and provides regulatory support as Leo needs it. Structure and boundaries are put in place within a highly warm parenting style. Leo responds well to this, but his need to control is never far from the surface, and he particularly resists the nurturing activities. It is notable that Leo responds well to the younger activities betraying the emotional immaturity that is so often masked by his pseudomaturity. After this, April and Don are helped to introduce more relationship-based play attuned to this younger emotional age at home. It is hoped that this will help to build Leo's safety in his relationship with his parents, increase regulatory support, and provide a platform for the direct DDP work planned for later.

Alongside this, some support is offered to school from the specialist education team while I continue to offer parenting support. In addition, an occupational therapist joins Leo's team to provide additional support with sensory regulation.

During this phase, Leo does appear to be developing increased security within his family. There are periods of growing stability and periods when Leo appears to be more dysregulated and anxious. The outside world continues to be challenging for Leo. In addition, there is an ongoing tension with Michael. Leo struggles with an older, capable brother and is jealous of the attention their parents give to him. This rivalry between Leo and Michael will continue as each tries to make sense of a sibling relationship within which one was born and one was adopted into the family.

Intervention Phase 3

When Leo is 5 years old, he is again struggling with escalating fears and anxiety. He has always known he is adopted and that Michael is not. With cognitive maturity this begins to trouble him in a different way. He struggles to make sense of the idea that some families are kind and some are hurtful. With increasing cognitive maturity, his feelings of shame and fear of abandonment are closer to the surface. These become harder to deny and more intrusive, affecting his reactions to routine frustrations. Increasing empathy and more awareness about how his current behaviors are experienced by others affects Leo. The shame from Leo's past and feelings of culpability around not being cared for by his birth family only strengthen this complex mix of emotion in the present. This is leading to big fears that his adoptive family will recognize his badness and abandon him too. His increasing cognitive abilities allow him to understand himself in more complex ways, and his attributions are largely negative. Leo's developing sense of identity as an adopted child is largely poor. As before, his anxiety and agitation manifests through angry and aggressive behaviors toward his mother. Now he can also notice himself getting anxious but finds it hard not to interpret this as being naughty. He describes getting hot and prickly on his skin and talks about having black bugs inside himself that make him naughty. Controlling behaviors redouble, and attempts by his parents to emotionally connect with him appear to enrage him. Leo is a sensitive, empathetic child who does not want to hurt anyone. His dysregulated rages at home and school fill him with shame and activate his worst fears. Leo does not want to be seen or understood.

As I continue to support the parents and increase my support to school staff, they all appear worn down by the ongoing challenges. In working with Leo's mom, we discover elements of her attachment history that are being triggered by her son's anger. She wants to stay accepting and available to him, recognizing that these are the times when he needs her most. She decides to get some support, from a therapist already known to her, to further explore this so that she can be more flexible when these triggers arise. She shares her self-exploration with me as it is important that I also understand these triggers and do not unwittingly make it difficult for her when I am working with Leo.

Leo is referred for a psychiatric assessment; this leads to medication to help with anxiety as well as some support for Leo from the community psychiatric nurse (CPN) that is aimed at building his resilience and emotional regulation. Over the next year, Leo settles and his regulation improves. He builds up to being able to attend mornings at school, and his physical aggression toward his peers decreases. Along with this, Leo is increasingly recognizing that he is struggling, and he is developing some trust that others might be able to help him with this. When his work with the CPN ends, Leo expresses concern. He wants to know who will help them "sort this stuff out now" and wonders if I can help him. I have been "hired," and we are ready to begin a more direct DDP intervention with Leo.

Intervention Phase 4

When I meet Leo to begin therapy, gone is the charming child of our first meeting, although I will see flashes of this as we work together and as I observe him with others. He uses the full charm offensive with the head teacher at his school, for instance. With me he wants to control in different ways. This 6-year-old comes in determined to show me who is in charge and with an apparent determination not to be understood by me. Even light "Connect and Chat" is difficult for him as I try to establish an intersubjective connection. This frightened child, who wants help to sort things out, is terrified of being known. I go slowly, follow where he leads, but persistently attempt some gentle leads as I follow him. I establish a rhythm to the sessions to help him feel safe with structured beginnings and endings. We do relational activities, drawing from Theraplay ideas (Booth & Jernberg, 2009), when talking is too much, but I continue to talk to him, about him, and just occasionally for him. "Talking for" can enrage him as it evokes his feelings. He finds my empathy difficult to tolerate, so I learn to tone it down and keep it factual.

For example, the following dialogue occurred when Leo told me about having a new bank account and his feelings about this being different from his brother's account. I follow this and explore with him why this is hard. His mom and I then lead to some thinking about jealousy and perhaps feeling less good than one's brother. He experiences connection from his mom around exploring these difficult experiences.

LEO: Mom wants me to keep my money so I can get older and I can buy stuff. I have a bank account. Michael has one but his is stupid.

KIM: I wonder why Michael's is stupid?

LEO: Because I get more money. Michael's losing because I have more money than him.

KIM: You both have bank accounts, and you are both saving some money, but Michael's is stupid. Is that why it's stupid, because he hasn't got so much money?

LEO: Yes.

MOM: [With a gentle tone] Or could it be because he's got a card and you haven't?

KIM: Ah, so you are a bit jealous. I can understand why you would be jealous, if he has a card and you haven't. Sometimes it's hard having an older brother who has things that you don't have.

Leo starts pushing one of the soft toys into his mom's face.

> KIM: I think, mom, that maybe Leo worries that you don't love him as much when Michael has things that he doesn't have.

Mom leans forward and gives Leo a hug. He tolerates this for a moment and then moves away demanding his drink. He opens the cupboards as if looking for something. Our conversation is over for now.

Leo's favorite activity is to build a den out of all the blankets, cushions, and soft toys in the room. He snuggles under these and can tolerate mom and I quietly talking about him, making sense of his experience in the present, with an occasional touching on the past.

For example, mom has told me that Leo got frightened when another child had a rage. Leo witnessed this but wasn't involved. In response, Leo ran to mom and started hitting her. As mom is telling me, Leo does all he can to distract us with demands that we fetch things for him. He then becomes focused on my locket, as he has in previous sessions, and whether I have a photograph inside. I follow his attention briefly, as we check once more that there is no photograph. Then I guide us all back to how frightening it was when the other child got so angry. Mom and I chat about how much Leo doesn't want to talk about this. Mom wonders if it is because Leo got cross with mom, and perhaps he doesn't want this to come out. We chat about how confusing this is for Leo when he has big feelings and he doesn't know what to do with them. He runs to mom to help him but then is frightened that she might hurt him instead. He had a birth mom who hurt him in the past. It is so hard to know if this mom now will help or hurt him. Leo is quiet in his den while he fiddles with one of the toys. Then it is enough, he demands we help him to fix his den again.

Over time, Leo can join us a little more in thinking about his feelings as my follow–lead–follow becomes a bit more intersubjective—he is allowing us to match his affect and attention is becoming more shared.

For example, as part of an activity, I have been making up a story about an elephant who goes to school but finds it a little bit tricky without his mom to help. Leo is very engaged with this and is helping me think about the things that the elephant will take to school and who he will pick to be his partner in the lessons. When I choose a name for the elephant, I unwittingly pick a name that has resonance for Leo.

> KIM: Oh, we don't have a name for the elephant. Shall we call him Harry?
> LEO: Yes, because Harry is my friend and he left. He plays basketball and is really quick. [With pride] He's better than me because I'm not that good.
> KIM: [Matching his animation] Wow, that sounds like a special friend.

Leo hides under the cushion.

> MOM: Is it hard thinking about Harry?
> KIM: [Talking more quietly and slowly] Did it make you feel sad thinking about your friend? He was at school with you and then he left. Is it sad remembering Harry? Ah, no wonder. He left and was so special, good at basketball and everything, and now he is not there. I would feel a bit sad about that.
> LEO: [Moves from under the cushion] I miss Harry.
> MOM: [Puts her arm on Leo and comments quietly] It is sad when friends leave, isn't it?

Perhaps fear is decreasing and Leo has some intention to be understood in very small steps. The affective–reflective dialogue still needs to be light on the affect, but a dialogue is happening. Leo often follows these more connected sessions with a need to get back in charge. Sometimes he mimics the dysregulation he can genuinely display, but this is an attempt to put distance between us. He resists our attempts to help him to regulate. If he runs out of the room, it is rarely if ever with real distress but a need to reassert that he is in charge. Leo's insight into this is apparent in conversations he has afterward with mom and dad. At times, his honesty about what he does is captivating. He also expresses his frustration that he has done this. Leo is experiencing conflict between wanting a relationship with me, to let me help him to sort things out, and his fear of letting me get close. I draw encouragement from his increasing ability to allow his parents to regulate him and his increasing tolerance of their curiosity and empathy about his experience. Change seems very little within the therapy room but is more evident at home.

Occasionally, we have magic moments of connection that are deeper and more affective.

My most fond memory is the day the session starts to go horribly wrong. We begin okay with some interactional play between the three of us. I mistime an activity and Leo struggles with the level of nurture we are trying to provide. His attempts to take charge deteriorate into a full-blown toddler tantrum. His distress is real, and our attempts to soothe him are rejected. Feeling helpless, mom and I look at each other: "What now?" Just at this moment, a crow flies past the window. Leo's attention is grabbed by this, and I take my own opportunity. I tell Leo that the crow is worried about him and has come to see if he is alright. Leo is intrigued. He gets up and moves to the window just as the crow settles onto the branch of the tree. I talk for the crow, allowing the crow to express my acceptance, curiosity, and empathy for what Leo is experiencing. Then the magic: Leo talks to the crow with a very convincing crow noise, and the crow caws back! As this cawing goes back and forth, a few times I keep on talking, helping Leo and the crow to find the affective–reflective dialogue that was so hard for him to tolerate from me directly. As the crow flies away, I comment that he knows Leo is okay now. We go back to our activities all more regulated by the experience!

As our work progresses, I develop a better understanding of the neurodevelopmental difficulties that Leo struggles with. As an articulate child, he often masks these behind his good verbal abilities, but his parents and I become aware of more profound speech and processing difficulties. As April and Don seek advice to help him, this piece of the puzzle falls into place, and we understand why school continues to be so stressful for him. It also explains why the more verbal elements of the therapeutic work are harder for him than the experiential. I learn to adjust the way I talk to Leo, more simply and with more checking that he understands.

As Leo becomes more open and engaged to the DDP work, I can help him to make sense of some of his current experience in light of past experiences. His security with his mom continues to grow, and there is some nice claiming through hide-and-seek, with Leo finding his mom—no easy task to hide in a small therapy room, but the symbolism is clear. Leo becomes more comfortable allowing himself to be younger and letting his mom nurture him.

Leo becomes more open to coregulation within sessions, supported by the Theraplay activities, but cocreation always remains more challenging. We do small bits of talking together, the three of us, as we try to make sense of experiences big and little that happened during the week. The biggest progress in this area is, however, at home, and it is lovely to hear of conversations he and his mom have that reveal his developing reflective capacity and willingness to cocreate with mom. This also displays his decreasing shame, as empathy for others, guilt, and remorse became more apparent.

A favorite example I have written about elsewhere is the story of a difficult day at school (see Golding, 2017). Leo manages to explore an incident when he has hit two other children and to make sense of this with the support of mom's acceptance, curiosity, and empathy. Leo then decides to make cards for the children in question, urgently needing to take these to the children straight away as he does not want the children to be upset all night. Leo is learning that he is a kind boy, that things can go wrong, and that he can help to make things right again. After he has delivered his cards, he tells his parents that he "feels good."

I continue to work with Leo and his mother, alongside parenting support with both parents, until Leo is 7 years old. He continues to find it hard to relinquish control and to get frustrated quickly if things don't go the way he plans. However, this becomes easier for him to manage as the sessions progress. I notice an increase in maturity and an increasing ability to let his mom help him to manage when he is experiencing difficulty. Leo is looking much more secure within his family.

Afterword

Although our therapy finished, the journey continues. I do a further brief intervention with Leo at his own request when he is 8 and wanting to understand his life story more fully. Supported by his mom and dad, we explore together what happened to him during his 5 weeks living with his birth family. His maturity and engagement with this is impressive. Afterward, he describes feeling sad and has some thoughts that maybe he shouldn't have asked the questions, but overall this has been a positive step in his understanding and development of a positive sense of identity.

At the time of writing, Leo is now 10 years old. His security within the family has continued to grow, but sadly, the right school for him has proved elusive, and the search continues.

I will end this case study with a recent incident described in his mom's words that demonstrates the progress that Leo has made.

More good news—well, good news in the way only a parent of a child with attachment issues could view it! We've been doing lots of car boot sales recently, and it was mine and Leo's role to count up the money. Sadly, having counted it up, when I left the room Leo stole £6. (This was last Friday.) On Sunday morning, he was insistent that we both count his money. I thought it odd, as I knew he only had about £1.40. Anyway, he brought his wallet in and proceeded to count out £7 and was about to start on the coppers. I asked where this extra money had come from, and initially he got angry—a sure sign of shame. I told him that I was there for him when he could talk about it, and after about 30 minutes he came and told me that he'd taken it. He struggled a lot with guilt—wanting to give everything he owned to me to make up for it, but I just kept repeating that everyone makes mistakes and how proud I was that he came to tell me and how hard that must have been. To be fair, he's super shocked now, because I've increased his pocket money but specified jobs he must do to get it, saying that his maturity in being able to put right what had gone wrong showed he was ready for that. I can't tell you how proud I was of him—for any child who'd mucked up like that it would have been difficult, but the leap he took . . . ! I have just dropped him off for his taster morning, and he was able to tell me he was scared and didn't want me to leave. Just amazing! So, therapeutic parenting does work . . . it just takes 8½ years!

CONCLUSION

Good beginnings, where the more cognitive information-sharing processes take place effectively, create a later context and atmosphere of shared awareness and complementary goals. This enables parent work and therapy sessions to focus on emotional connections and on setting necessary limits to behavior when required. Therapy involves weaving narrative threads together to make one story. The plotlines outside therapy are many, and different stories interconnect. Therapy can be seen as finding the threads that bind the story together. One thread is the work undertaken between therapist and parents. Another is the work undertaken with the therapist, parents, and their child. At any one time, the threads will be entwined in different ways. The thread of the therapist's work with the parents and child may be there for a long time or it may come and go. What determines the pattern is the therapist's connectedness to the parents through which she can enable the parents to best help their child. Sometimes the pattern also includes a thread between the therapist and the child as the child grows into an adult and makes choices to develop her own stories.

CHAPTER 6

The Complex Therapeutic Alliance with the Parents

The therapist has many roles when working with the parents of a child with developmental trauma. The therapist must focus on her relationship with a parent to ensure that the parent is safe, open, and engaged while relating with the therapist. From there, she must be ready to be a consultant, teacher, therapist, support person, coach, and mentor for the parent as needed by the parent and child. All the while, the therapist is engaged with the parent in a manner similar to how the parent is—or will be—engaged with the child. As the parent comes to feel safe with the therapist, the parent begins to enter into reciprocal conversations that lead to developing stories. These include stories about parenting and the parent's own childhood, as well as general stories involving areas of pride and shame in the parent's life. From there, the therapist is able to get a sense of the parent's view of self and her narrative. With this foundation in hand, the therapist then begins to develop with the parent ways that they may—together—assist the child in resolving themes related to developmental trauma and in developing new themes around the child's relationship with the parent. During this complex journey, involving the development of the therapeutic alliance, there are likely to be times when the relationship between therapist and parent ruptures. Perhaps the parent feels blamed in some way or is frustrated because the child is not yet receiving therapy. At these times, the therapist works hard to repair the relationship so that they can continue to work together to meet the needs of the child.

DEVELOPING THE THERAPEUTIC ALLIANCE WITH THE PARENTS

In this section, the importance of the therapist building a relationship with the parents based on trust and understanding is explored. This builds a foundation for mutual respect which will be important for supporting the continuing intervention. The therapist will be PACE-ful towards the parents, helping them to reflect on their attachment history, and supporting any blocked care which is apparent within the parents.

Getting to Know the Parents

The therapist will initially focus on the parents' experience of their child. It is this that brought the parents to see the therapist, so the parents need a space to share what is happening with all its challenges and frustrations. This begins the process of getting to know the parents. Their conversation may begin with anger, discouragement, fears, and even shame. And you need to listen, understand, and wait—without judgment, only playfulness, acceptance, curiosity, and empathy (PACE), probably without much playfulness. And when they have told this beginning of their story—which may be the hardest bit—they need to know that you understand how hard it is and how much it matters to them. From there you may notice a pause and an opening to explore their hopes and dreams when years ago they decided to become parents. This helps the parents to feel understood through a broader lens than that of their current challenges, to experience the therapist as truly getting to know them. This may help them to feel safer to show their doubts—their hopes and dreams may not come true. And from there they may become vulnerable. They show no blame now, no resentment, only pain. When the parents share this pain, and when you are able to hear, understand, experience empathy, and not judge them, the parents may begin to trust you.

During these early conversations, a parent needs to experience the therapist experiencing her as being a good person who is doing the best that she can and who cares about her child. The therapist's intersubjective experience of her positive intentions and qualities will make it less likely that the parent will become defensive when the therapist later explores and perhaps questions some of her ways of managing her child's challenging behaviors.

It is vital at the beginning of therapy that the parent trusts that the therapist values her motives and efforts for her child. It is vital that the therapist experiences the parent's strength and challenges and communicates that experience intersubjectively so that the parent feels safe. The therapist and parent need to become a team that is working cooperatively and with reciprocal trust that both are doing their best to meet the needs of the child. At times this can be very challenging. Therapists want to protect children, and when the parent tells stories of escalating consequences and mistimed interventions with little compassion for her child's history, it is likely to trigger the therapist's own alarm system and a desire to correct and lecture. It is at these times when the therapist has to hold most tightly to the transforming possibilities of PACE . . . a way of being that needs to run through all interactions.

Blocked Care

Parenting a child with multiple challenging behaviors lasting for a considerable period of time is very stressful. One of the greatest difficulties in providing care for the child who experienced developmental trauma is that the child does not seem to respond to the parents' care. Parents of traumatized children often say that they feel the child is simply a boarder in their home or that their child appears to want to live anywhere than with them.

Intimate relationships, whether between partners or between parent and child, work best neurologically and psychologically when they are reciprocal. The systems involved in caregiving in our brains are the same systems involved in attachment (Hughes & Baylin, 2012). The child's attachment behaviors involve wanting to be near his parent, experiencing pleasure in being with her, becoming skilled in reading her socio-emotional cues, and valuing the meanings of routines and rituals that make up their interactions. These attachment systems are activated by the equivalent systems in the caregiver's brain. When the caregiver starts to give up and fail to respond, the attachment behaviors weaken. The child turns even further away from seeking connection, and the caregiver's desire and readiness to initiate and respond also weakens. The parent becomes less interested in being near her child, she enjoys her time with her child less, she is less interested in reading the child's socio-emotional cues, and she experiences less meaning in their routines and rituals. The child's blocked trust leads to the parent's blocked care. This is not a sign of selfishness; rather, it represents the parent's natural response to the pain of continuing rejection.

Helping parents understand and recognize the neuropsychological state of blocked care helps them to make sense of an experience that has filled them with shame. They may have come to dislike and continually blame their child, made repeated efforts to exert greater and greater control over him, or finally given up. Their basic neurology has led them to a chronic state of self-protection, with little space for their child.

When a parent is experiencing blocked care, it is of value to provide the parent with psychoeducation about the nature of both blocked trust and blocked care. This may help the parent to remember that her child is a child not an adult and to have compassion for his history. This information may enable the parent to experience the rejection less personally and have more patience with the child's behaviors.

Sometimes such information is not sufficient. Then it is crucial that the parent rely on the therapist for care. The therapist can help the parent to reflect on whether she can rely on another adult—partner, best friend—who will become engaged with her in a reciprocal manner. If the parent's own attachment tendencies are successful in allowing another adult to care for her, then she is more likely to experience her own caregiving becoming active again. The following is an example of blocked care and the therapist's response.

"Somedays I just can't stand him! He looks through me like I'm not there—like I mean nothing to him! Adopting him was the worst decision that I've ever made in my life!"

Janelle adopted her 7-year-old son, Nathaniel, 3 years before. Since then, her life has only gone from bad to worse. She is increasingly isolated from her family and friends. Nathaniel seems to others a quiet, sweet, gentle boy who might be most parents' ideal child. When Janelle expresses her frustration over his distance from her and seeming indifference to relating with her, she generally gets looks of surprise that she is complaining about her son. As her frustration turns to anger, these looks turn to disapproval over her seeming rejection of her son. Even her husband, Jim, is starting to say that she might be expecting too much, that she needs to accept him as he is.

Karen, the dyadic developmental psychotherapy (DDP) therapist that

Janelle contacted 4 months ago, listens. Two months before, Janelle was hopeful that the joint sessions that had just begun would make a difference. Now she has doubts about anything being able to make a difference.

Then Karen says, "You give and give and give—as a good mother would do—and he seems to reject it, to reject you. Like he does not want a mother, only someone to meet his physical needs—anyone might do."

Janelle replies, "Yes, what am I doing wrong? What's so wrong with me? Aren't I better than his first mother who drank and slept all day and only spoke to him when she was yelling at him because he was bothering her?"

"You're so ready to give him what his first mother did not give him—what he probably was desperate for when he was a baby and toddler—and he seems to say, 'Don't bother! I don't want it!'"

Janelle cries out, *"He doesn't want me!"*

Karen expresses her empathy in her face and voice, matching Janelle's pain, experiencing it with her. As Janelle cries more softly, Karen sits quietly with her, tears in her own eyes. Karen whispers, "I see the mother you are. I have to help Nathaniel see who you are. And then maybe to help him to not fear letting you mother him."

"Why would he fear me?"

"He fears that as he starts to need you, you will not like his clinging, his crying, his neediness—and you will not want him anymore. He really doesn't believe that he matters to you. And you don't believe that you matter to him."

"What do we do to make him know that he does matter to me?"

"First, I help you to find the strength to keep being his mother when he keeps saying that he doesn't want you to. Then we accept, understand, and have empathy for his loneliness that lies under his pushing you away. Then I help you again to hold onto your strength to keep being his mother."

"Can I trust that you won't give up, Karen?"

"Yes," Karen expresses with confidence and with care.

"Then tell me what we do next," Janelle replies, carrying a bit of Karen's confidence in her voice.

Attachment History

When we are parents, our own attachment history is activated to a greater extent than when we are not in a caregiving relationship. Providing care in various situations is likely to activate memories (conscious or unconscious) of similar situations when we were being cared for. Our child's behaviors are also likely to activate memories of our own behaviors and our parents' responses to us when we were children. If our child now has very challenging behaviors due to his history of developmental trauma, these behaviors are likely to activate a range of memories from our own attachment history. If there are unresolved (or partially resolved) traumatic experiences in our own history, then we are at risk of becoming dysregulated, dissociative, and defensively or aggressively reactive if our child acts in ways that trigger those unresolved experiences.

Parents may feel threatened when the therapist asks about their attachment history, so it is best to approach this theme in an open and engaged way, responding with PACE to any defensiveness. Make it clear that all parents are asked about their attachment history because we all are influenced by our history in raising our children, and we are more likely to have our history activated by very challenging behaviors. Also, the therapist might let parents know that simply reflecting on our history and seeing the connections with our current reactions to our child's behavior is often enough to reduce the impact of the behavior on us. With reflection and understanding, we are often able to inhibit a reaction to the behavior, make sense of it, and then choose the best response. Of course, sometimes the unresolved experiences in a parent's attachment history may require more time and effort to be resolved before the parent is able to provide safety for his child in joint sessions. At these times, the parent may need to engage in his own therapy prior to—or concurrently with—joint sessions with his child.

Greg was becoming impatient with the therapist's thoughts about the challenging behaviors that his son, Chris, kept demonstrating: "Okay, I get it. He lost his grandfather and misses him. But it's been 4 months and he has to learn that life goes on and he has responsibilities. His grandfather was my father too, you know, and I've gotten on with my life."

The therapist responded, "I hear you saying that you understand your son's grief over the loss of his grandfather. And you fear that this grief might become an excuse to not do what he needs to be doing in handling his responsibilities. You want to support your son, and you worry that my focus on PACE for so long over his grandfather's death might prevent your son from facing his responsibilities."

"That's right. I think that we both need to say that he needs to just move on."

"Is that the message that you got when you were his age? I recall that your twin sister died when you were 11. What do you recall was your father's approach to helping you to handle things afterward?"

"After a month or so he said to just stop thinking about it. That it would be easier if I just focused on my homework and chores and maybe spend more time with my friends."

"How did he seem to handle the death of his daughter?"

"I have no idea. We never talked about it. He didn't seem any different. You know, I do recall just wishing that once we'd just sit down and be sad together. Then it wouldn't seem like I was the only one who was sad."

"What might have happened if your dad sat with you, maybe put his arm around you and recalled your sister with you?"

"I would have cried—really cried. Maybe he didn't want that."

"Why?"

"I don't know. Maybe it would have made him sad and he wasn't sure he could handle it."

"Have you sat like that with your son?"

"I guess maybe I've been afraid to. Afraid that I might start crying and that wouldn't be fair to him."

"Wouldn't be fair to him, because?"

"Because he needs to see me strong, so he can be strong and handle things like this in life when they come up."

"And you worry that if you are sad together it would make you both weaker?"

"I think that's what my dad taught me over the years—if you let yourself be sad, you get weak and then you won't be as strong as you need to be."

"Is that what you want to teach your son?"

"I don't know what I want to teach him."

"What about teaching him that if you are sad together over the death of this man who was important to both of you, and comfort each other over your sadness, that you will also become stronger together. More than if you try to handle your sadness alone, by making it go away."

"Maybe I'd like to teach him that. Maybe I'm not sure I can."

"Maybe I can help you to feel safe enough to be sad with your son. Maybe your father's death will help you to learn something that your father never knew how to teach you when he was alive."

"That would be something."

PACE with Parents

When we respond to parents' vulnerable or defensive behaviors with the attitude of PACE, we are both supporting them in their distress and helping them to make sense of it—what is going on for *them*—as they relate with their child. This will be their first experience of us and of PACE and its value. This *experiencing* of PACE will have far more impact than us falling into the trap of simply describing PACE, telling them or even perhaps lecturing them about PACE and why they should be doing it with their children.

Whether the therapist is providing parenting support or is meeting with the parents to prepare them for therapeutic work with their child, PACE will be a central part of this work. When parenting support is DDP informed, PACE will sit alongside problem solving. The therapist forms emotional connections with the parents, and this supports their joint reflections about parenting tasks or decisions. The practitioner will focus on curious exploration with the parents, and inevitably this will slow down the desire to problem-solve and reach for quick solutions without first understanding what is going on. Deep curiosity about the parents and their experiences, supported by acceptance of everything that is being discovered and empathy for the struggles and frustrations, allows parents to move into a more reflective stance from which they can begin to rediscover their child. This more reflective stance is also likely to assist the parents in regulating their emotional responses to their child's challenging behaviors.

Conversations—with PACE embedded in them—produce change without being about problem solving. This is the paradox of change through radical acceptance. Parents often unexpectedly discover a way forward as therapist and parents explore together behaviors, dilemmas, and evoked responses.

With PACE, the therapist first understands the parents' experience of parenting the child. What is the effect on them? When do they lose empathy or find it hard to stay with acceptance? What are their fears about the child's behavior? What meaning does it have for them? This helps parents to explore what triggers them into a defensive response toward their child, helping to break the negative cycle embedded in blocked trust being met with blocked care. This compassionate, attuned exploration allows parents to develop increased flexibility and energy to try something new.

Next, the therapist can help the parents to understand the child's experience too. Together they wonder about and explore what might be going on for the child in the present and how this is linked to the past. With this increased understanding, the parents will be better able to connect with the child. From a foundation of open and engaged connection, the therapist and parents can together think about the parenting of the child. Parenting becomes a process of connection and behavioral support that increases security for the child and in turn allows the child to become more flexible in his or her responses.

As the parents build trust in the therapist, the therapist will be able to explore each parent's most difficult experience. The therapist will have acceptance and empathy for feelings of shame, anger, fear, despair, or hopelessness that the parents may hold. He will provide coregulation for the parents, who, in not being judged themselves, will be able to stop needing to blame their child and be more able to reflect upon their experiences and make sense of behavior. Specific thinking about ways of parenting the child will emerge from this safety and curious exploration. The parents will find that the discipline, structure, and behavioral support that they need to provide for their child will be empowered by PACE. Discipline will be underpinned by understanding and acceptance, providing guidance and teaching for the child. The child will experience this type of discipline differently; it will surprise the child and over time help him or her to become more open and trusting, with a growing confidence in the parents' good intentions and secure in their unconditional love. PACE brings them all back to a place where they can begin to trust the relationship they are building together.

A therapist is meeting with an adoptive parent, providing her with some parenting support through a difficult period in her child's life.

THERAPIST: It has been tough then, seeing her getting so stressed and angry again. I guess it must be hard going back to this when things have been so much calmer.

PARENT: Yes, in a way it is harder than when she was like this all the time. We got used to it back then, it was every day. It has taken me by surprise this time. I just don't know how to deal with her when she is so angry toward me. I can't let her get away with some of the things that she says.

THERAPIST: Yes, I can see how that is difficult. I am guessing some of those things are quite hurtful?

PARENT: Too right. It's like we haven't made any progress at all. She doesn't want to live with us now; just like she didn't want to live with us the day she moved in.

THERAPIST: Yes, I can see how hard that must be. You've been working so hard to help her feel secure, and right now it feels like you have made no progress at all! I wonder what is most hard about it?

PARENT: I feel useless, like a total failure. Why did I ever think I could parent children?

THERAPIST: I remember, when I first knew you, it was a bit the same. You were feeling useless then too. Do you remember we thought about all the fertility treatment you had, and when it failed you thought that was your body telling you that you couldn't be a parent?

PARENT: Yes, and I remember how we thought it might have gone back even further, my mom always treating me as a useless daughter, and now I feel like a useless mother. I'm back there aren't I? I hadn't thought about it, but when Yazi started shouting at me, telling me I was useless and she never wanted me as a mother, I just went right back again, didn't I? Why didn't I see it?

THERAPIST: That makes sense to me. It's hard to see when you are in the thick of it. She does give you a mental battering, doesn't she? Hard for you to stay open to yourself or her when she is making you feel so useless.

PARENT: That's what I must do, right? It's not about how I punish her for being angry, is it? It's how I stay open so I can reach the stuff behind the anger. Thanks for reminding me.

DEEPENING AND EXPANDING THE THERAPEUTIC ALLIANCE

As parents learn to engage in open and engaged conversations with the therapist, they learn the value of having such conversations with their child. As they engage more easily in such conversations, they discover that their own life stories, perceptions, values, and beliefs have a great impact on their parenting and that their child's life stories greatly impact his daily behaviors. Through the experience of being securely held in the mind and heart of the therapist, parents come to understand the value of their child also being in their mind and heart. Through the relationship that they have with the child's therapist, parents discover why their relationship with their child is the key factor in whatever progress their child is likely to make.

After trust has been established, parents are able to rely on the therapist for directly learning new ways of engaging their child in therapy and at home. When they are not defensive, they are likely to respond positively to the therapist's coaching them, modeling for them, practicing with them, along with allowing the therapist to serve as an attachment figure and mentor for their journey toward increasing their caregiving skills with their mistrustful child. They might role-play with the therapist alternative ways of relating to the child during a conflict. They are likely to use the therapist as a model for how to express curiosity at their child's behavior while maintaining the necessary open and engaged, accepting attitude that will make it likely that their child will enter a conversation with them about the troubling behaviors or vulnerable fears. They are likely to be receptive to the therapist's efforts to coach them to inhibit their defensive reactions to their child's challenging behaviors so that they can remain open and engaged. And they might directly learn how to express empathy for the child's distress before making any efforts to reassure him or problem solve.

Once the therapist judges that the parents are able to actively participate in joint sessions with their child, the dyadic work can begin with the child being brought into the sessions. This is of course an opportunity for the therapist to begin to directly get to know the child she has been hearing about and is also an opportunity to observe the parent–child relationship and to develop a more detailed understanding of the strengths and vulnerabilities within it. Parent sessions interspersed with the dyadic work are an opportunity for parents to begin to explore their responses to the sessions, raise any uncertainties about them, and receive further coaching based on a lived experience of being in therapy with their child. Parent sessions also allow therapists to give direct feedback about the qualities they observe in the sessions with specific examples from attunement, PACE, and comfort and joy, which will support parents to strengthen their skills and ways of being that will help their child to grow.

When parents are able to be with their child in sessions offering PACE and safety, their presence will make a significant contribution. This will support the child in addressing their traumas and integrating their story and also in strengthening the bond between child and parents. Their open and engaged presence helps their child to feel safe when exploring themes of fear and shame. They may coregulate the child's difficult affective states while helping the child to develop new meanings about events that they were present for. When their child explores traumatic events, they are available to provide comfort in a way that the therapist would not be able to do. Such comforting further strengthens their child's attachment with them. After their child expresses their doubts and mistrust, their "PACE-ful" response increases their child's confidence and trust in them and their relationship.

MOVING FROM MISTRUST TO TRUST WITH GRANDPARENTS

The following composite case example is a story of working with grandparents. Often, children who have experienced developmental trauma reside with their kin as an alternative to foster care. While this story is inspired by many families Kim has worked with, the characters in this story are invented.

As I put the telephone down, I can feel a sense of satisfaction and hope rise within me. This is not my usual response to a call where I have listened to a parent in distress who needs to offload her frustration and fear that things will not change. Then again, Naomie is not a usual parent for me. I am privileged to work with many parents seeking the support of a psychologist. Naomie, however, only became involved with me because of her fear that otherwise she would lose her grandson. From a traveler (Roma) community, she remains distrustful of external services and the influence they can have over her. My privilege is in being allowed into her life, so that trust can develop at her own pace. She is kinship carer and grandmother to 7-year-old Stevie. It has taken 9 months for her to feel confident enough to ring me and confide that she is finding things tough. Trust has come slowly, and keeping the network onboard with a slow-paced intervention has been a challenge.

I think back to my first network meeting to discuss Stevie. Apparently tough on the outside, belying the anxiety within, Stevie is a challenging child who is being brought up by his grandmother, Naomie, and step-grandfather, William. They are conspicuous by their absence at this first meeting. This is a divided network, with strong ideas about what should happen with Stevie. School staff are struggling to manage a disruptive child in class who rarely arrives at school on time and sometimes doesn't arrive at all. They want him moved to local authority foster carers, away from the family that they believe is a bad influence on him. The family support worker, Cerys, is frustrated because she is finding it difficult to engage with the family and is concerned that Stevie is spending too much unsupervised time moving between his grandparents' house and that of Naomie's sister, Annie, who lives two doors away. She is also worried about the "accidental" informal meetings between Stevie and his father, John, which are not sanctioned by the social care team. The social worker, Gary, sits opposite me. I have worked with him before and trust his judgment. He shares some of the concerns being expressed but feels that Stevie deserves a chance to grow up within his family. He has a strong conviction that Stevie should grow up within his traveler community and feels that Naomie and William are committed to offering this, even though some of their parenting practices are of concern. He wants me to work with Naomie and William to enable Stevie to stay with them.

I try to be curious with the network. I wonder why it is hard for Naomie to get Stevie to school and on time; I also reflect on the support that Annie can give to Naomie. This curiosity is not returned, masked by the anxiety of the members of the network and their desire to see things happening more quickly. Getting nowhere, I switch to empathy for their concerns for this child and their desire to get things right for him. There are some shared goals here that we can all acknowledge. Supported by the social worker, I suggest that I try to engage Naomie and William with some parenting support, but caution that progress is likely to be slow. There is concern that I am not offering therapy for Stevie. I explain that this is unlikely to be helpful until the grandparents are more accepting of our help and understand and are comfortable with the DDP model. Attachment relationships are central to Stevie's difficulties, and he will need his current attachment figures fully involved in any intervention offered. Reluctantly, they agree to give my input a try and to attend further meetings with me. It is not the most auspicious start to an intervention.

My spirits sag further when I make my first home visit to meet with Naomie and William. They live in their own home, not far from the council-provided site where others of their family and community live. I am also aware that a couple of family members, including Annie, live on the same street. I imagine I can see the curtains twitching, feeling a stranger in this tight-knit community. As I stand and wait, I can hear the sound of dogs barking behind the door. I picture to myself lurchers or perhaps Staffordshire bull terriers. I realize I am going to have to question my own stereotypes and resolve to raise this in my supervision. They turn out to be two West Highland terriers, mother and daughter. As the door is opened, I briefly reflect on the strong community that surrounds Stevie and feel a twinge of sadness that this is so often not a feature of modern life in England.

This first meeting, as anticipated, is a tricky one. Naomie is polite but suspicious as she shows me in to their very tidy living room. I wonder if she has tidied up for my visit but then laugh to myself at imposing my standards on this lady. I suspect that cleanliness is a strong value for her. I can see a box of toys in the corner and photographs of Stevie on the wall. Stevie has a place in this home. I hear William and his grown-up son, Thomas, discussing their scrap metal business, but they remain in the kitchen out of my sight. I am aware that there have recently been some thefts of lead piping from the local church that are being blamed on the traveler community. I can understand that they will not welcome a *gorja* coming into their home.

The next 9 months is a slow building of trust with Naomie and William. I try to understand their family history from their perspective and to empathize with the difficulties that they have experienced with Naomie's own son, Stevie's father, John. Naomie's marriage at the age of 16 to John's father was not a happy one: I suspect some domestic violence, although this is not confirmed until I know Naomie a lot better. John and Mercy met at school and married, also at 16, when Mercy became pregnant. They did their best but they were very young, and Stevie's needs were often neglected. John could be quick to anger, and Mercy slipped into depression. Naomie, now married to William, tried to support them, and Naomi and William frequently cared for Stevie. They could not do anything, however, to stop the spiraling drug habits. Mercy and John were using these perhaps to manage deteriorating mental health without seeking outside support. Sadly, Mercy died from a drug overdose when Stevie was 3 years old. Stevie came to live with Naomie and William under an informal arrangement. William and Thomas tried to involve John in the business, but he became more and more troubled and out of their control. Child-protection concerns were raised as physical abuse by John against Stevie became evident, and Stevie was removed into foster care for a time while assessments of Naomie and William were undertaken. The formalized kinship placement was a vote of confidence in their commitment to Stevie, but they had to agree that John would not come to their home and would only meet Stevie during contact meetings set up by the social worker. They remain aware that Stevie could be taken from them at any time by a system that they do not feel part of. No wonder they are suspicious of my visits.

I listen without judging, am cautious and tentative about offering advice, and work hard to understand both a culture that is different from my own and a personal story that reflects the challenges of growing up in a minority group subjected to much discrimination. I find much to admire in the close-knit family bonds and strong values. I am concerned about parenting practices that involve a high level of shouting and perhaps too-high expectations. I observe how the isolation and suspiciousness within the local area is leading to a more closed and disadvantaged group and suspect that this in part is leading to increases in domestic violence and drug abuse. I notice how no one in the network around Stevie originates from a traveler community. I therefore introduce a foster carer, Kelly, whom I have previously worked with. She is a well-respected foster carer who is also from this community. I am pleased to see the help she can offer to the family, and it is welcome to see her support Naomie to attend the network meetings.

Slowly, I feel that Naomie begins to look forward to my visits. She seems more relaxed, and we find things to laugh together about. She teases me about my dislike of tea, an affront to her hospitality. The glass of water proffered by William when I arrive becomes a joke between us all. While I do not work directly with Stevie, I sometimes see him as he arrives home from school. He accepts my presence and understands that I am helping his grandparents so that they can take even better care of him. Naomie and William are warm and nurturing toward him; I also see a harsher side to their parenting at times, which I suspect contributes to Stevie's anxiety and fear that he could lose them.

Gradually, Naomie opens up about some of the doubts and fears she has in parenting Stevie. We explore his high level of separation anxiety, which makes getting him to school a daily nightmare. He is extremely attention-needing, and the respite from this when Stevie goes over to Annie's for tea or to play with her grandchildren is much needed. She knows that John is dropping in to see Stevie but is afraid to rock the boat. I wonder if these unplanned meetings are making Stevie anxious. Naomie is willing to consider this possibility. She will in time let the social worker help her to manage this so that visits are more planned, and Stevie can be supported to have good contact with his father.

Stevie regularly explodes in frustration and anger, behavior that Naomie and William interpret as naughty and disrespectful toward them. They become open to alternative possibilities that I suggest, and this leads to some decisions to try some different parenting approaches. I help them to learn how to respond with PACE, and Stevie is open to the curiosity and empathy they offer. However, frequently this is not sustained, and Naomie resorts to her former approach, which is based on punishment and coercion, while William withdraws. They are very reluctant to admit to not coping, and the triggers that I suspect they are both experiencing when Stevie has tantrums remain a "no-go" area. They still have high levels of anxiety that Stevie could be taken from them.

The telephone call from Naomie represents something of a turning point in this work. I listen, accept, and do not judge, although Naomie expects me to. She is tearful, close to her breaking point. I can see the possibilities of blocked care emerging, as she feels acute feelings of failure and disappointment in herself. I also notice that William is becoming more absorbed in his business and less present at home. I increase my visits to Naomie, and William is open to joining some of these.

Over the next few months, we explore together something of their own attachment histories and make sense of their current behaviors toward Stevie and each other when these are activated. Naomie learns that her own highly perfectionistic and demanding mother has left her with a strong need to get things right. Her sense of failure triggered by some of Stevie's behaviors echoes the disappointment she often experiences with her mother. Similarly, William recognizes that he was affected by a pattern witnessed with his own father, who would leave the family home sometimes for days or weeks, whenever there was discord. While William does not leave, he can emotionally withdraw if things become difficult, a pattern that increases Naomie's vulnerability and sense that she is getting it wrong.

During this time, I am consistently supported by Gary, an ally when others in the network complain that I am still not providing therapy for Stevie. There are changes, however, throughout the network, and we appear to be working better as a team. Cerys provides much needed practical support, which Naomie and William are more accepting of as they experience more acceptance and less judgment from her. I am pleased to see Kelly becoming a friend to Naomie, providing emotional support as well as practical help such as attending meetings and offering some respite when things are tough.

After this exploration, I notice an increasing determination in Naomie to parent Stevie differently, and I can see Stevie responding to this. William becomes a bigger source of support, but there is an increasing tension between Annie and Naomie. Recognizing how important Annie is to Naomie, I invite her to also meet with me. I am not surprised that Annie is suspicious about this but to her credit she agrees, and we have some very helpful three-way meetings.

While things improve a lot for Naomie, William, and Stevie, this is not an easy path. Stevie remains highly anxious, and his ability to regulate only increases slowly. His separation anxiety does moderate, making it easier to get him to school, and his episodes of dysregulation happen less frequently.

School staff are open to some training sessions to help them to understand the impact of Stevie's experience of developmental trauma on his behavior and capacity to learn. As they make adjustments to the support offered, Stevie becomes more engaged in school. They continue to need advice and guidance but are learning to help him to regulate in and out of the classroom, and they help him to engage successfully with a small group of friends. They notice that while Stevie will still get into conflict with teachers and with peers, he becomes able to talk about this to his support worker. His attention-needing in school does not moderate, however, and therefore an additional support worker is added to the team, so that neither of them will get too worn out by his ongoing needs.

Two years after my first contact with this family, Naomie and Annie have the confidence together to join one of our Nurturing Attachments groups. This will give them fortnightly support during school-term time over the next year and help them to further experience the DDP-informed parenting approach reflected in the house model of parenting (Golding, 2014a). William is too busy with his business to join but will attend a couple of evening sessions to better understand what Naomie and Annie are exploring. I am hopeful that with this support I can reduce my engagement. We have discussed therapy for Stevie but agree that for now they have enough going on. This will remain a possibility in the future, especially as Stevie begins to ask questions about his family. I am confident that Naomie and William will be open and honest with him, and that they will now feel able to ask for help when they need it.

CONCLUSION

Given the child's domains of impairment secondary to developmental trauma, raising him in a manner that meets his developmental needs and has an effect on his blocked trust is likely to be very challenging. The DDP therapist often needs to make significant efforts to ensure that parents are willing and able to provide the child with the care that they need. These efforts begin by establishing a therapeutic alliance with the parents, an alliance based on mutual respect and compassion and underpinned by the principles of PACE. Providing the parents with this support that they need in order to care for their child well is often the crucial component of successful therapy for the child.

As trust emerges within the therapeutic alliance, the parents are provided with modeling and coaching, teaching and guidance that will enable them to participate positively in the therapy sessions. They also receive knowledge and support to help them to provide their child with good care in their home as well. Ways of engaging the child in therapy are much more effective if they are congruent with how the child is being engaged at home.

These dual supports provided for parents in therapy and the home are based on the same principles that guide DDP for their child. Trauma is contagious, and parents who are looking after a traumatized child are likely to be experiencing many of the same feelings about themselves as parents as their child feels—I'm a failure at this relationship, I can't get anything right. Within DDP, both parent and child engage in the process of developing stories of hope and resilience, comfort and joy, and these new stories become an interwoven narrative that holds them both.

CHAPTER 7

Parenting Children with Developmental Trauma

Just as playfulness, acceptance, curiosity, and empathy (PACE) permeates the child's experience with his parents and therapist in therapy, PACE also permeates the child's life at home. Parents are curious about their children's inner life, seeking to understand and connect with this. They accept, without trying to change, the thoughts, feelings, wishes, fears, beliefs, and desires of their child and provide empathy for this experience. They provide playfulness at appropriate moments, allowing the child to experience joy in their relationship. Within PACE, the child in therapy is becoming skilled in reciprocal conversations that create new stories. The same child is deepening and expanding these stories at home with his parents. In this way, a more integrated sense of self emerges, which leads the way toward developing a coherent narrative.

The parenting attitude of PACE will support the child's developing sense of safety and exploration of self and other. To hold this attitude, parents need to have reasonable mentalization (Fonagy, Gergely, Jurist, & Target, 2002) and emotional regulation abilities. A key ability within mentalization is to be mind-minded: to understand and take into account the mental state of another person (Meins et al., 2002). When a parent can understand or make guesses about the internal experience of the child, it is easier for the parent to emotionally connect with the child.

Jonathan has just had his 8th birthday. He has done well this year: He enjoyed opening his presents without any disappointment, and he was able to cope with a family meal to celebrate. Over the next 2 days, however, he has been moody and sulky, not able to cooperate with the demands being made of him. He has also returned to more attention-needing behaviors—a side of him that his mom and dad have not seen for a while. It is dad's turn to settle Jonathan tonight. Jonathan is unhappy that mom is not there too. Dad thinks to himself that Jonathan managed his birthday so well this year. Perhaps this is the root of his behavior now. Maybe Jonathan is having trouble with the return to normalcy. Perhaps not being treated as special anymore has triggered old fears of not being good enough. Dad is pleased thinking this through. This is actually a step forward. Dad is seeing some tentative shoots of security in Jonathan managing his birthday and talks to Jonathan about this, expressing pleasure that Jonathan had enjoyed his birthday and also an understanding that Jonathan might wobble a bit now that things are getting back to normal.

Notice in this example that Jonathan's father remains emotionally regulated as he figures out what is going on for his son. The capacity for emotional regulation is also an important part of holding the attitude of PACE. Regulation enhances reflective function: Parents who can stay regulated or can notice the loss of this and bring themselves back to a regulated state will be more consistently present to the child. If either regulation or reflection is weak, then PACE will also be weak. This is a circular process. Regulation and reflection enhance PACE while the use of PACE further strengthens regulation and reflection.

OVERVIEW OF DDP-INFORMED PARENTING

As is illustrated in Figure 7.1, DDP-informed parenting, with PACE through its core, relies on the parents being able to offer their children a secure base. This is informed by an understanding of Attachment Theory. Parents will then help their children to develop a safe relationship, aided by an authoritative style of parenting offering unconditional love and acceptance. All of this provides a strong foundation for supporting the children with their behaviour whilst helping them to maintain feelings of security. These key ideas will be explored in this section.

Finding a Secure Base: Attachment Theory

Within dyadic developmental psychotherapy (DDP), parenting is informed by attachment theory (Hughes, 2009). This theory explains the range of attachment trauma themes that are commonly seen with developmentally traumatized children:

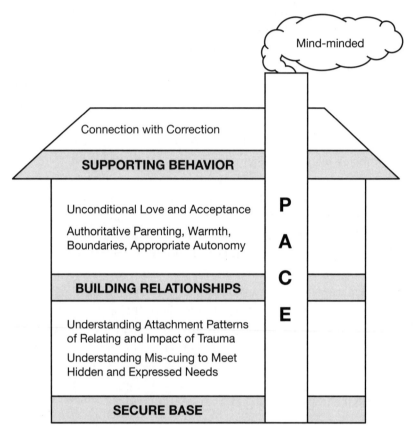

Figure 7.1 Overview of the dyadic developmental psychotherapy (DDP) approach to parenting. (Figure 7.1 has been modified from figure 3.6.4 in *Nurturing Attachments Training Resource* by Kim S. Golding, 2013, p. 331, with permission from Jessica Kingsley Publishers.)

1. These children believe that love is conditional not unconditional; they do not trust that their parents will be there for them "no matter what." The children do not feel good enough and expect to be found wanting.
2. Consequently, these children expect that their parents will reject them. They anticipate rejection not only because of how they are behaving, but also because of the range of thoughts and feelings that underlies this behavior.
3. These children therefore anticipate that they will be abandoned. Parents will not be available when needed.
4. These children manage these fears and beliefs by taking charge.

They become self-reliant or coercively in control. They cannot anticipate safe comfort, support, or guidance from their parents. Attachment breaks are frequent, and repair to these breaks is not straightforward.

5. Without comfort, support, and relationship repair, these children are not getting the attachment experience that they need. They do not develop emotional regulation or reflection abilities at the same rate as other children. Typically, these children are emotionally immature compared to their peers.

The dominant theme that connects this range of attachment trauma themes is that families do not feel safe to the children. Consequently, they do not express their needs in a clear way. Parents can understand the attachment insecurities of their children by understanding how their children miscue their needs.

Children who have grown up in an environment that lacks security learn to adapt their behavior in line with their expectations of parents rather than in tune with what they are experiencing internally. This means that they develop patterns of expressed and hidden needs as they cope with anticipated unpredictability or unavailability of parents (Dozier, 2003). If parents only meet the expressed needs, they will reinforce the pattern of insecure attachment that the child is displaying. Instead, parents need to meet the hidden needs as well as the expressed needs. This is sensitive parenting, but with a gentle challenge added. The child's expectations that parents will be unpredictable or unavailable are challenged so that the child can start to trust in the parents being there when needed.

Ten-year-old Crystal has just had a disappointment. Her father who has been overseas was due back this weekend. She has just been told that his return has been delayed. She appears unconcerned about this. She retreats to her bedroom where mom finds her, as usual intently reading her book. Mom sits on Crystal's bed and gently explores how she is feeling. "I am fine," Crystal proclaims, continuing to read her book. Mom persists but is angrily told to leave her alone. While Crystal is at school, mom pops a note on her pillow; she acknowledges Crystal's courage in managing the disappointment about dad's delayed return. She also comments that Crystal had made some great plans for this weekend to greet her father and how disappointing this feels. Later, mom finds Crystal quietly crying in her bedroom. This time she allows mom to comfort her.

Building Relationships

We know from longitudinal research that children's later adjustment, socially, behaviorally and in their good mental health and improved self-esteem, is correlated with the type of parenting that they experienced (Baumrind, 1978). This research demonstrated that highly authoritarian parenting, strict in discipline, led to young people who had difficulty showing initiative. They struggled to manage when freed from the shackles of this parenting. Highly permissive parenting, lax in discipline, led to young people who could be impulsive and who struggled to follow through plans; the lack of structure in early life made it hard for these children to provide themselves with internalized structure as they matured. Some children were neglected, experiencing harsh or lax parenting and little warmth or availability from parents. These were the children who had the greatest problems in adjustment as they were growing up. The best-adjusted children grew up to be autonomous, confident, and socially competent; everything we would want for our children. It was found that these children had parents who were warm and nurturing but also provided clear boundaries and structure for their children. They provided the children with appropriate opportunities to be autonomous, but this was linked to the developmental stage the children were at. These parents are described as authoritative.

It is this type of parenting we wish for in DDP-informed parents: Parents who are warm and nurturing, able to be curious about their children and therefore able to emotionally connect with them, accepting their inner life even while putting boundaries and limits on their behavior. There is, however, a further aspect to parenting developmentally traumatized children. These children have already experienced parenting that is counter to the healthy parenting of the authoritative parent. They have learned to mistrust parents and are often in states of blocked trust (Baylin & Hughes, 2016); they doubt their own lovability and thus experience high levels of shame; they fear entering reciprocal, intersubjective relationships; and they have adapted to all of this by miscuing their attachment needs. Parents of developmentally traumatized children need to provide therapeutically healthy environments as well as authoritative parenting. DDP-informed parenting takes these additional needs of the children into account.

Comfort, Curiosity, and Joy

Children in blocked trust remain angry with or shut down from relationships. They hide their more vulnerable states, avoiding the experience of sadness and shame. They cannot seek comfort from their parents. Comfort means being vulnerable, and the children hide from vulnerability at all cost. They do not feel safe enough to feel sad.

The children remain vigilant, narrowly focused on further signs of danger. This means that they also lose a wider curiosity about the world alongside the joy that comes from being able to relax and experience fun within relationships.

Comfort, curiosity, and joy are the big sacrifices that children with developmental traumas make to manage in a world that feels inherently unsafe. Parents need to help the children to relax their defensive responding so that they can become open to and engaged in social relationships. Within these relationships, children can discover the safety of vulnerability when comfort is available and accessible; the wonder of curiosity, as together with their parents they discover the world; and the fun of joy in relationships, being able to relax and enjoy relational moments of play.

These are the relationships that parents offer to developmentally traumatized children. Parents provide an ordinary experience of being parented that is authoritative: warm with structure and boundaries. Alongside this is an extraordinary experience that offers safety where there was danger, comfort where there was unavailability, and joy where there was pain. Children learn to trust and socially engage with safe parents. The intersubjective feels safe, and attachment needs are met.

Supporting Behavior: Connection with "Correction"

Connection

All children need emotional connection. Secure children receive this connection from birth: Long before parents have to be concerned with discipline, they are connecting with their children, providing them with love and nurture that is unconditional. This provides the children with an experience of parents as responsive and sensitive to their needs. They learn to trust in their parents and develop a conviction of their own lovability.

Infants mature into toddlers. With mobility and curiosity, these young children move out into the world, learning and experimenting. They need to be kept safe; parents provide discipline alongside the connection that is solidly present.

The trust that secure children developed in infancy moves with them as their world expands, encompassing behavioral support as well as connection. They believe in their own lovability and continue to experience parents as loving them unconditionally, even when restrictions are put on their behavior. The children trust in their parents' good intentions. The trusting child will test boundaries and protest restrictions, but ultimately he will develop prosocial behaviors as he learns and develops under the guidance of parents. This is how children learn to regulate their behavior, internalizing the values of the cultures within which they live. This is a healthy independence, built upon healthy dependence.

Developmentally traumatized children do not have the opportunity to feel emotionally connected to parents from infancy. This is the root of their trauma. They need connection but instead get fear, pain, or silence; love is conditional. Behavioral support if it happens can be chaotic, rigid, or a mixture of the two. The child develops mistrust as he doubts his own lovability and stops expecting parents to be responsive and available. The absence of a reciprocal relationship in infancy becomes the controlling behaviors of toddlerhood and beyond, as the children try to take charge of their own safety. The children do not believe in parents' good intentions, and the brain becomes wired for a socially dangerous world. This leads to blocked trust.

Parents improve or children move to new, healthier families. The children, however, remain in a state of blocked trust. They do not believe in the connection that is being offered. They perceive any correction, however gentle, as a sign that they are not good enough, not unconditionally loved, and that they will be abandoned by these parents one day.

Kim was once reading a simple children's book to a developmentally traumatized 9-year-old adopted boy. The book was called *Oh No, George!* (Haughton, 2014). It is a story about a dog who was naughty and couldn't resist all the things he knew he was not supposed to do: eating the cake, upsetting the rubbish bin, and so on. He tries so hard to resist doing these tempting but forbidden things. One day his owners are out, and he can resist no longer; naughty George! The owners return, I turn the page and read: "What will happen next?" Quick as a flash, this child tells me that the owners will get rid of George.

The fear of abandonment is ever present for these children.

Behavioral Support

To help children with emotional health and development, children need emotional connection combined with sensitive, attuned behavioral support. This provides the child with emotional regulation together with a different experience of being parented. Behavioral support sits on top of regulation and emotional connection, allowing children to feel secure with the parent despite the limits being put upon them. The emotional connection allows the child to develop trust and attachment security while reducing the experience of shame inherited from earlier experience.

This is two hands of parenting, what Dan Hughes has called a "connection with correction." Parents embrace their mistrusting children so that they feel safe in emotional connection and unafraid of behavioral support.

Comparison with Traditional Parenting Approaches

Attachment-focused parenting is different from parenting based on social learning theories. Social learning theory guides parents to understand behavior in terms of what is happening externally: the triggers and consequences. Parents can then use these in an attempt to ensure that some behaviors happen and others do not. They can, for example, reward a behavior they want to increase or ignore a behavior they hope will decrease. In this way, they can contain the child's behaviors, ensuring that they fall within acceptable limits. This behavioral management does not take into account the level of security or anxiety that the child is experiencing. It cannot build attachment security for a child traumatized within early relationships. The child's ability to connect emotionally, to feel good about himself and to experience less shame will not increase when behavior is contained but internal experience is not understood.

Within DDP, much more attention is given to what is happening beneath the behavior. The importance of emotionally connecting with internal experience is emphasized, and this is provided alongside support for behavior.

THE HOUSE MODEL OF PARENTING

Kim Golding developed the *house model of parenting* as a visual guide to understand parenting that is guided by the DDP approach (Golding, 2014a). This model is used here to explore the DDP approach to parenting developmentally traumatized children, an approach founded on principles of PACE. All children thrive when they experience emotional connection alongside behavioral support. Developmentally traumatized children can only begin to recover from developmental trauma when they experience this. The house model of parenting is built around this basic principle (Figure 7.2).

Secure Base

The secure base represents the safety that parents provide for their children. Safety has to be demonstrated clearly and explicitly. As throughout the house, PACE will be the parenting attitude that most clearly conveys this.

Building Emotional Connection:
Empathy, Attunement, and Relationship Repair

All children need attunement from safe parents. This is the secure base from which children can safely explore the world, returning to it as needed. When a parent is experiencing empathy, he will attune to his child. Emotions might be different—a child is upset, a parent is soothing—but affect will be matched. Affect is the nonverbal or bodily expression of emotion. When the parent is sensitive to the child's emotion, experiences empathy for the child, and matches the affective expression of that emotion, the child is likely to feel understood and become less upset and more regulated. This is attunement; the sharing of affect within the deepening intersubjective connection. This moves away from defensive responding toward an open and engaged stance within which experience can be made sense of.

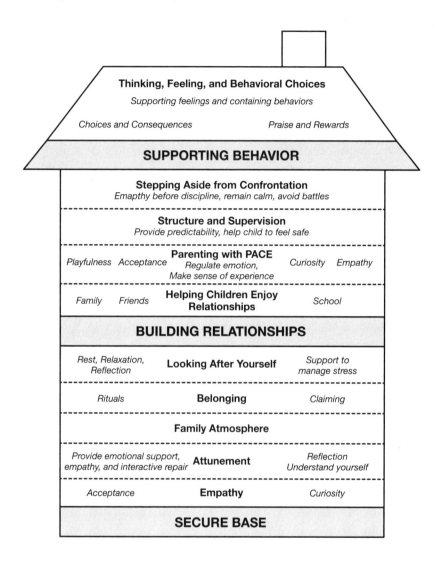

Figure 7.2 The house model of parenting. (Figure 7.2 has been modified from figure 2.1.1 in *Nurturing Attachments Training Resource* by Kim S. Golding, 2013, p. 142, with permission from Jessica Kingsley Publishers.)

Children with secure attachments are likely to have had many experiences of emotional attunement; they are comfortable with and expect empathy from others. Security comes from the connection that is consistent and provides contingent responses to the child.

Children who have been traumatized within early relationships are less likely to have had these experiences. They will be uncomfortable with attunement and find it hard to trust empathy. These children need to be gently helped to discover these. If the child is resistant; accept this. Acceptance and a gentle persistent presence will, over time, help the children to tolerate more experiences of attunement and empathy, although it may be some time before she seeks this when she is stressed.

RELATIONSHIP REPAIR

Sometimes parents find it hard to stay attuned and empathetic. Parents become defensive too. Parent and child become locked into a cycle of escalating defensiveness as they each react to the other. At these times, the parent needs to notice and to find his way back to open and engaged responding again. It helps if the parent can have acceptance and empathy for himself: "This is hard, the child is hurtful, and it is understandable that he has responded in this way." With this compassion for self, the parent can focus on his child once more.

An important part of this response is relationship repair. This is the parent's responsibility. The parent needs to convey to the child that whatever has just happened between them, the relationship is still safe. The child is loved unconditionally, and the parent will find a way to make it right again.

Attunement can also be lost when the parents provide some limits on a child's behavior. The child experiences the limit as lost attunement, and this evokes feelings of shame. This experience of shame can build quickly, escalating the behavior as the child experiences fears of not being good enough and anticipation of abandonment. When the parent provides a quick repair following the discipline, this can calm the escalating child. It reduces the shame and helps them both return to a state of attunement again. The conditionality that the child was anticipating is counteracted by the parent's demonstration that, for him, the relationship will always be the priority. The child is loved unconditionally. Over time, this repeated cycle of attunement–break–repair and reattunement will help the child to experience less shame.

Now, children will be able to experience feelings of guilt and remorse. They will seek their own ways to repair the relationships that they have potentially damaged. The children will learn how to manage conflict and mistakes and to make repairs of their own. They will be experiencing empathy for others and discovering the comfort of attuned relationships.

Hayley has arrived from school bubbling with excitement. They have been exploring World War I during class, and she wants to share what she has learned with her foster carer, Liz. She chats away, and Liz listens, smiling at her enthusiasm. However, as Hayley is talking, Liz becomes preoccupied. She wonders whether this topic is going to be a challenge for Hayley, given her experience of loss and separation. She feels cross that she was not warned that this topic was coming up. She suddenly realizes that Hayley is asking her if she can go on the school trip to France. "Oh, I don't think that will be possible, Hayley. You don't have a passport." Hayley erupts in anger and rage; it takes all Liz's energy to contain her. It is only after she has finally got her to bed that Liz reflects on the conversation. She realizes that the loss of attention, followed by the abrupt "no" probably triggered big fears for Hayley about not being good enough. The following day, Liz talks to Hayley. She tells her that she does not think she was listening very well when Hayley was talking about the things she had learned. She expresses that she is very disappointed that the lack of a passport means that Hayley is missing out on things. Hayley cuddles into Liz as she hears this. Liz continues to have empathy for how hard it is to be in foster care. She then lets Hayley know she has a little surprise for her. She has found the old gas mask that her grandfather used during the war. Hayley is captivated by this and eagerly asks if she can take it to school tomorrow. This is a request that Liz is happy to agree to.

Attunement and empathy, therefore, are an important part of PACE-led parenting, allowing the parent to emotionally connect with her child and to return to these connections when they are temporarily lost.

The Family Atmosphere

A family atmosphere that is safe, respectful, fun, and predictable is important to help children feel safe and secure. Within such a home, children can experience and feel comfortable with reciprocal interactions. This is not always the children's previous experience. The children may be more used to atmospheres of tension, hostility, fear, and isolation. Within such homes, the children fear reciprocal interactions and reject the influence of others. The child discovers that control is the route to safety, although a safety bathed in rigidity and isolation.

The child's resistance to the family atmosphere can be challenging. The child might seek to create an atmosphere of hostility and recriminations. This feels more normal and better matches the child's sense of who he is. It is easy to be pulled into this more negative atmosphere.

The parent becomes defensive, and conflict increases, which is a reminder of the child's previous experience, thus his fear increases. He redoubles efforts to be in charge of what is happening within the family home.

Although it doesn't always feel like it, ultimately the parents are in charge of the family atmosphere. They want this to be a positive experience for all family members. Even through the worst of the controlling behaviors of the child, the parents can choose to continue providing this atmosphere, inviting the child to join with this, but accepting when he chooses not to. In this way, it does not become a battle, but a backdrop to the child's life. The parents protect the atmosphere so that it is there when the child is ready to accept it. The child discovers that this home is different from his previous experience, and that while things can go wrong, it is possible, together, to make it right again. The world of reciprocal interactions and safety is opened up to the child.

Helping the Child to Feel a Sense of Belonging within the Family

Belonging within the family can be hard for children to feel after difficult early experience. Children may feel unwanted, rejected, or only accepted if they behave in a particular way. Belonging is something they have to work for rather than it being given to them by right. "You will only belong with us if . . ." feels very different from "You will always belong with us no matter what."

This is especially difficult when loss and separation have been a feature of previous family life. Children have learned the hard way that they do not belong. Joining a family rather than growing up within it can bring a range of challenges. In particular, children do not implicitly develop an understanding of family rituals and ways of being that operate within a family. They are uncertain about how they fit in, what is going to happen, and how they should respond.

Parents need to work hard to help a child gain a sense of belonging. They need to be explicit about family rituals and routines so that these are understood and enjoyed by the child. New rituals might be introduced that the child can be part of developing.

Parents might pay special notice to ways of claiming the child. Photographs, choosing bedroom decorations, having his own possessions as well as sharing family possessions all let the child know that this is where he belongs. Being involved in family events, even helping to name the new family pet, will build on this. Conversations and stories about the child being present in a projected future will build continuing security.

Remember too how hard it is for a child who joins the family late to hear reminiscences about the past. While a younger sibling can be unconcerned about an older sibling having existed before him, this can be much harder when the child would have been there if he had been born to this family. Empathy and acceptance of difficult feelings will be important to help the child manage these family stories.

Mary, a foster parent, prepared a memory book as part of celebrating her husband's 60th birthday. This would be a surprise for him at the family gathering that they were planning. Mary involved her foster son, Sam, in putting this book together and was careful to ensure that photographs of him as part of the family were included. She was surprised and disappointed at how difficult Sam seemed to find it when this book was finally revealed. He had done well participating in the celebration meal, and even managed to show excitement over the giving of presents, something that he habitually found very difficult. The book, however, seemed to trigger problems for him, and the special day was nearly ruined as a consequence. It was only several days later when Mary gently talked with Sam about this that she finally understood. Sam was upset because he was not present growing up alongside their biological children. He appeared abruptly in the family when the biological children were in their teens, and this created strong feelings for him of not being part of this family.

Looking after Self: Self-Care and Being Cared For

The final part of providing a secure base might seem surprising to parents so focused on the security of the child. It is, however, an essential part of security for the whole family. If parents don't take care of themselves, they are unlikely to have the emotional energy to continue to care for their children. Looking after the self relies on self-care; doing things for yourself. It also involves other care; finding people in your life who can offer care to you.

SELF-CARE

Self-care involves rest, relaxation, and time for recuperation. It can be hard to find time for this in the hectic life of parenting, which is combined with many other responsibilities. Without it, however, emotional resilience will quickly run dry. When self-care is poor, parents are at higher risk of blocked care. They are also more likely to respond to their child's blocked trust defensively.

Parents need to have PACE for themselves: time to play and also time to allow themselves to reflect; to be curious about their responses to others, including their child; and to have acceptance and empathy for any difficult experience they are encountering.

Hobbies and interests are an important part of emotional well-being, even if these might be low key and simple among the day-to-day business of parenting. Parents can also benefit from good physical exercise, sleeping, eating, and other self-care routines.

When self-care is poor, parents are at higher risk of blocked care. The term *blocked care* describes the difficulties parents can experience when parenting a child is very stressful, sometimes alongside other stresses in life (Hughes & Baylin, 2012). Blocked care in the parent is closely related to blocked trust in the child. When experiencing blocked care, parents are more likely to respond to their child's blocked trust defensively; they struggle to stay open and engaged, to approach or to enjoy their child. How well parents look after themselves and how well they seek support from others will affect how protected they are from blocked care and how easily they recover when it is present.

There is increased risk of blocked care when parents have unresolved difficulties within their own attachment histories, particularly if the child they are parenting presents reminders of this past experience. This is why a parent's understanding of their own attachment history is seen as an important part of being able to parent the developmentally traumatized child.

OTHER CARE

Other care involves having good social support in the parent's life. Parents need opportunities to meet with friends and to have time with their partners apart from the children.

Some friends are great for forgetting about the children for a time. They provide opportunities for some of the adult things in life: nice meals, theater, sharing interests. It is also important to have friends who can provide a listening ear—people that parents can be honest with about the challenges being faced. The best types of friend don't rush to reassure or offer advice when discussing these challenges. They have the attitude of PACE also; helping the parents to feel understood and to offer empathy for what they are going through. These friends can be used as a sounding board when parents want to reflect on their child. Curiosity shared can open up greater understanding that leads to deeper acceptance and empathy, both for the parents and for the child. Supportive friends and family are also an important source of support when parents are experiencing blocked care. Recovery from blocked care is much less likely without this.

MINDFULNESS

Mindfulness practice is becoming a popular approach for taking care of self and is grounded in good research (Siegel, 2010). Mindfulness is the ability to deliberately focus attention on feelings, thoughts, and experiences in the present moment and in a nonjudgmental and accepting way (Kabat-Zinn, 2004). In mindfulness, there is a letting go of any efforts to control what is reaching awareness. Without these mental efforts to change or control, we become more fully aware of the qualities and meanings of what is reaching awareness. This leads to a greater understanding of our inner experience and a developing ability to become mind-minded about this experience. Reflecting on internal experience can strengthen the mind-minded abilities parents want to use with their children.

RESPITE FROM THE CHALLENGES THAT CHILDREN PRESENT

Finding time away from the children can be a tricky issue for parents of developmentally traumatized children. Respite is often a feature of adoptive or foster family life, although the term itself can be problematic and tends not to be used in biological families. Children are likely to see the need for "respite" as a judgment about themselves, and attempts to dress it up differently can feel dishonest. Finding ways to build in these breaks in a normal and healthy way is important.

Time for self is important, and yet time away can increase children's insecurities and fears of abandonment. Similarly, it might be challenging for children to spend time with relatives or friends, even if these offers are made. This is a tricky balance that parents have to find. Leaving the children in the care of others is a normal part of family life. Children do go to visit grandparents and other family members; sleepovers with friends can be an adventure for the child while giving parents much needed time for themselves. Consistent and trusted babysitters can be an important part of the family network. All of these can be trickier to access when parenting a challenging child. Friends and family can be unavailable after a few times of trying to help out; babysitters can be hard to find. Invitations for sleepovers may not come, and when they do, the opportunity might have to be turned down as it may well be too challenging for the child to manage. It is worth the persistence of parents, however, as finding support that can be there when needed is an important part of looking after themselves. Building this in as a normal and consistent part of family life can also be helpful for the child, providing experiences of the parents or the child going and coming back, which reinforces for the child his sense of belonging in the family and reduces his fears that one day the parents may not return.

Caring for self and being taken care of are important parts of developing and maintaining emotional resilience as a parent. It can be hard to find time for this, but this is equivalent to putting an oxygen mask on before helping someone else; it is an essential part of parenting developmentally traumatized children.

Building Relationships

Helping children who fear relationships can be challenging. Children develop controlling ways of managing within the home, and this can extend to relationships outside of the home, causing continuing struggles. Parents introduce safety in relationship to children at home; helping them to find comfort in connection and demonstrating that this connection doesn't need to be lost even in conflict. This relationship experience will help the child mature and move out into the world of wider relationships.

Finding the Joy and Comfort of Relationships

Helping children to discover joy and comfort within relationships is the challenge that is presented to parents of children who have so far only discovered pain and fear. Blocked trust means that these children are adapted to react defensively to all relationships. Social engagement has been sacrificed as part of maintaining this defensive shield. Children become tough and do not notice the potential comfort that is on offer because they have suppressed any social pain that they have experienced. A terrible isolation is the cost as children strive to remain in control of the relationships within their life without being socially engaged within these.

Helping children to find enjoyment and comfort in relationships is an exercise in patience. Continuing to offer such relationships while accepting the child's resistance to these can be hard. This, however, is what the parents need to do. They demonstrate over and over that even if the child does not want the relationship now, the parent is going to continue to make it available to him.

Playfulness and fun can provide some lighter moments, but the parent needs to be patient. The child might engage for a short time but then needs to create distance again. Acceptance can be stretched when the parent has enjoyed some time with the child only to find herself rejected and hurt again soon afterward. With the persistent offering of such experiences and continuing acceptance of the child's need to reject at times, the child discovers the constancy and availability of parents. He might dare to enjoy relationships, making himself vulnerable to the pain when experiences have to end, because he is becoming more confident that comfort is available when needed.

The parent will need to take this slowly. Introduce low-key activities initially, and leave big days out until the child is more resilient within relationships. The parent notices when the child is finding it difficult and offers empathy and comfort. If offering this too directly is too intense for the time being, then it can be done indirectly. For example, the parent might express her empathy for the child to another person within the child's hearing. A pet or soft toy can be a helpful substitute if no one else is present. The parent demonstrates to the child that his reasons for finding this hard are understandable and holds hope that in the future, this will become easier.

RELATIONSHIPS OUTSIDE OF THE HOME

Helping children with relationships within the home can be difficult, but at least the parents can maintain some control over the experiences that children are having. Siblings can exhibit intense jealousy and aggression toward each other, but the parent does have opportunities to provide supervision and structure to these interactions.

When the child moves outside of the home, this difficulty goes up a level. Watching children who want friendships but don't know how to make or retain these can be heartbreaking. Children may have missed out on the gradual and supported exposure to their peers that naturally occurs within families. They may be emotionally immature, not yet ready for the peer relationships of their chronological age but forced to engage in these by a school system that deals in same-age groups.

The ways they have managed relationship difficulties are generally not tolerated by their peers, who quickly move away from the controlling, bossy child, preferring to find socially successful friends instead. The child is left socially isolated. It is not unusual for the adults who are with the child outside the home, be they teachers, coaches, or parents of peers, to be unfamiliar with the emotional and social needs of children who have experienced developmental trauma. These adults may maintain unrealistic behavioral expectations, and they may relate in a manner that generates anxiety and shame, further destabilizing the child's behaviors.

Parents can help their children by ensuring that they work closely with school staff. They make sure that the challenges the child is having are known, and especially draw attention to the child who needs social support but is outwardly displaying a veneer of confidence.

Outside of school, parents can find younger, more emotionally matched children for their children to relate to, as well as structured activities where supervision is available. It is helpful if parents can make relationships with the parents of these children so that these other parents can be helped to understand the need for a bit more structure and supervision for the visiting friend. This can help the children to have successful experiences relating to peers, extending their newly found ability to enter into reciprocal relationships within the home outward toward these potential friends.

PACE in Parenting

As much as possible, PACE is ever present in parenting. PACE helps the parent to attune with and connect to her child. It provides support to the child when discipline is needed. PACE continues to be there afterward, offering a connection that returns to attunement and helps with the repair of the relationship. Parents learn to notice when they lose the attitude of PACE and to find ways to move back to it.

PACE is a way in which parents can change their responses to their children. This is done with no immediate motivation to change the child. PACE is not a technique but a way of being with each other and the child. PACE aims to connect in order to increase security, but this is not done with an expectation that the child will change. An immediate intent to change the child suggests a lack of acceptance, which therefore is not holding the attitude of PACE. When the child experiences PACE as reflecting the parents' desire that he change, perhaps that they are being nice to him to manipulate him to "be good," the child is likely to experience this as the parents' disappointment in him. He is likely to respond with power struggles and a more intense need to be in control.

Involving the child in PACE can be helpful at the right time. For example, the parent might be curious with the child; deepening her understanding of what the child is feeling and thinking. Many children cannot join with this, however. This might be because they are feeling a high level of shame that needs regulating first. Alternatively, they might not be at a developmental stage where they are able to join in the parents' curious exploration. Parents will adopt the attitude of PACE regardless, being mindful of the children's current state and developmental stage in their expectations of them.

Structure and Supervision

Parents need to ensure that they give the appropriate level of structure and supervision to their children, being mindful of both age and developmental stage. Getting structure and supervision right builds security and trust for the child. This also reduces the amount of consequences that are needed within discipline.

Children who have experienced developmental trauma need a higher level of structure; they struggle with the spontaneous and benefit from the close, gentle presence of the parent. Trauma spoils the unexpected and the surprise. These children feel much safer with predictability and knowing what is going to happen. The more a day is planned, and the child is able to mentally go through with their parent what to expect, the more successful that day is likely to be, especially when the child will be encountering something new.

Often when the child's behavior is escalating, the parent can help by increasing structure and supervision. As the child becomes safer and more trusting with the parents, she can be offered more choices and freedom. The parent needs to be careful not to increase this too quickly, however, as it is easier to provide structure and supervision in the first place than to increase it because the child is not coping. The parent needs to remember to provide structure and supervision to the child as a gift to help her to feel safe and be successful rather than as a punishment for her "bad" behaviors.

With good levels of structure and supervision matched to the child's developmental age, the child will experience increased safety and be more successful living within the home.

Stepping Aside from Confrontation

When living with a controlling child, it is very easy to get pulled into control battles. The need for control represents defensive responding and a lack of trust. When we try and take care of someone who is habitually responding in this way, it becomes very easy to respond defensively in kind. When the child is controlling, parents need to work hard to maintain their own open and engaged attitude. Only this can de-escalate the patterns of defensive responding that are otherwise feeding off each other. When the parent is open and engaged, there is an open invitation for the child to enter this state also. This de-escalates situations and increases safety for the child.

Stepping aside from confrontation through calm, empathetic responses and a consistent attitude of PACE is therefore an important part of helping a child to reduce her need to control. This can help her to trust in reciprocal relationships and to be more open to the soothing presence of the parent.

Supporting Behavior

While connection is an important focus for parenting of children who have experienced developmental trauma, these children also need all the typical discipline of any child. Maintaining and returning to connection while providing limits, restrictions, and consequences is an important part of raising a child who also needs to recover from trauma. While consequences are necessary, their utilization may be reduced when parents remember the need for the right degree of supervision and structure alongside the setting of expectations congruent with their child's developmental age.

Thinking, Feeling, and Behavioral Choices

With any use of behavioral support, it is important for parents to understand how thinking, feeling, and behavior connect. Understanding the motivations behind behaviors can help a parent to remain empathetic in the moment. When empathy precedes discipline, the child will experience the limits as gentler. The connection with internal experience provides regulation: reducing rage, calming emotion, and helping the child to feel in control of her behavior again. This will also reduce levels of shame, as the child can experience remorse and want to make amends. Consequences for behavior are worked out collaboratively between child and parent, allowing the child to take age-appropriate responsibility supported by the parent. With this approach to discipline, the child is able to learn to deal with frustration and conflict and to feel safer seeking support for this. When parents understand the motivations for the behaviors, the reasons why the child has done certain things, the parents are in a good position to know what, if any, consequence is the best fit for this particular child and situation. Knowing the reason is not the same as giving the child an excuse; instead, it helps a parent to choose an appropriate consequence and to provide this with empathy for the internal struggles of the child—connection with "correction." Knowing the reason for the behavior can also help the parent review whether his support is sufficient to help the child succeed. The parent might well provide a consequence that changes the environment, possibly with a change in structure and supervision, rather than adding or removing a reward for the child.

Choices and Consequences

Children with developmental traumas have much less choice over their behavior because they become emotionally dysregulated so easily. Children need help to regulate, and then they will manage the natural consequences following their behaviors more easily. The connection that the parent tries to maintain during this will increase safety and help the child to use the parental support that is on offer. This is regulation-based behavioral support rather than shame-based behavioral management.

Children who have had unpredictable and inconsistent early care often find understanding cause and effect to be difficult. Consequently, they can struggle to understand the link between behavior and the consequence that follows. Instead of learning from consequences, this simply confirms what they always believed, that others are random and mean. Children will benefit from highly predictable parenting, matched to their level of emotional maturity, along with help to understand how behavior and consequences link.

Praise and Rewards

Providing praise and offering rewards are an important part of parenting. We want children to feel good about themselves and to receive rewards for their accomplishments. Ultimately, praise and rewards are helpful because children want to please their parents. When children mistrust parents, this is not the case. Praise and rewards can easily become signs of being evaluated, and the children increase their defensive responding as a consequence. Children can also be motivated to behave in ways that will avoid praise or will convince the other that they are unlovable. Behaving in order to ensure that others do not give one praise can be perplexing to those of us used to children whose incentives are to behave in ways to feel loved and to meet with approval.

Praise at its best is an expression of our positive experiences of the child, not a rational judgment about her. Children will benefit from descriptive, rather than global, praise and from low-key rewards, as long as the focus remains on helping the children to experience connection within relationship. As the children discover that they are acceptable to their parents and start to trust and feel safe with parenting, then they will be able to benefit from very normal types of parenting that focus on consequences, praise, and rewards.

CONCLUSION

Dyadic developmental parenting is an important part of helping children to recover and heal from developmental traumas. This relies on parents using both hands of parenting to connect emotionally alongside empathy-led "correction" through behavioral support. PACE is the central attitude to build these connections so that children can experience safety where they previously experienced threat and trust where they have only learned mistrust. The parent cannot change the child, but she can change her own responses toward the child. As the child is truly accepted for the child he is; and as what he does is understood with empathy, then trust and safety will build. Only then will traumas heal and the child be helped to engage in reciprocal conversations and develop new stories that enable him to find out who he is and what he can become.

CHAPTER 8

Providing Safe Settings: Dyadic Developmental Practice

What maltreated and traumatized children most need is a healthy community to buffer the pain, distress, and loss caused by their earlier trauma. What works to heal them is anything that increases the number and quality of a child's relationships. What helps is consistent, patient, repetitive loving care.

—Bruce Perry, M.D.

Children who have experienced developmental trauma and disrupted attachments, whether or not therapy is provided, often require a range of services in social care, child mental health, education, and residential care. The delivery of these services, fully integrated with the principles and interventions of dyadic developmental psychotherapy (DDP)—attachment focused, trauma informed, developmental, and systemic—is known as *dyadic developmental practice*.

At the center of dyadic developmental practice is discovering what everyone involved can say or do to be most helpful for a child and his or her family. What will have the most positive and enduring effect on the life of the child and his or her important relationships?

REASONS FOR DYADIC DEVELOPMENTAL PRACTICE

Dyadic developmental practice is important in the healing and recovery of traumatized children for a variety of reasons.

1. Raising a child with developmental trauma is very challenging for his parents, including his foster carers, adoptive parents, or other primary caregivers. While supporting them is central to DDP, parents may also benefit from a variety of integrated services in order to be able to function in a stable therapeutic manner. When DDP itself is not offered, dyadic developmental practice may be the main factor that maintains the success of the child's life in his family. The DDP practitioner often has to be a consultant, trainer, mentor, and support person for many adults in the child's life whether or not she is also the therapist for the child and his parents.

2. Within DDP, the child's safety and trust of the parent and therapist are developing. This may become undermined when the child finds the stress and conflicts occurring in other relationships in his daily life to be traumatic. Without support, well-intended teachers and social workers may unwittingly evoke fear and shame when relating with these children. Within dyadic developmental practice, all professionals are encouraged to develop a common framework of understanding and an approach that underscores the pervasive impact of developmental trauma and the need to emphasize safety within a strong attachment-based relationship. Variables involved in DDP and DDP-informed parenting will also be important in dyadic developmental practice. These include the coregulation of affect; interactive repair; developing the skills of reciprocal conversation and the new stories to replace those that were developed within the child's trauma; and understanding the need to discover the meaning of the child's behaviors before deciding how to respond.

3. Children who have experienced relational trauma will relate in a defensive manner that tends to evoke a parallel process in others. Children who experience themselves as being hopelessly unable to ever change are likely to relate in a manner that causes others to become convinced that the child will never change. The child whose developmental trauma has evoked within him states of rage relates in a way that leads others to also fall into rage. The best example of parallel process in children who have developmental trauma is the reality that the child's experience of blocked trust places the parent at risk to experience blocked care. Those in the community network are at risk of experiencing blocked care as well. The reality of this parallel process is well known in psychotherapy as an important dynamic that the therapist is at risk of falling into unless her supervision helps her to remain aware of it. Other professionals may not receive such training and supervision, thus increasing the risk that such a parallel process is likely to occur. Without close attention to these processes, systems around the child will become reactive rather than reflective, disconnected rather than integrated.

4. Splitting is another psychological reality that affects relationships among those providing services and care to children who have experienced developmental trauma. Splitting occurs when it is hard to hold on to or integrate opposing or contradictory feelings, thoughts, beliefs. Self and others are seen as either good or bad. The relational patterns of these children often evoke differing opinions and conflicts. The professionals involved with the traumatized child who is not making progress are likely to begin to experience shame over their sense of failure. One of the most common patterns that humans use to protect against shame is to seek a source of the failure outside of themselves. The teacher thinks the child would be doing better if the parents raised him better. The foster carers think that the child would be doing better if the social worker made different decisions. The social worker thinks that the child might be doing better if the therapist was more skilled. The therapist thinks that the child would be doing better if the teacher was more trauma-informed. Around and around the failure, shame and splitting goes, and at each step, the needed integration and comprehensiveness of the services is another step further from becoming real.

5. Given the realities of parallel process and splitting, conflict among the professionals in the network around the child is likely. Each may have great compassion for the child who has experienced horrific traumas, and each may become increasingly convinced that their insights and plans would be more helpful than those suggested by others. The resultant risk is for an increase in the level of defensiveness among those involved in providing the child's services, a breakdown in working relationships, and a movement away from a coherent, shared plan with short-, medium-, and long-term goals. Dyadic developmental practice strives for those involved to relate with each other using playfulness, acceptance, curiosity, and empathy (PACE). When successful, the various individuals are likely to remain open and engaged with each other in exploring the reality of disagreements, trusting that each is doing what she thinks is best for the child. PACE increases the likelihood that those involved will be open to the skills and opinions of one another, holding differing views while trying to find a common thread to jointly work with. PACE is a way to relate with others and develop emotional connections among the child's community of support that becomes the primary way of communicating.

For example, at a network meeting the DDP practitioner notices that the social worker, who has moved a foster child three times, is becoming annoyed that the child's behaviors are still very challenging. The DDP practitioner helps the social worker to avoid blaming by wondering what that must be like for her. Alongside this, the DDP practitioner expresses empathy for the social worker's fear that it is going wrong again. Or the DDP practitioner exhibits understanding with empathy about how a teacher who has 30 students responding well to her classroom approach might feel exhausted—and blamed—when asked to remain open to trying something different for one child. With the practitioner's PACE and compassion, the teacher is likely to stick in there and try again.

6 Developmental trauma is likely to have a significant impact on the child's development. Services that are likely to be the most effective are those that are matched with the child's developmental age, not his chronological age. Educators especially benefit from training on the social, emotional, cognitive, and neurologic impact of developmental trauma on the child.

The DDP practitioner emphasizes the importance of ensuring that organizational and team interventions are relationship based. She relates with others with the same principles as practiced in therapy, emphasizing that PACE is not a tool or technique. It is a way to relate with others and develop emotional connections that becomes a familiar way to communicate. This applies equally to caregivers, service managers, teaching assistants, social workers, or therapists. All need to be aware of the meanings of the child's behaviors and how these meanings are embedded in the child's lack of safety, his difficulties with reciprocal engagements, his story that is laced with fear and shame, and his fragmented sense of self.

CONTEXT FOR DYADIC DEVELOPMENTAL PRACTICE

There are a range of interventions that can be provided as part of a Dyadic Developmental Practice model. These will be briefly discussed here. Following this we present more detailed examples of some of these.

- Network consultations or team around the child meetings with parents and representatives of the services and networks involved with the child and family.
- Working with school staff and other key education professionals to develop trauma-informed and attachment-focused teaching environments.
- Training, supervision, and consultation to a wide range of organizations, teams, and professionals, including local authorities, schools, residential schools, residential homes, mental health professionals, social care teams, and social workers.
- DDP-informed parent-training programs for parents and professionals, individually or in group settings (Golding, 2014a, 2017).
- Parental consultations with parents only or with their support social workers, as described in Chapter 5 .
- Dyadic developmental psychotherapy, as described in Chapter 4.

While any of the above interventions may be combined, they are all interventions in their own right. We have pictured how these various interventions connect with each other through a simple model of concentric circles (see Figure 8.1). When all the circles around the child and family are DDP-informed, therapy with the child supported by his parents is likely to be more successful.

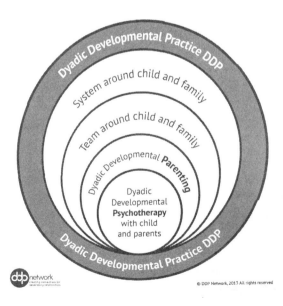

Figure 8.1 Dyadic developmental practice: Connections between interventions. (Figure 8.1 is used with permission from Julie Hudson, DDP Network website, 2013.)

EXAMPLES OF DYADIC DEVELOPMENTAL PRACTICE

We will now provide some more detailed exploration of the ways the Dyadic Developmental Practice model has been used for interventions with networks, schools and in organizations.

Network Consultation

In network consultations, the DDP practitioner focuses on developing interactions and interventions that support how parents, foster carers, residential workers, teachers, or social workers care for or work with a child. These include use of PACE—an attitude of "relationship first," for developing reciprocal, intersubjective interactions and making emotional connections with a child before setting limits around concerning or inappropriate behavior, and making sure that relationship repair is attended to. Great efforts will be made to ensure that expectations and structure are appropriate for his developmental (not chronological) age.

Consultations invite representatives from all services that are involved with a child, as well as the child's caregivers. Clearly structured one-off consultations can be successful, and regular consultations are most effective when a series of meetings is planned well ahead with clear chairing and agreement upon actions by specific individuals within realistic time frames.

Network consultations focus on making sense of the specific circumstances for a child in a wider social, cultural, and systemic context. Participants consider the child in the present and make sense of behaviors and patterns of relating and how these have been influenced by past experience. This understanding can lead to new and shared ideas for supporting and caring for the child. A DDP practitioner may consider individual factors in the context of knowledge as to how it can be that abuse happens, how sexually abused children are so effectively silenced, and how members of a family of origin can love yet also neglect and harm their children.

By working inward (see Figure 8.1), ongoing parental consultation or parent group work is provided within a network-agreed model of parental support; the school is also involved in this planning. If DDP is provided, dyadic developmental practice creates an agreed context within which relationship-based therapy takes place. Potential impact issues of therapy, such as an increase in challenging behavior at school, are predicted and understood rather than seen as a valid reason for a school to request that therapy be put on hold. If therapy is not currently planned, this is discussed with the network, with explanations for those who want to rush to provide this. An informed network can make good decisions about when and how to introduce therapy.

Safety increases because as many people as possible in the network are involved, knowing their perspectives are included and taken seriously. DDP principles of PACE are central in all relationships among the members of the network.

The DDP practitioner considers how to inform and include the child. Leaflets are helpful and should include photographs and developmentally appropriate words. A DDP practitioner may write to a child, with a copy to the parent, and suggest a time to visit so they can meet for the child to hear firsthand about what is planned. Consultation summaries or a child-centered letter can be sent to a child after meetings. Depending on the child, he can be invited to attend some or all of a meeting to see what happens.

Dyadic developmental psychotherapy is a narrative approach. The sharing of stories can lead to a shared understanding and shared ways forward. The consultant, using a PACE attitude, facilitates a safe environment within which these shared stories can emerge. Written summaries of network consultations are prepared through the co-creation of these narratives about the child, parents and the system, which have been shared within the consultation. It is a challenge for the DDP practitioner to ensure write-ups and minutes are accurately composed in such a way that keeps the child in mind. Write-ups are nonevaluative and nonjudgmental. They take much thought; it is time well spent as this aspect of the work has value in a context of missing information and frequent transitions.

Following is a brief extract from a network consultation summary addressed to prospective adoptive parents and copied to those who attended as well as other key professionals:

> Maintaining a family atmosphere of calm authority, acceptance, and making emotional connections before setting behavioral limits.
>
> You both know and can feel the importance of doing this within your household. It is however easier said than done on a twenty-four hour a day basis. When this becomes just too hard and you feel

everything slipping away, it is important that you both know who to call on. We considered a range of people who might support and advise you out of working hours, for your self-preservation. You decided who you felt the most helpful people would be and we gave you information about how to contact them.

Consultations can focus on a wide range of themes and concerns. Here are some examples:

- Agreeing on a model of intervention and ways to work together.
- Deciding who makes up the network team.
- Discussing the pros and cons of respite care.
- Making decisions about contact.
- Respecting the independence of mentors and advocates while including them in network decisions.
- Making foster placement decisions when things may appear good enough rather than highly concerning.
- Meeting to discuss disruption involving adoption.
- Providing reasons for joint agency funding decisions.
- Discussing transitions.
- Making referral decisions when a child doesn't meet referral criteria that are based on diagnostic categories.

Dyadic Developmental Practice in Education

Dr. Sian Phillips, a Canadian trainer, consultant, and practitioner in DDP, summarizes the impact of early relational trauma in the following contribution to this section.

Early relational trauma can have a huge impact on the developing architecture of the brain. Children who have experienced abuse and neglect really struggle to develop a healthy brain. These children then come to school and unfortunately are poorly understood or served by our current education models. Our schools' business is to impart knowledge and learning skills. Unfortunately, for children who have experienced trauma and neglect, their brains do not have the luxury of operating smoothly at a cortical level. These children are typically driven by their sympathetic nervous system, which keeps them at high alert for danger and any possible vulnerability. Alternatively, they are in a dissociative state. Neither state is compatible with learning. School, learning, peers, and teachers can all represent danger to a child who has experienced ongoing abuse and neglect.

Because fear remains high and emotion regulation is poor, these children, not surprisingly, present with challenging behavior. Physical aggression, verbal aggression, stealing, lying, social difficulties, defiance, attention difficulties, inability to learn from consequences, and lack of remorse are all common to children with disorganized attachment.

Our education system has often responded by further shaming the child through suspensions, expulsions, and restrictions. Teachers, parents, children, mental health workers, and protection workers become frustrated with the ineffectiveness of these responses. Behavioral or cognitive-behavioral approaches are only successful with children who have secure attachment and enough cortical resources to allow for self and other awareness and have little effect in their use with children with complex developmental trauma (Dozier & Rutter, 2008). Children in care have much less success in school. They do worse in all cognitive and social measures, typically drop out of school early, and struggle with learning and mental health difficulties.

Contributing to the Creation of an Attachment- and Trauma-Informed School

For the DDP practitioner, school staff are an integral part of a child's network and will be invited to network consultations. In addition to consultations, DDP practitioners can provide in-service training on developmental trauma to education staff and can present an attachment perspective on relationships and behaviors.

Following are examples of how a DDP practitioner may contribute when working with educators to create an attachment- and trauma-informed school:

Making sense of different behaviors between home and school, such as when a child is violent and oppositional within his adoptive home yet a model pupil at school. In the absence of trauma–attachment explanations, parents may be seen as to blame and the source of the problem by school staff.

Helping a school to design an individual plan for a child that may be outside of, or not adhere to, the school's core principles of consistency of limits and equal behavioral expectations for all pupils. Teachers may reasonably say, "We can't treat this child differently because it wouldn't be fair to the rest of the class; we would lose control of our authority." These are important points but are not a helpful stance when considering how to help a developmentally traumatized child reach the state of attentive calm required to learn.

Considering all options when a child tells school staff about abusive behavior by her foster carers or adoptive parents. This is not to suggest that they are not harming their child; rather, it is acknowledging that it is not uncommon for children to tell their teaching assistant, teacher, or the school caretaker about how mean her parents are when this does not reflect reality (the splitting referred to earlier). The child may have many motives for doing so that might be understood from a trauma–attachment perspective.

Helping an older primary school child keep school staff in mind during holidays; here, staff recognize and accept that the child can't hold onto a sense that his teachers will still be there when he returns. This might be done by teachers sending postcards and photos to the child during school holidays.

Supporting teaching assistants and considering their importance to the capacity of a child to get through the school day and to be regulated enough to settle and learn.

Factors to be mindful of include the impact on a child of teaching assistants being on leave or ill or leaving the job, and the value of having two teaching assistants to reduce the impact of stress. Considering who supervises teaching assistants is important so they can be helped to, for example, make sense of times when children tell them about their past or current family life, asking this not to be shared; that they are special to them; that they can't trust anyone else. The teaching assistant can think that she is in a special exclusive relationship then feel tricked and embarrassed when things change if they are not helped to understand such behavior from a trauma–attachment perspective.

Considering the impact on foster carers of school-related

consequences continuing into the evening at home when evenings are hard to manage.

Considering the impact of how information is passed between school and home and vice versa. This includes school-gate conversations, homeschool books in the school bag, or use of e-mail.

Considering how, in the first terms at secondary school after transitioning from primary school, increased safety needs and the emotional needs of the child may be met through "check-in" times with consistent designated staff twice a day such as at arrival at school and at end of lunchtime. The likelihood of getting lost between classes and being unable to organize self, books, and homework needs to be anticipated and nonstigmatizing support made available to the child. With so many different teachers to get to know, notebooks or cards about "This is me" from the child can be a helpful aide for teachers who don't yet know the individual needs of the child. It can be helpful to prepare teachers for these to be shown and not to be seen as an excuse.

Working with residential schools; for instance, managing transitions between foster home and residential school or the different expectations about attachment-focused care between the foster or adoptive home and the school, such as how to manage bedtimes (more on residential care is included in Chapter 10).

Louise Michelle Bombèr, a teacher, trainer, and therapist in the United Kingdom, has written extensively about the core features of an attachment-friendly school and related strategies and practical tools (Bombèr, 2007, 2010; Bombèr & Hughes, 2013). In the Appendix of this book, two school programs are included as examples of dyadic developmental practice: one in Kingston, Canada, and one in Nottingham, England.

Dyadic Developmental Practice as the Core Service Provision Model for an Organization

Some child and adolescent mental health services (CAMHS) in the United Kingdom adopt a DDP-informed model for their children in care, fostering, and adoption programs, and some incorporate the term *developmental trauma* into referral pathways.

Some local authorities and independent agencies in the United

Kingdom integrate DDP principles into their core service model. Local authorities in London and the north of England have commissioned DDP level 1 and level 2 training for staff to enable teams to implement dyadic developmental practice and DDP-informed parenting approaches with consultation from a DDP trainer or consultant. Local authority staff have also undergone training for the facilitators who implement DDP-informed parenting approaches, such as group work programs (Golding, 2014a, 2017).

Some local authorities employ or contract clinical psychologists or other therapists to provide relationship-focused therapy within the care planning, court work, children in care provision, and fostering and adoption support teams.

Examples of dyadic developmental practice as the core service provision model for organizations are included in the Appendix. These are a local authority in London, England; Adoptionplus, an adoption agency developing a social care service in London; and Play Kenya, which provides homes for children near Nairobi, Kenya.

ORGANIZATIONAL CERTIFICATION

The Dyadic Developmental Psychotherapy Institute (DDPI) board of directors has established a robust organizational certification process that enables organizations such as adopting and fostering support agencies and residential and educational establishments to become certified as DDP organizations.

Children Always First, a fostering agency in Worcestershire, England, is included in the Appendix as an example of a certified organization.

AN EXTENDED EXAMPLE OF DYADIC DEVELOPMENTAL PRACTICE

Luke lived with his mother and father until he was 5 years old, when he was placed in foster care after being neglected by his parents, who both misused drugs. A male family friend often looked after Luke from an early age when his parents were not at home. This adult regularly sexually abused Luke from the age of 2 years. As he grew older, Luke was told by the adult that Luke would go to prison if anyone found out. Before Luke moved to foster care, this adult told Luke that he would always know where Luke lived, and if Luke told anyone, he would come and kill Luke's parents. It was clear that Luke was emotionally and physically neglected, and Luke has spoken about being hit to his foster carer. There were numerous indicators that Luke might have been sexually abused, but nothing was clear. Luke has never told anyone about the sexual abuse. Nine months ago, aged 8, he moved to live with Carol, his prospective adoptive mother, who is a single parent. Luke is referred because of his aggressive behavior and sexualized behavior at home.

Network Consultation

Alice, the DDP practitioner, arranges a network consultation with agencies and teams around Luke. These help make sense of Luke's current behavior in the context of his past experiences. They consider interventions to help Carol parent Luke and set limits. They prepare for a time when Luke may talk more about his abusive experiences, including possible sexual abuse. Hypothesizing takes place without assuming Luke has been sexually abused. The curiosity component of PACE helps ensure everyone keeps an open mind and explores every explanation for Luke's perplexing behavior. Alice is careful to ensure all other explanations for Luke's preschool behavioral and physiologic presentation are considered. It helps to include the local pediatrician in initial network consultations.

In network consultations, Alice leads and asks those present to share their knowledge about the wide range of developmental, behavioral, physical, and emotional factors that can be associated with neglect and abuse, including sexual abuse. This enables people in Luke's networks to make tentative guesses together about his current concerning behaviors. With knowledge about how adults carefully groom children and use threats to silence a child, people consider how hard it might be for Luke to talk about such experiences, if they happened. It also helps with understanding how it could be that Luke is at risk of engaging in sexual activities with other children.

Another factor network consultations consider is the significant loss of key information when children are removed from their family of origin into foster and adoptive families or residential care.

Before working with Luke's network and with Carol, Alice requests, receives, reads, and collates all available past information about Luke. She asks for permission to read Carol's assessment to become an adopter. Carol is unsure at first, but on hearing the reasons why this is helpful, she agrees.

Alice meets with the network to think together about the chronology of events and to make sense of the long list of concerning behaviors that indicate that Luke might have been consistently sexually abused as a young child. This includes reviewing the extent of Luke's sexualized behaviors in his preschool nursery. Carol's adoption support worker liaises with past social work teams to ask specific questions and invites Luke's social worker to the next network consultation. The timing of the meeting takes this into account, and the network agrees to be flexible about the date to enable him to attend on the date he next visits Luke. Luke has not been formally adopted yet and receives visits from his social worker.

During consultation, communication using PACE enables Luke's teacher to feel supported in voicing her unspoken concerns at seeing Luke near the girls' toilets during break times. Ideas are shared with her regarding keeping Luke and the other students safe with added structure and supervision, without shaming Luke.

The network proactively plans for how they will support Carol given his aggressive behavior toward her and if Luke talks further about his early experiences. Action includes agreeing on funding for Carol's friends, a couple without young children, to regularly care for Luke both in their home and in Luke's home. Although making a case for funding is hard, the reasons for requesting this are understood and agreed to. It is recognized that responsibilities accompany making a decision to place a child of Luke's age with a single parent. It is also recognized that this level of additional support needs to be in place as soon as possible and not introduced as a consequence of any increase in concerning behaviors by Luke. Before they begin providing care for Luke, Carol's friends are provided with sufficient knowledge and interventions for Luke to improve their ability to provide him with appropriate care.

Actions agreed to also include a school-based safety plan regarding clarity for Luke about what is acceptable in terms of break-time behavior. The words to use with Luke explaining this to him are agreed to between Carol, his local adoption support social worker, and the school representative.

A summary of the network consultations is written up by Alice and circulated to everyone present, including relevant team managers, the head teacher, and independent reviewing officers. Alice is careful to respect confidentiality. She includes agreed-upon phrases incorporating PACE and lists actions and who agrees to undertake each action. It helps Alice whenever she writes reports, letters, and summaries to keep in mind the image of Luke reading this at a later date.

DDP-Informed Parenting

Parental consultations led by the DDP practitioner enable the adults to consider how to care for a child, focusing on consistent support, safety, and self-regulation for the parent as well as the child. This can also be provided via group training programs (Golding, (2014a, 2017). Parental consultations provide parents with a consistent relationship through which safety develops.

Alice meets with Carol regularly, often with her adoption support social worker.

Alice knows from reading Carol's adoption assessment that her father was strict and sometimes hit her. Her parents divorced when she was 10 years old. Carol tells Alice and her social worker that when boys bullied her at her secondary school, she felt she couldn't tell her mother in case she upset her. Carol suddenly realizes that aspects of Luke's threatening behavior toward her remind her of one of the bullies at school. This helps her make sense of why certain things Luke says really upset her. Later she says this connection seems to increase her confidence when setting limits with Luke.

Luke begins to talk more with Carol at home about being hungry, being hit, and being left alone at times when he was younger. Carol is at a loss as to how to respond to Luke. He talks about being hit in such a matter-of-fact way, and she finds this disconcerting. If she asks him questions, he just goes quiet. Specific words to use when responding to Luke are considered, using PACE. Other possible experiences of Luke are considered alongside potential responses evoked in Carol. Carol is helped to learn how to connect with Luke's experience, to accept all his wishes, thoughts, feelings, desires, and motives that are underneath his observable behavior. Carol learns how to "talk for" Luke as she parents him.

Carol learns about DDP: how to wonder about possible thoughts and core beliefs with Luke, showing that if they might be true, they will not harm their relationship. Carol gradually becomes more confident with emotionally accepting Luke's experiences and using PACE to connect with him around these experiences, however they affected him. Carols learns to set limits with

Luke clearly and consistently. After setting limits, there is often a strain on their relationship. Carol is given examples of how to repair the relationship after breaks in the relationship. When she has a bad day and wants to scream, she phones her adoption team social worker, her friend who looks after Luke, or Alice. If busy, all respond to say when they are available to call back.

Learning to love a child that one meets later in life, as Carol has with Luke, involves the overwhelming and often scary awareness that the child's pain becomes the parent's pain. This process can become another factor in making it hard for a child to tell his parent about past experiences he believes will upset his parent. Hypervigilant children notice parental distress and may only share experiences they perceive the adults can emotionally bear. This is a separate factor from "not telling" due to fears that their parents won't love them anymore. Children have often not been taught that parents can cry, be sad for them, and still be emotionally strong and want to hear more. They don't talk more because they don't want to upset their parent. This can effectively continue to silence a child, even more so with sexual abuse, as this interacts with the child's belief that he won't be believed anyway.

As parental consultations continue, Carol talks about how Luke begins to tell her more about his experiences such as about his memories of being left to cry. Luke then stares at her in ways she finds uncomfortable. Carol is helped to make sense of Luke's hypervigilance toward her emotional state. Carol's adoption support worker is also present during parental consultations, and so when they meet up, she can continue to help Carol with feeling uncomfortable around Luke. Carol is involved in planning as well as designing individualized safety plans, such as rules about doors being open when friends come over and rules about masturbation in private and in public. Alice talks more with Carol about the model used for DDP, and both feel the time is right to start sessions where Alice meets with Luke and Carol together.

Dyadic Developmental Psychotherapy

Dyadic developmental psychotherapy with a prospective adoptive family works with the child and the adult together. Therapy aims to help the child feel safe enough to explore new ways of connecting and forming relationships, to shift his or her habitual mistrustful ways of relating to different ways that can begin to trust enough to tentatively explore intersubjective relationships. At the same time, DDP coregulates the emotions associated with past traumas and assists the child to cocreate new meanings of those events. As the impact of the trauma decreases, the attachment to the prospective adoptive parent increases, and vice versa.

The focus on acceptance, being curious, and exploring the child's experience in the moment enables ways of working that do not focus too early on reassuring children that the abuse was not their fault. If done too soon, this denies their experience. It is important to explore how it can be that a child feels it is his fault and to show empathy for how tough the child's life must be to feel that he is to blame, being sad for the child that his life has been and continues to be so hard.

Luke often wonders how or when to tell his social worker and his adoptive mother more about his early experiences. He has no idea what words to use or where to start. He knows that once his adoptive mother knows, she will find out just how trashy he really is. She will find out what he used to do to the girls in nursery, and then he will have to leave again. Luke decides he will go with his new mom to see Alice. He is curious about what she is like. His mom meets with her a lot, and he wants to know what they talk about.

In therapy, Luke's way of checking out whether his mom will still let him live there if he starts to tell her more is a little confusing to the adults.

> LUKE: It's not fair. I deserve more love.
> ALICE: Well! That's a big thing to say. You deserve more love than you get now?

Luke nods.

> ALICE: Do you think your mom should love you more?

Luke covers eyes with a blanket. He looks at mom quickly and away again.

> LUKE: I love her more than she loves me.
> ALICE: What's that like? Thinking you love her more than she loves you.
> LUKE: Good.
> ALICE: How come it's good?
> CAROL: I'm confused.
> ALICE TO LUKE: Help me understand. Is there a part of you that worries that Carol doesn't love you enough?

Luke nods.

> ALICE: Because you just said, "I deserve more love." "Love me more."
> LUKE: Everybody needs more love.
> CAROL: So, it feels like there is never quite enough.

Luke nods.

> CAROL: That must be tough.
> ALICE TO CAROL: [Slowing down, with empathy] So you feel you are giving him all this love and it still feels to Luke like it's not enough. That is hard.

Luke cuddles into his mom, looking down and covering his eyes.

> ALICE TO CAROL: Mom, maybe Luke feels that no mom can ever love him enough to keep on loving him when she gets to know him really well. [Alice pauses for a while.] Could there be anything that has happened to Luke that would mean you stop loving him and want him to leave?
> CAROL: No, nothing.
> ALICE TO CAROL: Could there be anything that Luke might have done that would make you want him to go away?
> CAROL: No, nothing.
> ALICE TO CAROL: Do you think Luke believes you?
> CAROL: No. I know Luke doesn't believe me. How could he believe me? He has only known me a few months, and he has been lied to, let down, and hurt by so many adults. He tells me sometimes that he is bad inside in a way that no one can see. I just hope that one day Luke will begin to believe that he is so lovable. That he will begin to see what I see. You know, though, until then I'll just keep telling him.

Asking a newly in-love adoptive parent to be open to feeling the pain of the child she loves, putting to one side her anger, her guilt at not being there to protect, is so hard. For parents to do this, the professionals who support the parents also need to be open to their own feelings.

> ALICE: And just now when we were talking about you being a small boy learning how to look after yourself, and I saw you cover up your eyes, like that [shows visually], and quite quickly after that I saw you pick up your phone again [Luke smiles], do you know what I thought happened?

Mom is cuddling Luke; Luke is under a blanket.

> LUKE: What?
>
> ALICE: Maybe you felt that scary feeling again. You wanted to make those feelings go away. You tried to think about something nice. I wonder if that's right?
>
> LUKE: Yeah.
>
> ALICE: That makes so much sense. I suppose in here we try to think about those scary feelings and that's why your mom is here to help you with these things. And my guess is your mom is really sad she wasn't there for you as a little boy; that you learned to look after yourself. Thinking about you as a baby, learning that people weren't going to stop hurting you. That no one was there to help you.

Carol nods and murmurs in agreement, looking at Luke.

> ALICE: Thinking about you as a baby and that people weren't going to come to you when you needed them.

Luke looks at Alice intently.

> ALICE: When you were a little baby, crying.

Luke turns to look at his mom, who kisses him on the forehead. He snuggles in more.

> ALICE: You learned to manage everything all on your own. You were just a small boy. That must have been so tough for you. No wonder it is so hard for you to let your mom help you when you feel like that now. That it is far easier to get cross with her. You found a way to deal with it on your own. You found a way to get through.

At bedtime the evening before his next session, Luke starts to tell his mother fragments about his experiences of sexual abuse. He makes her turn away from him and not look at him. Luke's nightmares return that night. He is reluctant to go to school or let his adoptive mother out of his sight. He agrees that she can tell Alice in their session the next day. This is the start of Luke gradually telling about his experiences of sexual abuse.

In parental consultations with Carol, which her adoption support social worker continues to attend, Carol's sadness, confusion, disbelief, and despair is listened to, explored, and accepted with PACE. The associated pain, loss, hurt, anger, and fear for Carol is openly talked about.

As Luke talks more about his experiences in detail, Carol talks in parental consultations about her struggles to manage her overwhelming feelings of anger. She wants to physically hurt his mother and father and has dreams about visiting them to do so. She can't inhibit thoughts that she had taken on a child who is going to become a sex offender as an adolescent. These thoughts also are responded to with PACE, and as they are shared with Alice, they gradually can be accepted for what they are, and they become less terrifying and less frequent.

In therapy, Luke starts to talk about the threats made to him; that if he told anyone, the man would come and get Carol. His behavior fluctuates between being aggressive to his mother and not wanting to be away from her. The family friend comes over more often and looks after Luke so his mom can get some time to rest and reflect.

Luke gradually experiences that no one comes to kill his mother. He learns that his adoptive mother does not want him to leave. He protests but accepts both his mother and his teacher setting firm limits around his behavior. He experiences his teacher still liking him, and his adoptive mother is still warm and loving toward him. He slowly begins to come to Carol for a cuddle, not expressing rage, after she has limited him, much like toddlers do.

He talks more in therapy about his memories of being sexually abused. He agrees to his social worker coming to therapy sessions. He knows a special meeting called a strategy meeting takes place and that his social worker wants him to talk to the police. He knows the police are working out if they can do something. He talks to the police and is really frightened. The police tell Luke they believe him but there is not enough evidence for a criminal prosecution. He feels relieved.

Luke's aggressive behavior fluctuates and gradually lessens. He talks openly that his urges at school to go into the girl's toilets aren't there anymore. He accepts, though, that his supervision at school continues.

Soon after Carol formally adopts Luke, network consultations come to an end. Therapy has stopped. Luke knows it can start again if this might be helpful. Parental consultation continues once every 2 months as various concerns about Luke at home and school remain.

Luke is now 11. Luke is assessed as requiring a specialist school for his secondary education. After 2 years of collaborative work between Carol, Alice, and health, education, and social services, Luke starts at a school with residential provision. Luke is attending as a day pupil. Alice with Luke's primary school does an extensive transition to his special school. Attendance means an hour's taxi drive there and back each day. Luke has allocated teaching assistant time in addition to the standard help supplied by the school. This is hard to make a case for as small classes are provided in recognition of all the children's difficulties in settling to learn.

Luke attends school for 6 weeks. He settles in extremely well and is seen by his teachers and his teaching assistant as a model pupil. The teaching team in the school consider that his needs have not been appropriately assessed and are wondering whether the extra teaching assistant can be used in a more effective way with another child.

It is Tuesday morning, and Alice has an e-mail from Carol, who has just been told by the school that Luke's teaching assistant found a small sharp kitchen knife on Luke. When the head teacher asks Luke about this, he says that three boys offered him drugs during the break in return for sex, and that he had said no. He says he had told them he was going to tell the teachers, and at that point they threatened to beat him up, so he made sure he had a knife on him to protect himself. He also tells the head teacher that his mother shares her drugs with him at home so he doesn't need drugs from the boys at school.

During the follow-up telephone call, Alice accepts Carol's worries about this and her hurt and confusion around Luke making these things up about her and drugs. Carol feels in despair as his attendance at this new school is seen as a fresh start with hope that he will manage his education as an adolescent.

Immediately after talking with Carol, Alice sends the following e-mail to the head teacher, Luke's adoption support social worker, team manager, and the manager of the local social services referral and assessment team.

I am copying you all in as this warrants careful consideration. I hope this is alright with you all. I am responding by e-mail as I feel the situation warrants a response to the teams working with Luke. Nothing in this e-mail makes any assumption about the validity of the stated experiences of Luke or the other boys. It is meant as a reflective response about interactions and processes.

Your school will need to follow their procedures. This may involve social services liaising with us all about how we can work together.

It might be helpful to remember what we talked about last month in our school consultation. This is a new, exciting, and scary experience for Luke. It is the first time he has attended a school and not had his mother providing a nearby secure base. Luke had the same teaching assistant for 4 years in his last school. He knew her well and liked her. He is missing her.

At his previous local school, his behavior and emotional state was shared at the end of the school day between his teaching assistant and his mother. While Luke protested a great deal, it was apparent that he relied on this to ensure that those caring for him were able to work together about how to help him manage.

The current situation is a new experience for Luke in that in your school, there is no direct contact between his new teaching assistant and his mother at the end of the school day or at any time during the school week. This is not a situation he is familiar with. Luke says he likes this change but it creates anxiety. He needs to work out how communication does happen and how much control he can have over information that is shared between school, his family, and his social worker.

Without getting into the possible truth of what has happened, one possibility is that Luke is clearly communicating to all the school staff that they need to "know him" and all parts of him, despite his outward protest around sharing information. He will need to see how you respond to this and check out for himself whether (in his opinion) your school knows how to help him and make sense of him as well as educate him. Luke does this with all new people in his life. Any change makes him anxious; with him likely to return to past ways of coping that are now unhelpful for him.

His tutor and I talked about this when we met last month. It is a possibility that this recent behavior is his way of checking out how much information his social worker and I shared with his tutor last week and whether his tutor talked to the teaching staff such as you, his head teacher. Luke has found an effective way of doing this.

It is also a quick way of communicating to the staff at school that he is special and giving them a message about the process of having a teaching assistant. It is one way of ensuring that he keeps his teaching assistant and has an adult looking out for him at all times.

We also talked last week about how hard it is to know a child from someone else talking about him. It is most effective to know a child through direct experience of having a relationship with him. As we know, he finds waiting intolerable as it creates so much anxiety. I suggest that this is investigated calmly and quickly with an agreed outcome shared with Luke as soon as possible even if this outcome is that we don't know what happened.

Luke is a long way from home during the daytime, and that will decrease his sense of safety in terms of managing the outside world. He needs to know that the new interesting people he is meeting at school can really make sense of him and can look after him. He also possibly needs to check this out himself by discovering how you all respond to him now.

Please don't hesitate to ask me to be directly or indirectly involved if that might be helpful.

Alice organizes a network consultation at school within a week. An agreed-upon response was made. Alice met with Carol and Luke for four more therapy sessions. It is discovered that the boys were out of school during that day on a trip. Luke quickly tells both Carol and his head teacher that he made it all up. He says he is often scared at school and doesn't want to give up carrying his knife, just in case. With empathy for his fearfulness, he is told this is not possible.

The school agrees not to reduce his support. They increase the times he meets with a consistent designated teacher during the day to check in about how the day is going. Luke settles accepting the limits involved in the safety plans.

Alice resumes organizing network consultations every 3 months for 9 months.

As Carol (and Luke) learn to believe that his school can be trusted to look after him as well as educate him, the extended times they are apart each day means she discovers what she does with "free time" for the first time in years. Carol misses Luke when he is away all day and now looks forward to him returning home.

Over the next year, Luke's concerning behaviors decrease, and he regularly tells Carol when he has a bad or good day at school. Alice continues to offer six monthly parental consultations with Carol. She meets with Carol and Luke for therapy when they all feel this might be helpful.

This happens after Luke's nightmares return when he experiences the changes in his body as he starts puberty. Alice and Carol talk together, using PACE, as Luke listens, about how tough it must be for Luke that, unlike his friends, his developing sexuality gets mixed up with remembering his experiences of sexual abuse when he was a small boy. They share their sadness for him about how unfair this is, which Luke accepts and joins in with how angry he still is about what happened. Alice and Carol notice with Luke how he can now be angry about things without also getting aggressive with Carol. Luke nods, smiling a little, saying he still thinks about taking it all out on Carol. Carol and Luke work out ways that he can let her know when he wants to hurt her and changes his mind. Luke agrees he will try this.

Over the next 6 months, Luke's aggressive and sexualized behaviors significantly decrease. Luke now tells Carol when he feels strong or confusing feelings bubbling up. Alice continues to offer six monthly parental consultations with Carol and occasionally meets with Carol and Luke.

CONCLUSION

The key aim of dyadic developmental practice is to expand the focus from the child and his parents to the community network around them. This network may expand or contract on the basis of the emerging needs of the child and family. Thus, when an adolescent with developmental trauma begins to hit his parents, rather than simply telling the parents to call the police, within dyadic developmental practice a member of the police department is asked to become part of the network in order to integrate their services to those already being provided. The challenges faced by a child with developmental trauma become the challenges faced by his parents and eventually also the challenges faced by his community. Dyadic developmental practice is a proactive means of addressing these complex challenges in a manner that is integrated, trauma informed, and attachment based. Strengthening the relationships that all individuals who relate with the child have with him and each other is the goal of dyadic developmental practice.

CHAPTER 9

Interventions with Specific Populations of Children and Young People

This chapter demonstrates the use of dyadic developmental psycho-therapy (DDP) interventions with many populations of children and young people who have experienced developmental trauma. The age range described goes from the preschool child to the older adolescent who does not want to be parented. The children and young people described range from those with learning and neurodevelopmental difficulties to those who are violent to their parents or who have been sexually abused or exploited. We have also chosen to demonstrate how DDP is able to be integrated with another therapeutic modality: Theraplay (Booth & Jernberg, 2009). While the central features of DDP remain constant, their various ways of being expressed are determined by the unique features of the child, family, and community context.

PRESCHOOL CHILDREN

Sarah, 2 years old, is standing with her prospective adoptive parents when the therapist comes into their home for the first home visit. Sarah gets a bag with some of her clothes, takes the therapist's hand and walks toward the door. Her meaning is clear—I am leaving this home and going with you. This shocks her prospective adoptive parents who had been thinking how well things were going.

Harry, 4 years old, comes to his first therapy session with his foster father of 6 months. His other foster father hoped to come but has been called away with work for two nights. Harry sits on his dad's lap. He moves to the doll's house and nearby beanbag. Within a few seconds, Harry unzips the beanbag, climbs inside, and zips it up. The adults move to the floor continuing their talk and including words that accept Harry's need to feel safe and warm when he is in a new place meeting a new person. Harry says that his daddy has gone away forever and he wants him back.

Sam, 3 years old, has just been away for a low-key weekend to a hotel in a large town. It was her prospective adoptive parents' wedding anniversary, which was celebrated by a small meal with family and friends. When Sam comes home, she wants to know when she can change her name. Sam was sure she had met the judge when away and she is now adopted. She is inconsolable when she is told this is not the case.

Dyadic developmental psychotherapy is an effective intervention with children as young as 2 years. The parents of infants and toddlers who have experienced difficulties secondary to trauma and attachment disruptions certainly may also benefit from DDP-informed parenting interventions. In each of the scenarios above, DDP has been provided. Preschool children readily engage with storytelling and creating narratives when feeling safe, comfortable, and sitting close to those who care for them. With preschool children, the therapist might assist the child's momentum in developing the story by emphasizing nonverbal expressions of interest and enthusiasm followed by sudden comprehension. DDP sessions include a comfortable sofa, cushions, blankets, access to soft toys, puppets, paper, crayons, storybooks, and sometimes music. These can be helpful for children of all ages and are particularly needed with the preschool age group.

Preschool children are susceptible to behaving in ways they perceive will please adults and also take on the words of adults. It is how they learn language. It is helpful for the therapist to notice words embedded in the child's own story that are unusual, such as "eyes like a bear" or "he smelled like smoke" and are unlikely to have been said by caregivers or social workers. It is helpful to incorporate such words or phrases into narratives.

When working with preschool children, it is important to take into account their cognitive development. The way that young children make sense of information and communicate with us is different than that of older children. They are also more open to the influence of what adults tell them. This does not mean that they cannot join the therapist in co-constructing experience, however. If they feel comfortable with the therapist, they can have less concern about talking about events than older children do. It helps them to tell the story of an event if they are allowed free recall. This means allowing them to tell us what they remember in their own words without too much influence from us. The event does need to have some meaning to them, but if it does they can provide a logical, accurate, and surprisingly well-structured report. This recall can be helped further if the child has toys available to play it out. The use of these toys can even help a child who initially has little recall of the event.

For example, an articulate 3-year-old boy uses a toy tractor and car to tell the story of how a car he was traveling in ran into a muddy ditch and had to be pulled out by a tractor. He relates this with no help from the adult, becoming engrossed in the story he is relating: "Tractor in the mud. Get car out with tractor. Tractor pulls car out of mud. Out of the mud. On to the road. In we get. There."

DDP therapists will need to consider how they talk with the child. Long complex questions and the use of pronouns will reduce the child's storytelling ability, but the child can be helped by several short questions. It is also important to remember that very young children will be limited in their vocabulary. A 2- to 3-year-old child for instance will generally put two or three words together, conveying some basic meaning but drawing on a limited set of concepts. If you listen to young children talking, you will notice that they tend to use nouns and verbs (the content words) while leaving out pronouns, articles, and prepositions (the function words). It is not until 5 to 6 years of age that children will be consistent when they answer direct questions concerning why, when, or how. Concepts such as what do you know, remember, guess, or forget can be confused until around the age of 6. These ages are just a guide, and many developmentally traumatized children are immature for their age.

The need to use a conversational tone rather than speaking in monotone is more evident with preschool children than with older ones. The preschool children will become bored in less than a minute, and their attention will go elsewhere when we use a flat, serious tone. They need a prosody that is very melodic, with flowing rhythms, pauses, crescendos, and whispers to become enthralled by the conversation and be open to your influence.

Remember that whereas preschool children when retelling an event may ignore features that you feel are important, they tend not to create a false picture when talking about a memory using their own words. When asked, they often add relevant and true details and are more likely to miss things than to add things that are not true. Specifying the time of events will be difficult; concrete sensory memories and visual memories are more likely to be recalled such as a smell or being dark or light.

Lim, a 3-year-old, goes to the grocery store with her foster mother. She settles in the seat of the grocery cart, laughing as they choose cereal. She suddenly screams and looks terrified. Her foster mother can't work out any reason why. She cuddles and soothes Lim, then carries her, pushing the cart with one hand. Lim calms but seems frozen, with her eyes moving everywhere. Five minutes later, the same thing happens. This time, Lim is sick. Her foster mother notices something. The same man is nearby as before, and she recalls smelling his aftershave again, a well-known, heavy-smelling brand. She remembers learning that smell is powerful and processed in the oldest, most primitive part of the brain. She knows Lim was hurt by men when little. She leaves the grocery store and the shopping, goes home, and soothes Lim.

This experience is brought into the next therapy session, and the therapist and foster mother talk about this together, being curious. This includes Lim's foster mother showing what happened in a gently reenacting way, not mentioning the aftershave smell. Lim watches them and then joins in. Wrinkling up her nose in disgust, she says "Nasty smell. Hate smell." Her foster mother had guessed correctly that the smell had been the trigger.

Dyadic developmental psychotherapy involves cocreating narratives, weaving together current and past memories and behaviors to enable new meanings to be made, and exploring experiences, remembering to take a developmental perspective. Preschool children's core beliefs and internal worlds depend on who supports and helps them in their lives. Their version of events may be qualitatively different from that of an adult, particularly features of an individual, such as age, height, and size. Remembering qualities of specific voices are difficult for children of all ages. If your primary carer is your brother who is just 4 years older than you, the beliefs you develop will reflect this.

How a young child makes sense of his early experiences depends on the verbal and nonverbal messages given by those who cared for him. Being shouted at and told you are a waste of space at age 3 as you spill a cup of tea you carefully made for your father will have a significant impact on how you see yourself, tea, and fathers. A 4-year-old shut in a cupboard all day with no food after wetting himself, left alone to manage his experience of shame without repair, is likely to believe he must be very bad.

In the development of basic trust, young children tend to believe that adults can be relied on to do what is best for them. It is extremely confusing for young children to understand the possibility that trusted adults might act in ways that are unpleasant. For children under 7 years of age, authority figures can be seen as having a right to be obeyed because of larger size, power, strength, or status, and children rarely question the rules they had been taught by such adults.

A child's experience of being asked by an adult not to tell anyone about a specific activity is influenced by his or her relationship to the adult and by developmental factors. Preschool children are less likely to have learned social expectations about breaking promises and keeping secrets. In a safe setting and with trusted caregivers, preschool children may forget previous promises about keeping secrets. Using direct questions is helpful when talking about embarrassing, poorly remembered or secretive events. This is particularly relevant if a child has been threatened in connection with talking about his abuse; for example, "If you tell anyone, I will know and I will come to get you." Particularly powerful threats include "God will see and tell me" or being told the adult will come and kill the person the child tells.

When talking with children about their perceptions of potentially abusive experiences, remember not to make assumptions about how they will make meaning of your use of "good" and "bad" events. For children under 7 years of age, morality is often defined on the basis of the consequences of the behavior in question, not by the intention of the other person. An adult giving sweets or toys is likely to be judged to be a good person by young children. A gentle but inappropriate touch may not be interpreted as "bad," especially if performed by a trusted and therefore "good" adult. Such perceptions mean that preschool children may spontaneously tell about abusive experiences in conversations about everyday life. Although morality can still be closely linked with "niceness," it is not until children reach 8 or 9 years of age that they begin to understand that even trusted adults behave in ways that are not necessarily morally correct. Even then they can continue to believe that this must be because of their own badness, beliefs that can resonate well into adulthood, even when rationally they know this is not the case.

Dyadic developmental psychotherapy aims to explore the child's reality and beliefs—to go into the child's moment-to-moment experience using conversations steeped in playfulness, acceptance, curiosity, and empathy (PACE). This means that a preschool child's unusual memories, thoughts, and beliefs can be explored and accepted without judgment, evaluation, or comparison with normal expectations. Once fully explored, any "making sense of" conversations that aim to cocreate a different narrative is likely to have more meaning for the child.

Following is an example of a therapy session with Ben and his prospective adoptive mother. This is based on an intervention carried out with a parent and child many years ago. The family background has been changed, but many of the words are based on an actual therapy session with permission of the parent and the child, who is now an adolescent., This shows how DDP can be an effective therapy for preschool children.

Ben, age 3 years, joined his prospective adoptive family 9 months ago. He had two foster families after leaving his family of origin at age 11 months. Ben comes to a therapy session after a one-night visit with his prospective adoptive parents to meet their good friends. On returning home, Ben's aggression returned, as did his nightmares. This is a transcript from a therapy session 2 days after they returned home.

BEN: I found a lovely mommy. I'll never go hungry. I'm going to put her in a cage all year.

THERAPIST: She's a lovely mommy and she strokes your hair. I wonder when you knew this mommy was going to be such a lovely mommy? Did you know when you first met her?

BEN: No. I hoped she was going to be a lovely cuddler, and she is.

THERAPIST: I am so pleased for you that you found a lovely mommy who is lovely cuddler.

BEN: Cheeky mommy.

THERAPIST: And she's cheeky too.

MOM: I learned my cheekiness from you.

THERAPIST: And you want to put her in a cage. I wonder how it could be that you want to keep your mommy in a cage?

BEN: Then I could keep her forever. Yes, don't go.

THERAPIST: What would happen if you didn't put her in a cage?

BEN: She'd turn into pony. My little pony.

THERAPIST: She'd turn into a pony.

BEN: And she'd run away.

MOM: I don't think I'd want to do that. Why would I want to do that? Why would I ever want to run away from you?

Mom naturally tries to reassure Ben. The therapist continues with exploring the experience of Ben.

THERAPIST: Is that what mommies do, Ben? Do they always run away in the end?

BEN: Yes, they run and run and run and they can't stop. They always get away.

THERAPIST: You know what Ben? I'm sitting here feeling so sad because you've had mommies that have got away.

BEN: Yes, Karen got away.

Karen was a previous foster carer who loved Ben.

MOM: You've done so much thinking about mommies this week. You had a really hard time this week, and you were so scared about going away and then you became really upset about coming home. You cried a lot as you didn't want to come home.

MOM TO THERAPIST: We felt so sad for Ben.

THERAPIST: Did you want to stay there with mommy and daddy?

BEN: No. With Tom and Fiona (the couple they stayed with for one night).

THERAPIST: With Tom and Fiona.

BEN: Yes with them. They would make a very good mommy and daddy.

The therapist has worked with Ben's adoptive parents about the need to possibly explore this experience with Ben and how hurtful this will be for them emotionally.

THERAPIST: Maybe you think it's time to have a new mommy and daddy?

BEN: Yes, it's time.

THERAPIST: You've had this mommy and daddy for quite a while now.

BEN: Yes, I wish I had another mommy. I wish I had mommy Karen as my mommy.

THERAPIST: It's so sad you don't have mommy Karen any more. It's so sad. Maybe it feels like she turned into a pony and ran away.

BEN: Karen's not there anymore. She's not there anymore.

THERAPIST: That's another mommy that left, that turned into a pony and ran away, and that's so hard for Ben.

BEN: Another chance. Give us another chance. Give me a chance mommy. Don't turn into a pony, mommy. Don't run away mommy.

MOM: I'm not going away.

BEN: You are. You are.

MOM: I'm not going away. I'm going to give you millions of chances.

Mom again naturally tries to reassure Ben. The therapist continued with exploring the experience of Ben. She will telephone mom after the session, as this will be so hard to hear. No amount of preparation and anticipation makes this any easier to experience emotionally as the new parent.

THERAPIST: Mommy, Ben thinks you are going to turn into a pony and run away and leave him.

BEN: You are. You are.

Mom remembers to talk about going with the experience in the moment, resisting giving reassurance too early as this can stop Ben from exploring and being open about his internal world. She remembers PACE and to be accepting of Ben's feelings.

MOM: Sometimes you say, "Go away." Then I know you are feeling scared inside. I love you so much. You know, one day it might be that you stop having these feelings and really begin to believe that I won't run away. That I will look after you, no matter what.

THERAPIST TO MOM: Oh my, can you imagine what it's like to have someone who is such a lovely mommy; is a lovely cheeky mommy and yet believing that they will run away?

MOM: It must be so hard.

THERAPIST: And maybe sometimes the sadness of losing Karen feels so big. It hurts so much. Maybe Ben can't bear to feel that pain again especially with this mommy, because she is so lovely. Such a good cuddler.

BEN: And she didn't even say good-bye.

THERAPIST: No, she didn't even say good-bye.

Karen had not felt emotionally able to say good-bye to Ben as he left her home. This was a significant event for Ben. The storytelling tone, the acceptance, curiosity, and empathy combined with the narrative thread led him to bring this into the story, spontaneously. When adults had tried to talk about this before, Ben had always said nothing, often putting his hands over his ears.

THERAPIST: And Karen didn't even say good-bye.

The therapist and his mother continued the theme, with Ben listening. This is "talking about," showing empathy for Ben's sadness at missing Karen so much and his hurt and confusion that she never said good-bye. With Ben's mom rocking him and stroking him, a narrative thread was co-constructed using Ben's words about a cage and a pony and running away. Ben's mom was able to talk with the therapist about times when Ben told her he was a horrible baby and that nobody could have loved him; that he thinks it was all his fault. Toward the end of the session, mom and Ben say:

MOM: I will never let you go.
BEN: I will never let you go. I will never let you go at bedtime. We will cuddle and cuddle and cuddle all night.

This therapy example starts with the child bringing in his own embedded concept, a cage, which lends itself to developing abandonment themes. Often this is not the case, and the therapist needs to be active in developing stories that cocreate meaning for preschool children and their parents. The therapist and parent put together the history, the content of recent and past events, and develop possible meanings.

For example, when a 4-year-old girl bites her 2-year-old adopted brother, the therapist gives a context to this event and is curious about what might be happening for her that led her to bite her brother. Using big wondering, high interest, and building suspense, bringing in a little of the history and using "talking about," the therapist says to the adoptive father:

THERAPIST: Maybe, just maybe, Kylie feels you love Joshua more than you love her! She gets into trouble and gets told not to do things. Maybe she sees your cuddles with Joshua and your soft words and only hears your sharp voice to her. Maybe she feels you have so much more love for

Joshua than for her. She feels hurt and cross and then she bites him. You need to let her know that this isn't okay. And when you do this, maybe Kylie remembers all the times when she felt her other daddy loved her little brother more than her. Sometimes just being with him and seeing you care for him must be so hard.

CHILDREN AND ADOLESCENTS WITH LEARNING DISABILITIES

Dyadic developmental psychotherapy is an appropriate intervention for children and adolescents with learning disabilities because it is premised on the need for the therapist and carer to understand, relate with, guide, and support the unique child regardless of that child's differences in all areas of social, emotional, psychological, cognitive, neurologic, and physical functioning. The child with learning disabilities may need a particular way of engaging, communicating with, and guiding his behaviors, but so does each child and adolescent. That being said, the following are assumptions that the DDP therapist and carer have with regard to a child or adolescent with learning disabilities:

- The extent of the learning disabilities may become less. They may result from developmental trauma, and as the impact of that is less, the learning disabilities may decrease.
- The learning disabilities may be permanent. Successful treatment of the trauma may have little direct effect on the learning disability. However, the DDP principles may enable the adults in the child's life to reduce the impact of the learning disability.
- The fact that the child or adolescent has learning disabilities does *not* mean that his behavioral challenges may only be addressed with external reinforcers. When there are assumptions that the child will not benefit from reasoning and cognitive skill development and that he cannot generalize from one situation to the next, these assumptions may only be valid because of the limited way that we are "teaching" these skills.
- The child or adolescent with learning disabilities may need an extra focus on issues relating to safety, emotional regulation, attributing negative motives to others, feeling shame, and communicating his inner life. These issues, also important with all children who have

experienced developmental trauma, are likely to be even more prevalent with young people with learning disabilities.

In providing interventions for children and adolescents with learning disabilities, the following might well be kept in mind:

- There needs to be a thorough assessment of the individual's skills and challenges so that we do not expect too much. These assessments might include speech and language, sensory processing, cognitive functioning, and adaptive behavior. A learning disability is defined as having significant impairments (within the lowest 2% of the population) in adaptive behavior and cognitive functioning. If there have been successful interventions for the young person's developmental trauma—with signs of improvement in reflective thinking, theory of mind, empathy, and impulse control—then a reassessment of the classification of learning disability may be indicated.
- Interventions might best start with the young person's strengths, then adding other interventions to support skill development in other areas also. Thus, it might be wise to begin interventions around sensory integration and relational attachment issues and integrate Theraplay and DDP interventions in small bits.
- Therapeutic focus might best be on recent, concrete events, as timelines might be very difficult. At the same time, carers need to keep the child's history of key events, moves, and relationships using detailed records and pictures.
- There needs to be fewer themes to hold in mind, with more breaks and available things to do or eat. Stories involving trauma or shame-related themes need to be especially short, with much support given, if they are to be integrative. Developmentally sensitive resources that include images, photos, and videos, as well as storybooks with younger children in mind, may be of great value.
- PACE is especially important to generate safety, attention, and an open and engaged attitude to prevent or reduce challenging behaviors.
- Dyadic developmental practice involving caregivers and the network is especially important in order for the child with learning disabilities to experience the safety that comes from consistency of relationships, appropriate expectations, and activities.

- The network needs to keep in mind the stress or even traumas associated with having learning disabilities in addition to the challenges due to developmental trauma. While we need to assist the individual in addressing the impact of developmental trauma, we cannot forget the impact of the day-to-day challenges (frustrations, shame, fears, sadness, loneliness) of his learning disability.
- A member of the network needs to have particular expertise in understanding and addressing the needs of children and adolescents with learning disabilities.

With the child or adolescent with learning disabilities, it may be more important than usual to convey much of the meaning of the story being developed with nonverbal expressions. These include facial expressions, voice prosody, and gestures all synchronized with similar expressions in the child. The interest and understanding of the story often emerges as the therapist builds suspense, uncertainty, active wondering, and follows suddenly with the surprise of a new way of looking at something. This surprise involves both what the event might mean (your parents didn't know how to teach you, and you thought that you deserved to be hit) and also what the child and parent might do differently to solve a problem:

> THERAPIST: I wonder . . . I wonder . . . maybe . . . maybe . . . when your mom sees that you're ready to scream . . . she might . . . spin around and say in a big voice with big eyes, "Should I scream for you?" And you will spin around and in a big voice with big eyes, say "No!" And she'll spin around and say in a small voice with sleepy eyes, "Then what can I do?" And then you will surprise her and say one of three things: "Hug me." or "Count to 10 backwards while I count to 10 forwards. Go." or "Touch my nose while I touch your nose and we'll count to 3."

Any suggestions, problem-solving ideas, or information must be presented in this active, engaging manner, not in a rational manner with a monotone voice.

Safety needs to always be in our minds as we cannot take it for granted that the child with a learning disability is feeling safe during the routine conflicts, disappointments, changes, surprises, and transitions of living. In their ongoing nonverbal communications, the adults in the child's life need to be conveying that they are safe and that the child is safe . The adults need to strive to consistently maintain the open and engaged attitude that communicates that they and the child are safe. They need to have the habit of relating with PACE. When they are having a hard day, react unpredictably with anger or impatience, and when they are busy with other responsibilities and need to say "wait," they need to be aware of the child's response and repair the relationship at the first sign of trouble. The clearer our attitude toward the child expressed nonverbally, the more likely that the child will not misinterpret our thoughts and intentions toward him.

Joey was a 9-year-old foster boy with a moderate to severe learning disability. He tended to be both impulsive when he became anxious and compulsive with regard to his daily behaviors. He had been sexually abused by his mother until he entered foster care when he was 6 years of age. He was referred to a DDP therapist because of his compulsive behavior of touching his foster carer's breasts whenever he had any physical contact with her. Explanations, restrictions, and rewards for appropriate touch were not effective, and the placement was in danger.

During the fifth treatment session, after they had been chatting about some enjoyable recent family activities, the foster carer, Yvette, began speaking quietly and sadly about a problem that they had in the family that involved Joey touching her breasts. The DDP therapist immediately conveyed empathy for them both over this problem and wondered how it might have started. Joey had good eye contact with the therapist, showing interest in the story that the therapist was developing. The therapist wondered about where Joey might have gotten the idea about touching his foster carer's breasts. After more wondering, with sudden animation, the therapist recalled how Joey's mother had wanted him to touch her breasts and Joey must have thought that all moms would want their children to touch them the same way. The therapist maintained the intensity of the story while saying that Joey's mother was wrong, other mothers do not want their sons to touch them that way, and there was another way of hugging and being close that both mothers and sons enjoy when they learn it. After making this point a few more ways, with excitement the therapist asked Joey and Yvette if they would like to learn the other way. They both agreed, and the therapist then showed Joey how to hug a mom or a dad, and he had Joey practice with him. Joey was very focused on this, taking the practice quite seriously. When they thought that Joey was ready, he hugged Yvette the way that he had been taught. Yvette expressed delight and asked to have two more hugs. Joey was excited and pleased at what he had learned and asked if he could hug his foster dad the same way. They agreed that for the next week, Joey would only hug his foster mom or foster dad when the other was present to give him ideas if he wasn't getting it quite right. Joey liked that idea, and he often initiated hugging time when both were present. He continued to be proud of his new skill, and he seemed relieved that the problem with his foster carer had ended. He no longer had to worry about upsetting her. Yvette could now give him the physical affection that was so important to him without worrying.

CHILDREN AND ADOLESCENTS WITH NEURODEVELOPMENTAL FRAGILITY

There are multiple reasons why children who have experienced developmental trauma are also at increased risk of neurodevelopmental fragility. The trauma experience itself can have a pervasive impact on the developing brain and nervous system; this often leaves the child "wired for danger" and in the process can leave sensory integration, emotional regulation, and cognitive abilities underdeveloped (Cook et al., 2005). Developmental trauma has a major impact on the social world that the child is growing up within. As a social species, we are dependent on healthy social relationships, and without these, important experience that influences a child's neurodevelopment is missing (Siegel, 2012). For a child to be able to integrate sensory and emotional experiences, he needs supportive parents and safe and healthy touch. For example, a child is soothed and regulated by being cuddled and will then be better able to make sense of his experience. When touch is missing or is connected with harsh, frightening experiences, the soothing and regulation will not happen, once again affecting neurodevelopment (Coan, 2016). In addition, the mother can be having experiences or taking substances that affect the developing fetus. Drugs and alcohol are particularly damaging. Fetal alcohol spectrum disorder (FASD) and fetal alcohol effects (FAEs) are notable examples of this (Ross, Graham, Money, & Stanwood, 2015). The impact of stress during the pregnancy—experiencing domestic violence for example—can additionally lead to the fetus being bathed in elevated levels of cortisol. This in utero experience can lead to compromised neurodevelopment (Davis & Sandman, 2010). Finally, among the population of parents who struggle to parent successfully, there is likely to be a higher level of learning and neurodevelopmental difficulties. Many parents with learning difficulties will parent success-fully, but risk is increased because of their own neurodevelopmental struggles (Cottis, 2009). It might be speculated that these difficulties can be passed on genetically such that higher levels of learning difficul-ties can be represented within this population of children.

Dyadic developmental psychotherapy interventions therefore need to begin with assessment of the neurodevelopment of the child and the development of attachment and relationship difficulties. Thorough assessment can help parents to understand their children and the nature of the difficulties that they present.

A question that is frequently asked is whether the difficulties a child is displaying are due to attachment experience, autism, or fetal alcohol exposure. Clinical experience suggests that this is not easily answered. This is because there is a transactional relationship between the devel-opment of the difficulties such that emotional development, including attachment, and neurodevelopment each affect the other. Disentangling these is a fruitless task. However, parents can be helped to understand the pattern of strengths and difficulties displayed by the children in their neurodevelopment, thus helping the parents to tailor support as needed. This can also be helpful to guide teaching staff in the child's school. As parents and teachers more fully understand the difficulties of the child, they are less inclined to dismiss the children's behavior as naughty and therefore will modify the support that they are offering. For older children, psychoeducation can also be important to help them to understand their differences and difficulties, reducing their own sense that they are bad when they cannot regulate their emotions and their behaviors. We may never know the precise causes for the difficulties a child is displaying or their relative impact, but we can develop interven-tion strategies. It is important to go at the child's pace and not to get annoyed or frustrated if these produce little gain. Even when difficulties are neurologically based, progress through experiences is still possible.

For parents, understanding the nature of their children's neurode-velopmental difficulties can be a helpful piece of the jigsaw puzzle that the child presents to them. The DDP therapist needs to also remain aware of how painful this can be. Complicated reactions of grief for the child they thought they were parenting and of disappointment in understanding that their hopes and dreams for the child will never be realized need to be fully understood and supported by the therapist. Not knowing what to expect in the future or how much progress is possible can also be difficult. Parents will understandably be concerned that they could reach a plateau with no further progress possible. This can lead to worries about the young person remaining dependent upon them with the consequent loss of the older age they were envisioning and fears about what will happen after their deaths. If all these worries and fears are not fully understood with acceptance and empathy, they can hinder the therapy with the child.

Dyadic developmental psychotherapy will need some modifications to accommodate the additional challenges of the child. The therapist will need to anticipate slower progress and not become disheartened by apparent lack of progress. Additional time with parents can be helpful as they explore with the therapist what has happened in sessions and make sense of where neurodevelopmental challenges are affecting progress. It is also not uncommon for parents to report some progress at home but not seen in the therapy room, providing some reassurance that the therapy is beneficial.

For example, a therapist is working with a child who has a diagnosis of autism. The child struggles to respond reciprocally and tends to dominate the session with discussion of insects, his particular special interest. The therapist does her best to respond to this intersubjectively and to use the interest as a platform to help the child to experience safe relationships with his parents. She leaves many sessions, however, doubting that anything useful is occurring. She is therefore surprised when she meets with the parents to hear their reports of a more connected relationship with their son at home. They are experiencing him becoming closer to pets, siblings, and themselves even though this is not evident in the therapy room.

Modifications may be useful in engaging children with autistic features in DDP.

The DDP therapist needs to understand and accept that a child with autism will demonstrate more inflexibility and rigidity and a narrowed range of interests. This acceptance is often based on being sensitive to and entering into a nonverbal rhythm with the child wherever his attention is currently focused. This is a rhythm that includes synchronized movements and activities, fine-tuned continually, and with more space than is common. Less eye contact and touch will also be helpful. This continual fine-tuning enables the child to feel an engagement that is not too stimulating or intrusive.

With this acceptance, the therapist can work at establishing some reciprocity with the child without frustration. She can accommodate social communication difficulties, remembering to go slower, be simpler, and provide more explanations of what is happening within the relationships that the child is experiencing within the sessions. The child is likely to provide fewer nonverbal cues, and so the therapist might check in with him more often. Monologues can be especially difficult to manage within a therapy session. The therapist can, however, share attention with the child and work to shift the monologue to a dialogue. This will mean slowing the child down, interrupting his descriptions with curiosity, and being extra animated to convey excitement, thus helping the child to notice and engage in the relationship with the therapist. As the child becomes more used to these reciprocal relationships, they can later be used to explore current experience ("I wonder why you got cross with mom") and even past experience ("I wonder if thinking about insects helps you not to think about your birth father hitting you?")

Exploring an obsessive interest can enhance the connectedness felt between parent and child; for example, being excited together playing card games, playing with cars, or watching the washing machine spin. Moment-to-moment attunement can lead to new brief connections never felt before by the parents, which introduce the children to relationship experience. The therapist can help the parents understand the importance of these reciprocal moments however trivial or meaningless they might feel. The therapist will also accept and empathize with the parents' understandable desire for so much more with their children. Understanding the misplaced hope for longer-term change in the parents is so important, allowing the parents to experience the joy of the moment for what it is.

Children with autistic difficulties can have a special interest that has been informed by their experience of the world as frightening. It then becomes an obsessive interest in its own right and can cause difficulties for the child. For example, one child who grew up in an atmosphere of domestic violence developed an interest in knives. Storytelling around this obsessive interest only increased this interest in an unhealthy way. It may be better to work with the child to replace the interest with something healthier; for this child, he was able to swop knives for superheroes.

We are increasingly becoming aware of the damage that can be done when children are exposed to alcohol in utero. This can be a hidden disability, not easily understood, but children are often left with difficulties organizing and using information, despite normal levels of intelligence. This can leave children with attention difficulties that affect language, memory, and planning and initiating activities, as well as difficulties regulating emotions. As with the children with autism, these children need adaptations to DDP interventions. For example, these children are helped by a lot of repetition so that they can hold onto new learning. While such repetition can be frustrating for the adults, it is important to approach these with enthusiasm and interest and not with a sense of drudgery.

The therapist needs to be mindful and accepting of the difficulties the child with fetal alcohol effects has, but not be put off by these. These children will respond to PACE and intersubjective engagement. Progress is likely to be slower, and the parents and therapist will help each other not to fall into despondency when progress is not evident. Ongoing assessment and observation of the level of functioning of the children helps therapists to work with them in a way that offers experience of consistent success. Therapists accept and affirm that this is the level the child can manage without expecting more. They will, however, introduce bits of challenge in very small steps. The therapist thus invites the child to try while accepting if the child does not try or tries and fails and supporting the parents to accept these efforts without conveying frustration or disappointment. It is important to remember that these children can experience high levels of shame and awareness of their difference, which, combined with their poor early parenting experience, can leave them with a sense of their own inadequacy and sense of badness. If the impact of alcohol exposure is not recognized and understood, this sense can easily be reinforced, especially by the use of behavioral strategies that focus on evaluation and reinforcement contingencies designed to get the child to behave in ways that are acceptable to the adults but may be out of reach of the child. The DDP model involving a high level of PACE can be very supportive with this difficult experience, helping to regulate the shame and leading to a greater awareness of why the therapist is struggling for the child and those supporting and parenting him.

Generally, when working with children with neurodevelopmental fragility, the therapist can anticipate that the child will be easily triggered toward emotional arousal coupled with poor regulation abilities. The child might experience more frustration in not fully understanding the relationships he is experiencing or what is expected of him. He might also find it especially hard to let the therapist and parents help him to regulate again. More time in therapy will be focused on developing regulation abilities and helping the child to trust in the parents to help with this. This can involve exploring relational activities that can help to soothe and regulate a child. Children might benefit from increased structure to the session, with regular starting and ending activities, and extra support to manage the transition into and out of the session. Integration with interventions involving sensory integration and Theraplay can also be helpful. The therapist will be advised not to move too quickly onto helping the child to reflect, but to ensure that good routines and appropriate regulatory support are in place first.

As the therapy progresses, the therapist can introduce some talking to the child while continuing to move between talking and the experiential, thus reducing the verbal demands on the child. "Talking about" can be very helpful, enabling the child to feel more distance, and hence to feel safer. The child listens without any pressure as he is detached from the emotional content of the theme. It can be harder to check that the child is involved, absorbed as he is in his own world, so the therapist should be alert for small, often nonverbal indications that he remains engaged. "Talking for" will also be important but for shorter times, and the child is likely to need more active breaks. The therapist holds the theme in mind, returning to this when ready. The movement between chatting with child and parents and activity can produce its own structure and rhythm to the session.

The therapist will also need to know what level of emotional intensity the child can manage and not be discouraged when this appears to be lower than with children who do not share neurodevelopmental fragility. It might be helpful to find ways to connect with the child that respect this lower emotional intensity; for example, reducing eye contact. As therapy progresses, it is likely that the therapist will be able to stay with reflection for longer. The therapist will need to pay close attention to how much the child can manage and what additional things can help him to remain connected. This might be sensory support such as a back rub or giving the child something to chew, supported by regulating activities such as drawing or building with Lego blocks. Notice, however, that for some children, touch is not regulating. These children might respond better to having some space between themselves and the therapist or parents. Comfort and support is experienced from the voice of the adults rather than their touch.

With regulation in place, the therapist can focus on developing the story with the child and parents. She will need to pay attention to her tone of voice; some children need a harder, factual voice tone with light and indirect empathy so that their easily triggered fight-or-flight responses are not activated. Others respond better to softer tones and increased empathy, which helps the child to experience vulnerability and to receive comfort. Whichever is optimal, the storytelling tone of a DDP session will be soothing and regulating. The therapist will also need to ensure that she brings a playful, animated atmosphere to the session, as the child might understand and manage reciprocal moments of joy more easily than those of sadness. The animation and fun signal safety very clearly to the child who finds it hard to understand social interactions.

This safety is enhanced by the acceptance from both therapist and parents for the child's difficulties. The therapist is advised to be alert to loss of acceptance in the face of understandable longings for things to be different and for the child to have an easier time in the world. Parents will be helped to stay accepting through the "PACE-ful" support of the therapist. Therapists also are vulnerable to this loss of acceptance as affection for the child deepens. PACE during supervision will be important to keep the therapist on track too.

Working with children with neurodevelopmental difficulties can be challenging as they present a complex mixture of socio-emotional and executive functioning problems. Progress can feel slow, so small successes need acknowledgment and celebration. Trusting the process is never more important, and at a pace that the child can manage. It is not uncommon for the children to make progress in bursts, perhaps needing more time for consolidation in between. It can feel like little is happening, but these periods are important. Caring for neurodevelopmentally challenging children can take a toll on parents. They will need good levels of emotional and practical help along with help to support the therapeutic work with the children.

CHILDREN AND ADOLESCENTS WITH ADHD

Attention deficit/hyperactivity disorder (ADHD) represents a lack of organization, regulation, and integration of various aspects of an individual's cognition, emotion, and behavior, and as a result it presents significant challenges to a child or adolescent's functioning. There are various explanations as to the cause of ADHD, and most likely there is more than one explanation. There are some studies that demonstrate a relationship between attachment disorganization and ADHD (Green, Stanley, & Peters, 2007). Attachment disorganization at age 5 predicated ADHD symptoms at age 7 (Bohlin, Eninger, Brocki, & Thorell, 2012). These findings were found to be stable, when the same group of children who still showed attachment disorganization at 8½ were found to demonstrate ADHD symptoms a year later (Thorell, Rydell, & Bohlin, 2012).

When children begin to dysregulate, they greatly benefit from having their parents coregulate their affective expressions, which leads them toward calming down. Sometimes children with ADHD have parents who are intrusive by provoking or teasing when the child becomes overaroused. When this pattern of intrusiveness was combined with high family stress and chaos, there was a particularly high incidence of ADHD. In fact, when that intrusive parenting factor was combined with high family distress, "predictions to ADHD symptoms became quite strong, dwarfing endogenous measures of neurological status or temperament" (Sroufe, 2016, p. 1004). Having said that, it is important for the DDP practitioner to remember that more than likely, many children have ADHD entirely for neurologic reasons with no contribution from parental factors.

Dyadic developmental psychotherapy, involving the full range of psychotherapy, parenting, and practice, has been successfully applied to children and adolescents who manifest ADHD. In the therapy session, the DDP therapist matches the affective expressions of the young person in order to coregulate the often agitated and disorganized cognitive, affective, and behavioral states. The DDP therapist is likely to match the agitation with animation, joining the intensity and rhythm of the child's expression. At the same time, the DDP therapist focuses his attention quite actively, taking the lead in initiating and maintaining the focus on a particular theme or activity. The child with ADHD is most often not able to engage in focused attention on their own. The lead of the therapist is not based on rational directives or commands but rather on enthusiasm and compelling interest. The therapist leads the focus of the child's attention but is still receptive to modifying it in response to the child's congruent initiatives. Also, the therapist is likely to often switch to another focus when she sees that the child is starting to disengage from the joint focus. By doing this, the therapist is integrating the child's disorganized attention into the therapist's organized attention. There is a temptation to remain calm with a child with ADHD, but that often leads to the child's more intense affect not being contained. The child most often needs the therapist to be regulated and animated, not regulated and calm.

The animated focus of the DDP therapist on two to four themes and activities is often sufficient to hold the young person's attention and create a meaningful intersubjective experience with him. However, this brief period of time is often not sufficient to enable the child to attain the same degree of regulated attention throughout the day. It is important that his caregivers and teachers adopt a similar approach of active engagement. Passively following the child's focus of attention from one thing or event to the next often only creates more disorganization and agitation. However, insisting that the ADHD child follow a rigid schedule often creates ongoing power struggles and defiance. The caregiver and teacher need to know their child well in terms of interests, attention span, and signs of dysregulation. The ADHD child does need repetition and structure—an external organization for his mind and body, as his internal organization is weak. The adult needs to be proactive with the schedule, holding the focus of attention with compelling interest and then leading the transition to another focus when the child is nearing his limit.

It is also important to remember that given the symptoms of ADHD, we need to ensure that we are not asking too much—too much reason, self-control, delay of gratification, self-directed activity. We need to anticipate and expect a bit less than what we think the child is able to do—cognitively, affectively, and behaviorally—rather than a bit too much.

When the child's or adolescent's ADHD symptoms are affecting many areas of his functioning, many of his activities at home, school, and in the community, there might be value in considering other interventions as well. Sensory integration therapy along with concrete, repetitive, rhythmic, or gross motor activities may be of value for both attention and regulation. The challenges that the child faces need to be met with PACE and great effort to design an environment that reduces failure and shame. Medication may also need to be considered.

Finally, it is important to note that sometimes the externalizing symptoms of ADHD may represent efforts of the child to distract himself from the anxiety, sadness, and shame that is secondary to experiences of abuse, neglect, and loss. At times, the successful treatment of developmental trauma has led to a significant reduction in the ADHD symptoms in a remarkably short time. However, it is important not to expect such a change because with other children, though the impact of developmental trauma is definitely less after DDP, significant ADHD symptoms remain.

CHILDREN AND ADOLESCENTS WHO ARE VIOLENT TOWARD THEIR PARENTS

Parents caring for children with developmental traumas have to manage a range of difficulties, many of which are related to behavioral challenges that the children are presenting. Possibly the behavior that is most likely to trigger a breaking point within families is when the child is violent, especially as the child grows bigger and stronger and the violence becomes more targeted. For example, a study of adoption by Selwyn and colleagues (2014) found high levels of violence associated with adoption family breakdown. Eighty percent of adoptive parents of young people who had left the adoptive family home gave violence toward parents or siblings as the main reason. The levels of violence displayed by the young people led to feelings of threat and intimidation and undermined support networks. Parents reported living in fear. They often struggled to tell therapists, other practitioners, friends, or extended family of their experience because of the level of shame they were experiencing.

Many children who demonstrate high levels of violence in adolescence will demonstrate high levels of dysregulation and physical aggression earlier in their childhood. Often these children are struggling to trust being parented. They can especially resist being comforted, as this requires them managing feelings of vulnerability and signaling this to parents. When feelings of vulnerability have been met by children with fear, pain, and silence earlier in childhood, the children will grow up finding ways not to experience vulnerability so that they do not need comfort; these children are not safe enough to feel sad. A consequence is that they do not get the relationship experience that would also help them learn how to handle frustration and other distressing feelings. They have not had early coregulatory support with a safe adult, and consequently their ability to self-regulate is weak. As they have also learned to avoid or resist seeking support from parents when distressed, they never make up for this early lack of nurture. When a child cannot turn to adults to help him manage strong feelings, then he will end up dealing with these difficult feelings alone and in maladaptive ways, such as through violence.

Parents can be supported to put in proactive interventions to prevent the onset of violence with these younger oppositional children who are struggling to manage strong feelings. This will involve the use of PACE and other DDP principles to help the children become used to parental support and coregulation, so that they learn how to manage conflict and feelings of anger. The parents can then support the child to convey his feelings through words rather than being acted out through behavior. It is hoped that with this support, the child will learn to trust and seek support as needed and therefore not escalate to the more challenging and violent behaviors.

For example, Ren is 8 years old and living with his aunt, uncle, and his younger sister, Sakura. He has very low frustration tolerance and especially struggles when his aunt is giving attention to Sakura. This will often result in verbal aggression and trashing of the room but hasn't yet escalated to physical violence. The aunt, supported by a DDP therapist, learns to respond to Ren with PACE alongside clear behavioral limits. One day, Sakura is demanding a lot of her aunt's time. Aunt is delighted and accepting when Ren tells her how angry he is feeling because of this and even more delighted and accepting when a little while later he adds, "And I feel sad, because it feels like you love Sakura more than me." Ren does not trash the room, and he and his aunt have an enjoyable time together before bedtime when Sakura is finally asleep.

Dyadic developmental psychotherapy interventions can therefore be successful in preventing the escalation of difficulties when early oppositional and aggressive behavior is evident. The parents are helped to understand the shame and mistrust of their children and to respond to these with PACE and regulatory-based behavioral support. As the children experience being understood and safe in emotional connection, they will develop increased trust and security, and levels of physical aggression will reduce. This can halt the progression to violence against people emerging in adolescence. Most important, these children learn to turn to their parents at times of need. They are helped to be vulnerable with their parents, and when they do express feelings through aggression, they are supported to regulate the shame that is experienced as a consequence. They experience safe dependency and can draw on this as they grow and develop, especially as they struggle with the challenge of developing independence in adolescence. Parents are a safe source of support, available as needed.

Adolescents who have not developed trust and security and who display this via violent behavior can need DDP interventions at times of crisis within the family. The DDP therapist works with the parents and child at a time when neither feel safe with the other. A priority of the intervention will be to help the parents to feel safe again so that they can help their young person to feel safe. This will require high levels of parent support alongside therapy with the child and parents. DDP interventions in this situation are likely to be more intensive. Weekly or twice-weekly sessions will provide capacity for parent-only sessions alongside parent and child sessions. The family may also need this support to be supplemented with daily telephone calls at least in the initial stages of the intervention. If a support worker is assisting a therapist to offer this intensity of support, it will be important that both are consistent in their use of the DDP principles. Parents will need high levels of PACE-led support for themselves before being able to focus on their child's internal experience. Only with this foundation will parents be able to think about how they might adjust their parenting to the needs of this young person.

Psychoeducation will be an important part of this support. An understanding of how trauma can affect the nervous system in ways that lead to hypervigilance and a heightened fight-or-flight response will start to make the violence more understandable for parents and young people. Parents can also notice how their own nervous systems are responding in kind, with more quickly dysregulated states of anger becoming quickly triggered by this young person.

An important part of helping parents to gain this understanding will come from an exploration of attachment history as parents understand how their current responses to the child can be caught up in past relationship experience. The ways in which anger was expressed or denied in the parents' own families of origin will prepare them well or poorly to deal with anger in the children that they go on to parent. When parents have trouble coping with children who are angry, the parents are less likely to be able to prevent an escalation into violence. Escalating patterns of anger can, however, be interrupted when parents understand how their responses link to their past experience. Now parents can learn to remain open and engaged toward their child even at these most difficult of times for them.

Therapy sessions will help provide some containment and also exploration for young people and parents. It is important for the therapist to talk with the network, parents, and child about how intimidation or aggression will be handled within the sessions, whether directed toward the therapist or the parents. The young person needs to understand what will and won't be tolerated and how limits will be put in place. This will contribute to everybody's feelings of safety during the sessions. An oppositional young person is likely to test these limits, and so this will be anticipated, with the adults planning how to manage this. Some young people might use violence to try and stop therapy, particularly if they have done this in the past with other approaches. Again, planning ahead about how to manage this will be helpful.

Anxiety is likely to be high for both parent and child, as each anticipates the next outburst of rage. The raised anxiety itself can increase the likelihood of more rage. "Walking on eggshells" is a term often used by parents to describe what it feels like living with these difficulties. DDP therapists can also be affected by this raised level of anxiety, feeling the pressure to help such distressed families. Supportive supervision for the therapists will be important to help them remain regulated so that they can help the family with this raised emotion.

It is likely that parents will need more active coaching in maintaining a PACE attitude within sessions and at home, given the complex emotional reaction that they can be experiencing toward the violent behavior. The therapy sessions can then help to restore a sense of safety for the young person and the parents as emotion is coregulated and experience cocreated.

The therapist will also need to keep a close lookout for signs of shame in the young person or the parents and will need to work hard to regulate this. Families where child violence is high are very prone to quickly triggered shame as each has a sense of failing. The young person will have encountered many people who suggest that he is unacceptable or bad, and this often resonates with deeply held beliefs about the self. The therapist will need to slow down, ensuring that regulation is provided as needed and noticing any ruptures in the relationship with quick, adult-led repair for these. The storytelling voice of the therapist becomes an important way of helping the distrustful young person remain engaged in the session. These interactions can be explored in some depth in parent-only time so that the parents are helped to deepen their understanding of their young person and the support he needs on a day-to-day basis.

The therapist needs to be alert to signs of blocked care in the parents and to increase her support as needed. Therapist presence for the parents can help them to remain present to their young person at the times when they are feeling most challenged. The young person is likely to reject this presence and to be distrustful of the parents' PACE attitude, especially in the early stages of the intervention. While they won't often show it, the young people will feel bad about the violence that they are displaying and experience themselves as undeserving. Being cared for when they have been violent to others can be confusing. Parents will need to be supported through the young person's resistance to what they are trying to implement and to hold on until the young person is ready join with them.

A big challenge for the DDP intervention is managing the ongoing violence, which parents need immediate help with. The therapist and parents will need to work together to plan ways to manage these episodes as they arise. Parents are helped to apply containment and safety strategies. This will include supporting parents to ensure that they are providing needed structure and supervision. Often, boundaries have slipped because of the fear and intimidation that is present from the young person. Parents will also learn to use repair strategies following episodes, when this can be the last thing the frustrated parent feels like doing. This helps to reduce the shame that the young person is feeling so that he is more likely to experience guilt, remorse, and want to make restitution.

Parents need support: calling on others for help and combating a natural tendency to want to hide what is happening within the family. Having people who can come around to help can be an important part of diffusing situations. Additionally, it is beneficial if this support is proactively in place rather than only being a consequence of escalating violence. This involves identifying trigger points in the day, such as when the child arrives home from school, so that the helpers are routinely in the house to offer support. Parents will often resist putting this type of support in place. They can experience feeling like a burden to friends and family, like they are asking too much. The therapist will be accepting and empathetic toward these understandable worries while also gently encouraging the parents. A meeting with the parents and helpers can allow some of these worries to be aired, leading to the parents feeling more comfortable about asking for high levels of support over the short term. It is helpful if this support network also understands the DDP principles and can support the parents in holding onto a PACE attitude.

Parents will also need help to talk with the young person after incidents. With such difficult behaviors, it can be especially difficult to stay with the young person's experience, fully understand and accept their inner experience, and to use curiosity and empathy to help the young person to reflect also. The natural urge is to move straight to a discussion of why the behavior is wrong and what will be the consequence. The young person will already have a high level of shame, and talking about an incident too early only reinforces this. The young person is then not in a state to reflect and plan how to make amends. It can even trigger further episodes of violence. As the young person experiences support and understanding of his internal experience, he is more likely to be able to then reflect on his behavior in a way that leads to the experience of remorse and to a wish to make amends. Now he is ready to plan restitution. Parents will need to support the young person to follow through with any actions that he wants to take and to help him repair the relationships that might have been harmed because of the violence. Consequences tied to such relationship repair will be an important part of helping the young person to manage the aftermath of incidents.

Commonly, the violent behavior that the young person is displaying will also be present outside of the family, for example at school. Education staff will also need help to manage these situations and to implement the same DDP principles with the child as the parents have. This can also help parents and teaching staff to be on the same team, providing support for each other.

Clinical experience suggests that as young people begin to shift from pervasive shame to the beginnings of guilt and remorse, they start to feel bad about current and past violence inflicted on others. This is similar to the impact of interventions used with adult sexual offenders. As they begin to develop victim empathy, it is not unusual to need a suicide watch in prison for their own safety. Young people can experience increased risk of depression, self-harm, and suicide attempts as they struggle with these feelings.

For example, Lexi is an adolescent who is beginning to move from the habitual violence that she has used to survive in a world where she cannot believe in her own lovability and cannot trust in her mother's unconditional love. As she makes some tentative moves toward a healthier relationship with her mother, within which she is beginning to allow herself to be vulnerable and to seek comfort, she is haunted by the memory of her mother's broken arm, which led to Lexi being moved into foster care for a time. This tests her new-found confidence in her lovability. One day, as she perceives her mother's parental authority as a sign that she has been discovered as irretrievably bad, her fear builds to the point that she lashes out and unwittingly catches her mother in the eye. When she sees the black eye her mother is left with, she has a constant reminder of her relapse toward violence. She begs her mother to kill her because she can't bear how bad she feels at the hurt she has caused. Lexi is moving toward a future that is very different from her past, but she will need all the help and loving support that her mother can give her if she is to reach this future.

As is so often the case, child-to-parent violence rests on the parent's capacity to enter into a state of mind toward the child that is regulating and de-escalating. This can be a challenge when levels of violence are already high and strategies to manage the violence are being sought. The work with the parents to help them to understand themselves and their reactions to their young person is an essential part of helping them to stay regulated and therefore to support the young person to reduce levels of violence. A DDP intervention has to meet this need, including immediate support to the young person, as safety is built up, then therapy alongside the many strategies that can be helpful with parents and young people will have a chance to work. These will include behavioral support, regulatory support, and different parental behaviors in response to the young person.

CHILDREN AND ADOLESCENTS WHO HAVE EXPERIENCED SEXUAL ABUSE OR EXPLOITATION OR ENGAGE IN PROBLEMATIC SEXUAL BEHAVIOR

There is general consensus that intimidation, humiliation, and violence is not acceptable. Whether sexual activity is seen as acceptable depends on context, culture, relationship, age, consent, and power imbalance. We struggle to find words to adequately describe the impact of interactions where sexual activity is seen as unacceptable or harmful. Child sexual abuse (CSA), rape, problematic sexual behavior, child sexual exploitation (CSE), and child prostitution are examples. Sexual abuse is the term used in this chapter. Accepting the impact of the experience of sexual abuse can be hard for communities, services, and individuals. We break down an individual's experiences involving terror, pain, shame, intrusion, and rejection into manageable pieces. Acronyms such as CSA or CSE can distance us from the experiences the words are describing.

Governments occasionally allocate short-term funding in the aftermath of critical reports or public inquiries that uncover specific sexual abuse previously unknown to the public. One recent example in the United Kingdom is funding made available for the development of child exploitation services following independent inquiries. Such action helps to raise public awareness. It can also act as a protective factor for society, enabling the mistaken belief that this form of sexual abuse is recent and limited to certain groups. Another recent example in the United Kingdom is the Independent Inquiry into Child Sexual Abuse (IICSA). This 5-year inquiry has a wide scope. It aims to investigate whether the public bodies and other non-state institutions in England and Wales have taken seriously their responsibility to protect children from sexual abuse. It further aims to make meaningful recommendations for change in the future.

The capacity of societies to take on the extent of sexual abuse is still developing. The effective silencing of children and adolescents by those who abuse is a significant factor. Sexual abuse relies on the behavior remaining hidden and unbelievable to adults who might see potential signs of sexual abuse or hear the actual experiences as told by children. The phrase "hidden in plain sight" describes recent uncovering of long-term persistent sexual abuse by male celebrities.

The DDP practitioner aims to keep these wider factors in mind when working with children who have experienced sexual abuse as well as how sexual abuse involves the misuse of trust often combined with the development of pervasive shame. The lack of gender-based statistics and research data contributes to a lack of awareness of gender differences. There are differences between girls and boys in how male perpetrators use gender-based threats in an attempt to make sure children do not tell anyone about their abuse. Powerful threats for boys include the use of homophobia, such as "If you tell people they will think you are gay." This works in a society where being gay has negative associations. Additional factors for boys occur if they are visibly sexually aroused during the abuse, as fear and shame can become associated with their sexual functioning. The acceptance in PACE enables tentative exploration of such shame-based experiences as well as the core beliefs that develop about self, such as a child believing "I must have been bad" or "It was my fault."

Chapter 8 describes an example of dyadic developmental practice including therapy where a child has experienced sexual abuse.

Key information can be lost when children move to foster or adoptive families or to residential care. In DDP, a focus on "co-construction of narratives" enables adults to help children develop sensitive, accurate, and legally robust narratives so that the children can make choices about how much to share of their histories. Professional and parental fears are common about either asking children too much or too little. They can worry that responding with PACE to children beginning to talk about their abuse might be seen as leading the children to the police. In the United Kingdom, regular multiagency training used to be held that focused on working with children who have been abused. Such training enabled carers and professionals to develop confidence in talking with children in ways that didn't lead them but didn't shut them down. This training has almost disappeared in the United Kingdom, but strong beliefs still prevail about whether or not initial conversations started by children should be continued.

The DDP practitioner can help by attending strategy meetings. These are meetings where police and social services work together with parents and other professionals. They consider how to proceed where there are concerns that a child has been abused and new information is coming into public awareness. One role of the DDP practitioner can be to ensure that those most likely to be trusted by the child are supported by the police to help the child share in any way the child chooses. Another role is to challenge, with PACE, misplaced ideas that the process of collecting criminal evidence overrides helping children to share their experiences once a child takes the often huge step to begin to talk. Open discussion and acceptance of such fears are an integral part of dyadic developmental practice. Fears of doing harm by asking about past sexual abuse make it more likely that the subject is avoided. DDP using PACE enables parents and professionals to safely consider together words to use when communicating with children.

Care is always taken when "talking about" and "talking for" a child to avoid "putting words into children's mouths." Tentative curiosity explores whatever the child's memories might be. All possibilities are accepted with empathy for just how hard this was and still is for the child.

This is relevant for Imran, a 15-year-old boy who remembers being made to become involved when his perpetrator sexually abused other children when he was 7. He tells his foster carer this. He doesn't tell her he thinks he will be arrested because he was also an abuser. His perpetrator told Imran this, making such beliefs more likely to persist. His therapist proactively wonders whether Imran might be fearful that his parents will reject him once they know everything; that Imran might fear he will be seen as legally responsible for behaviors; that such a belief would be understandable; that it will be so hard for Imran to believe when they tell him he will not be arrested. He was a little boy who believed this was what all families did.

Of all the experiences that contribute to developmental trauma, sexual abuse most consistently involves the misuse of trust. This may not become apparent to a child until later, for example, when young children have been groomed to the extent that sexual abuse is just another part of their lives. The impact may not be felt until they are older and discover that other children did not experience this. This can come to light in confusing ways; for example, if a 6-year-old girl moves to a foster family, starts a new school, and sexually abuses a peer in school as her way of being friendly.

Dyadic developmental practice has much to offer when working with children engaged in problematic sexual behavior with other children. Intervention as early as possible once the behavior is known about is crucial. It is never more important to integrate attachment-focused interventions, with caregivers creating emotional connections as they set clear behavioral limits as to what is and is not acceptable behavior. It is particularly important to include network consultation alongside therapy and to work closely with police as well as social services.

If a child lives with her birth family and has engaged in such behavior with another child in the family, a sibling or cousin for example, planned foster care placement with agreement by the child's family of origin can provide a safe environment within which the DDP practitioner can work collaboratively with the child or adolescent, the child's family, foster carers, and the network. There are often legal implications to consider, and key factors in joint service delivery include continual linking back to other services and agencies, such as the police, youth offending services, and child mental health services. Continual assessment is required for the following:

- Risk in the context of a child's emotional, developmental, and attachment needs, such as risks to and feelings of other children; risk in sibling interactions; and risk in school placement.
- Placement factors: Is the family atmosphere becoming sexualized? Is the placement continuing to meet the child's needs? Are supervision requirements able to meet safety rules and contracts?
- Interaction of family of origin and sibling factors with placement and foster carer factors.

Resource and policy implications need to be incorporated into the model, such as supporting the foster carer to work alongside the family of origin as key agents of change, building attachments, and assessing risk in the context of "safe care." The impact of this work on workers requires consideration as do supervision needs.

The DDP practitioner can also contribute to:

- Assessment of risk in the context of assessment of the psychological, emotional, social, and developmental needs of the child.
- Identification of placement needs.
- Assessment of the capacity of carers to meet placement needs.
- Assessment of the training and support needs of carers, and how these will be met.
- How these differing needs can be addressed.

Foster carers can be supported to provide a contained protective and supportive family environment that allows the child to develop positive relationships and build up protective factors. This can reduce the impact of risk factors and provide a child with practice in coping and in reducing negative interaction cycles.

Network consultation provides reflective space to explore the meaning behind all the child's behavior, in the context of development, early and past parenting, relationships, abusive experiences from and toward others, and attachment patterns.

Consultation increases understanding, enables continuing shared assessment of risk, and increases awareness of the extent of difficulty in the child's early history. Sharing and agreeing on risk can place a child's sexually problematic behavior in a context that may make it seem less worrying and more manageable.

The DDP practitioner can enable slow progress and challenging behavior to be seen as stemming from the child's difficulties rather than the foster carer's inadequacy. Foster carers can be supported by all the network to make sense of understandable feelings of failing or that the placement is wrong for the child. She can recognize potential skills of foster carers, in the context of training and regular, consistent support. She can validate a carer's practice and increase confidence so as to help the foster carer to continue the placement. The school can be supported to make difficult decisions as to how they provide an environment that may need to support both the child who has engaged in the behavior and the child who has been abused. School staff may need to be supported with the dilemmas regarding which child may need to change school and how to help another school feel confident to educate the child and keep other pupils safe.

The example of work with an adoptive family in Chapter 8 includes a child who engages in sexually problematic behavior.

The DDP practitioner sometimes helps organizations find homes in which parents and carers are assessed as safe for children who have been sexually abused. She provides interventions enabling the adults to learn how to care for children through DDP-informed parenting. She provides therapy with the child and the adults together, enabling the child to form as secure an attachment as possible to her new caregivers. Therapy aims to help a child feel safe enough to try out new ways of connecting, to ask for help, and to trust enough to tentatively explore intersubjective relationships.

Parents are helped to be open to feeling the emotional pain of the child they love when hearing distressing and unbelievable experiences described, putting aside until later their murderous anger at former parents and their guilt at not being there to protect. They are helped instead to respond with PACE to their child. This is never easy either to do or to help parents to do. Professionals who support parents need also to be open to their evoked feelings. Regular effective supervision is essential.

Dyadic developmental practice provides a framework that integrates these factors, ensuring network and parental consultations regularly take place when providing therapy. Children are more likely to share their memories when they perceive that the adult can take on their experiences without becoming overwhelmed. DDP-informed parenting focuses on safety and communication using PACE. Parents provide a family atmosphere that actively shows that wishes, feelings, desires, perceptions, and motives underneath behavior are accepted and not evaluated or judged. They learn that this does not mean accepting inappropriate behavior, and they learn how to connect with their child's experience before putting in place necessary behavioral limits. Parents learn how to "talk with" , "talk for" and "talk about" their child both in therapy and in their day-to-day interactions.

When children consistently experience this parenting approach, they begin to develop a sense of safety and acceptance and may feel safe enough to risk telling adults more about past experiences. Young children who were developmentally too young to be effectively silenced by threats and secrets begin to do what young children do when they feel safe and unconditionally loved. They talk about their memories. An older child may consider it is worth taking the risk to share. An adolescent may test out how adults will respond many times before deciding to share. Parenting with PACE makes it more likely that an adolescent will continue to test responses out until the time feels safe enough to describe what happened.

As with all therapy with children, DDP includes discussions about confidentiality. These are not one-off discussions. Children need to be clear about, and hear repeated over time, what action adults will take if the children talk about adults who sexually abused them or they talk about their own experiences of engaging in sexual activities with other children. This is particularly relevant with DDP where the approach may mean children unexpectedly feel safe enough in a therapy session to talk about past experiences without having planned to do so.

Dyadic developmental psychotherapy therapists routinely request consent to video-record therapy sessions to ensure effective supervision. Sexual abuse can involve video-recording of children, and the need to be sensitive about this when asking for consent to video is important.

Therapists also need to be aware that video-recorded sessions, where a child talks about experiences of sexual abuse that are previously unknown, may be requested or subpoenaed in any criminal prosecution. Clear protocols about video-recording are essential, as is openly discussing this possibility with children, parents, and professional networks.

In a therapy session, an 11-year-old girl tells her adoptive parents that her grandfather made her "his princess," which she now recognizes included repeated sexual abuse. She says it made her feel special and loved more than her sisters. She also says one of her foster parent's adult sons sexually abused her. At this point, it is helpful if effective networks are already in place. Parents, social workers, the police, and the DDP practitioner need to work together to support the child emotionally while carrying out all statutory assessments as soon as possible.

At such times, teams and services can proceed to decision making that is based in fear combined with either too low or too high an intensity. Making sense of such actions within a social and political context that finds it hard to take on the full extent and impact of sexual abuse enables the DDP practitioner to genuinely respond in network consultations with PACE. This is essential to find a way to agree on decisions that are helpful to the child's long-term mental health outcomes.

Routinely including network consultations alongside therapy means support services can be prepared for the psychological impact on a child when the child talks in detail about past experiences involving high shame and effective developmentally sensitive threat. Anxiety and terror arise from beliefs that threats will be fulfilled and the adults who care for the child will reject him once they really know how bad the child is. This can result in a child being unable to engage emotionally or behaviorally in day-to-day life, including going to school.

At the same time, parental fears for and about their child may escalate, decreasing confidence. Routine parental consultations mean these fears can be spoken about, listened to, and acted upon. DDP focuses repeatedly on ensuring safety for the parent as well as the child. DDP-informed parenting provides an intersubjective, as-safe-as-it-can-be relationship through which the unimaginable is imagined. The associated almost unbearable pain, loss, hurt, anger, and fear is openly experienced and talked about in parental consultations.

With both network and parental consultations routinely in place, whether or not therapy also occurs, it is more likely that parents and professionals will make helpful decisions when a child manages his psychological distress by behaving in ways that confuse and frighten adults.

Abby, a 14-year-old girl living in her birth family, offers sex to the policeman investigating her report of rape by the adult son of a family friend. This disclosure is later withdrawn. Abby often comes in late and refuses to talk with her parents about anything. Abby's friends talk about visiting the flat of an older man with Abby where other men visit them. In the absence of knowledge about sexual abuse and given how hard it still is for society to fully accept the impact of sexual abuse, professionals may make sense of Abby's behavior in ways that see her as culpable, that she is wasting police time, with no need to consider a child-protection plan. Different care-planning decisions are made when Abby's behavior is made sense of in terms of being sexually abused, acknowledging that Abby is not yet ready to accept the perspective that her boyfriend, whom she still loves, exploited and abused her.

With a robust safety plan, and her perpetrator in prison, Abby later in therapy tells her parents that she once thought she was pregnant. This was why she said she had been raped. She wanted to keep the baby and marry her boyfriend, who said he would marry her, just not yet. They needed more money first. Through tentative curiosity and "talking about," her therapist includes a social and political context when using PACE and making sense of Abby's current behavior. The therapist says to Abby's parents while Abby listens:

THERAPIST: No wonder Abby finds it hard to walk into town or even come downstairs. Everywhere she goes reminds her of what happened to her. The advertisement on the bus, her favorite TV program, that song, that magazine. She can't escape by going out; she can't feel safe anywhere. And now she can't even see her best friend, not only because he is in prison, but because she is beginning to get that best friends don't ask you to have sex with other men for money. Even when Abby uses her phone, the advertisements pop up, the pornography sites, even the news. It must seem endless. The only place she just might feel safe is when playing her favorite game in her room. Here she can create her own world. She can create a strong avatar; create a world she wants to live in. Maybe what you can do for Abby now is let her know that you will be there for her, downstairs, when she feels ready to face a world that must look very different to her now.

It is important to help children develop core beliefs that they are not to blame for their sexual abuse. In DDP, the focus on acceptance, being curious about, on deepening the child's experience in the moment, and resisting the natural human response to reassure all enable ways of working that do not focus too early on telling children that sexual abuse was not their fault. If done too soon, this denies the child's experience. It takes much more than being told by an adult that sexual abuse was not your fault to alter such beliefs. When a child first takes the risk of sharing memories, it is important that others explore with interest how it could be that she feels it is her fault and show empathy for how tough her life must be to feel that she is to blame. Be sad for her. Most important, be emotionally strong enough to bear witness to her story.

OLDER ADOLESCENTS WITH LITTLE MOTIVATION TO BE PARENTED AGAIN

Because older adolescents with developmental trauma are not likely to have had much experience being well cared for by their parents, it is little wonder that they would not want to begin to rely on parents as they are approaching adulthood. Children who do not trust their parents because their parents have long since betrayed that trust learn that they must rely on themselves. They may not be that successful in meeting their developmental needs, but they have no other choice. They have stopped seeking comfort and support from parents. They also have stopped seeking experiences of reciprocal enjoyment. There is less pain in not seeking something that you will not get than in seeking it and not getting it. It is easier to "go it alone" than it is to be disappointed by another reaction of rejection. It is easier to be "tough" and "independent" than to be vulnerable and lonely. Adolescents who are not interested in being parented again are certainly not going to be too interested in relating with a therapist. The therapist might be seen as someone worth getting to know if she can show the adolescent that she is happy to explore things that the adolescent is interested in. These might include getting along better with his girlfriend, finding his biological parents, or finding ways to enroll in a continuing education program if he failed in his prior years of attending school.

The first goal of DDP with older adolescents who do not want to be parented again is for the therapist and parent (or another significant caregiver) to remain in an attitude of PACE. They do not try to convince the adolescent that he is making a mistake and that he should take advantage of this last opportunity to be able to be a child. Being a child was actually never that great for him, which is part of his rush toward being an adult. With the attitude of PACE, the DDP therapist focuses on getting to know the teen and the journey that he has taken so far. The therapist is understanding and accepting the challenges he has faced, the choices he has made, and the defenses he has developed. Given the extreme lack of safety and limited opportunity and support that he habitually faced, the life that he developed was most likely the best possible life that he could have developed. He found strength and survival through intimidating, manipulating, or staying apart from others. He probably often saw turning 18 as being the special day when he would be left alone, could do what he wanted—not what others wanted—and would pick his friends and not have to please anyone.

With PACE, the adolescent may feel understood and accepted—possibly one of the few times in her life. She is not being judged. When the adolescent accepts the playful interactions with the therapist and caregiver, she is likely to feel that they enjoy being with her, can relax with her, and that they are not focused on "serious" talk meant to fix her. The DDP therapist is likely to understate empathy in her voice when hard events are being explored. Rather, she is matter-of-fact in her tone, commenting on how hard something must have been but not bringing much emotion into the expression. The adolescent is not likely to want to feel vulnerable then, and an emotional tone is likely to evoke vulnerability. The DDP therapist will be curious about how the adolescent thinks that her childhood and adolescence have affected her. Without judgment or pressure, the therapist will wonder how the adolescent plans to make a life now, with possible educational limitations, as well as a lack of support, either financially or emotionally. The therapist might comment on possible community supports that might be available if she sees a need for them. Again, there is no judgment if the adolescent chooses not to take advantage of any specific services or opportunities.

By emphasizing playfulness, acceptance, and curiosity, the therapist and caregiver are enabling the adolescent to experience a relaxing, enjoyable, mildly supportive relationship with an adult who is not judging her. This way of relating is probably close to what the adolescent had in mind when she thought about turning 18. The message being communicated is that the therapist and parent are interested in the adolescent and would like to be supportive in any way that they might be as the adolescent is developing her independence.

When the adolescent is struggling with her emotions (anger, sadness, fears), relationships with peers (conflicts, seeming betrayals, moves), or behaviors (failing to keep commitments at school or work, in the home or with peers), the therapist discusses these with her with the expression of worry for her, not frustration or anger. The primary message is that increasingly the choices belong to the adolescent, and the therapist and parent want to be of help on the journey, because it is a hard one. When there is a conflict between the older adolescent and the parent, the adolescent's perspective is discussed with PACE, and if the parent does need to insist on particular behaviors, it is done with acknowledgment of how hard it is for the adolescent to still experience the parent's rules. In both expressing worry for the adolescent about current challenges and in making clear the frustrations of the parent's rules, the parent and therapist are expressing empathy. Empathy given over the adolescent's current situation is likely to be easier for the adolescent to accept than empathy given for past traumatic events.

The DDP therapist and parent are focusing on the adolescent experiencing a relationship with them that is based on PACE, respecting the adolescent's self-reliance and avoidance of vulnerability. The adolescent might then realize that she is able to preserve her independence and also have a relationship with someone who cares for her and does not judge her. As the relationship deepens, the adolescent may discover that she is safe enough to be sad, to be vulnerable with the parent and therapist. She is able to rely on them and also maintain her self-reliance. It does not have to be either/or. Rather, within a relationship based on principles of PACE, she discovers that it can be both/and. She does not lose her hard-won strengths when she is able to be vulnerable with someone she trusts. Rather, she actually becomes stronger. This is a deeper sense of strength than that of her earlier self-reliance. With this strength she might even choose to rely on her DDP therapist and parent to explore past traumas, reducing the shame and fear associated with the ghosts from her past.

Of course, other adolescents may choose to remain self-reliant throughout their hard times and move into adulthood without accepting much support from a parent or therapist. However, if their decision is understood and accepted, if they are not "wrong" in refusing therapy at this time, they might choose to do so in the future when they have a different perspective on being an adult and relying on others. If they have a good experience of a therapist understanding and accepting them at 17 when they refused therapy, they might be more likely to seek therapy when they are 27.

Jenny was 17. The last 12 months with her foster carer, Anne, had gone okay. Anne fed her, gave her a place to sleep, didn't bring up her past, and did not bug her too much about her schoolwork (even though it was not going so well) or the chores (even though she often put them off). Jenny was surprised that there didn't seem to be as much drama in her life as there had been in her other foster homes. Anne was different. She didn't judge Jenny and seemed interested in what Jenny thought and felt and wanted. And Anne had a wicked sense of humor for an "old lady." And just six more months and Jenny would be on her own. No more being a foster kid. She'd get a job and maybe get a place to live with one of her friends from school who hated her family.

One evening after dinner, she and Anne were talking at the table. She had her cake and Anne had her tea. Nothing special, it was something that they started doing before Jenny would go off to her room and her social media and Anne would take care of cleaning up. This time Jenny stayed to help with the dishes without thinking about it. Afterward, Anne combed and braided Jenny's hair after Jenny had casually mentioned that she felt like looking different for school the next day. It felt nice, and she especially liked telling Anne the next day how that boy she liked had even noticed and wanted to count her braids!

A few weeks later, Anne's brother Al stopped by after work. Jenny and Al did not get along too well. When Anne went into the kitchen, Al started with his questions about whether or not Jenny was following the rules and getting her schoolwork done. When Jenny would not answer him, he yelled that she had better grow up and learn to be responsible or she'd always be a lazy loser like her mother. Anne came in from the kitchen and said just as loudly, "Don't you talk to my daughter that way!" Al wasn't happy, he pouted a bit, and then went home.

Jenny stared at Anne. "You called me your daughter!"

Anne became tense, "I'm sorry that I said that if it made you uncomfortable."

Jenny replied quietly, "I don't remember anyone ever calling me that before. At least not that way."

Anne asked, "What way do you mean?"

Jenny stared at her, "Like you were protecting me. Like you are proud of me."

Anne came to her and gave her a hug. She whispered in her ear, "This is your home. You are my daughter. And I always will protect you. And I always will be proud of you."

As the days and weeks moved along, Jenny thought less and less about moving. She started talking about wanting to go to school to become a medical technician. She wondered if she could stay living with Anne if she decided to do that. She was scared when she asked, though she thought that Anne would probably say yes. She wondered that night why she had been so scared. She knew. First, she was scared that she might be losing her independence. Second, she was scared of losing Anne.

AN EXAMPLE OF INTEGRATING MODELS: DDP AND THERAPLAY

So far in this chapter, we have been exploring how DDP can be flexibly adapted according to the particular difficulties that children and families are experiencing. Adaptations can be further increased by combining DDP interventions with interventions drawn from other models. As long as the two approaches have complementary aims and objectives, this can be highly effective. In this section, Viv Norris, clinical psychologist, music therapist and certified Theraplay and DDP trainer, illustrates this with the example of how DDP can be combined with Theraplay (Booth & Jernberg, 2009).

> *Theraplay has a lot in common with DDP and can be integrated easily. They share fundamentally the same theoretical base, and both centrally include the main attachment figure within the work with a common aim to deepen the relationship between parent and child. There are some key differences: Theraplay is primarily nonverbal and focused on the here and now rather than on the cocreation of narrative or overtly linking present with past, and it is more structured and practitioner led in its overall approach. In thinking about the attitude of PACE, Theraplay would include all four elements, but the curiosity element is much more focused on understanding the nonverbal responses of the child and parent rather than being a curiosity about the sense a child may make of his experience or about making overt links between present and past. This means that the more verbal curiosity of the DDP element will be relied on to explore the shame and fear that links with the traumatic events of the child's past.*
>
> *Theraplay draws on a sequence of relationship-based play activities, led by the practitioner, as a means of connecting the child and parent and supporting them across four broad*

dimensions: structure, engagement, nurture, and challenge. There are various reasons as to why including Theraplay within an intervention or prior to a DDP intervention might be considered useful. These include, among others, children who need regulation support prior to being able to process their experiences; children who use talking and cognitive strategies as a way of avoiding intersubjective connection; parents and children who are really struggling to enjoy each other or play together; and children and parents with cognitive or communication difficulties and in situations where the child is very reluctant to talk about his experiences. The way in which Theraplay is combined with DDP is variable.

In some situations, it may be preferable to begin with a sequence of pure Theraplay sessions; for instance, to help the parents to support their child in his gaining a bit more control over his body (this work may include input from an occupational therapist). Once the child is steadier physiologically, it becomes more possible to transition toward more affective–reflective dialogue, and the work moves toward DDP. In another situation, Theraplay might be used to form a clear structure to begin and end a session with, including more DDP in the middle, often around the snack part of the session. A further variation is to begin with Theraplay, and, as trauma themes emerge, which they frequently do when playing, then the practitioner uses this opportunity to move into some DDP spontaneously. The most important consideration is obviously what is going to be of most benefit for the child and family. The potential effectiveness of combining these approaches is highly dependent on the practitioner's skill and experience and requires a deep knowledge of both the Theraplay and DDP models. Both DDP and Theraplay can be utilized as separate, stand-alone therapies. The powerful impact of integrating them relies on the practitioner being well versed in the potential of each intervention so that decisions about how to use them together are well made.

Two general considerations often indicate that Theraplay most usefully precedes DDP. First, from a neurologic point of view, Theraplay is focused on early stages of functioning: on primary intersubjectivity, how to create nonverbal here-and-now connection between two people, development of short sequences

*of patterned interaction, and development of the vitality match-
ing at a nonverbal level that children may have missed. It is also
highly focused on observation of nonverbal behaviors and trying
to understand and interpret children's cues and incongruent
behaviors (for instance, smiling while bracing the body), and a
significant element is aimed at physiologic regulation: supporting children to go up and down in excitement levels, to stop and
start activity, to share moments of delight and calmness, and
to give them organized and safe experiences of being led. This
combination of experiences comes developmentally very early,
forming the building blocks of relational development that under-
pins development of verbal expression, reflection, and narrative
exploration. Although the DDP approach encompasses many of
the above features (for instance, in its use of a melodic tone of
voice, affect matching, and constant monitoring of experience
of safety), the Theraplay approach is more physical and direct
and can particularly help children with significant regulation
difficulties prior to moving into DDP work. Second, a practical
consideration in terms of combining the approaches is that it is
generally easier for children to move from a more structured to a
less structured approach than the other way around.*

*There are some contraindications in combining the approaches,
most obviously that if not done well, the work can lose a sense of
coherence, which leads to lower levels of safety for the child. There
are also situations where responding in a playful way can be
very unhelpful, for instance if a child is highly distressed, and in
this situation, use of acceptance, empathy, and moving into some
exploration of the child's experiences will be much more manageable and meaningful for the child. Similarly, parents may
struggle to be playful. This might, for example, be linked to the
experience of blocked care. They may also experience doubts that
difficulties will be overcome with the positive focus of Theraplay.
In these situations, the therapist is likely to spend time with the
parents, using a DDP approach to explore these issues. This can
be before introducing Theraplay to the child or alongside this
work. In both the Theraplay and DDP approaches, the decision
about which elements to explore and how to combine them will
depend on the practitioner's ongoing monitoring of the child's
and parents' states.*

The combination of these approaches is illustrated through the following case example of Arif. This example is based on a real intervention, with permission of the family

Arif has experienced a great deal of trauma in his early years. He is now a physically large, overactive 9-year-old who finds it extremely hard to settle and focus, his attention shifts from one activity to another, and he is impulsive, destructive, and often violent, usually to his adoptive mother. He often introduces topics of conversation that might appear helpful to explore further, such as being bullied or unable to sleep, but any attempts to engage in dialogue are quickly rebuffed, and he moves on. His adoptive mother has become scared to move toward him in case she is hit. Having initially attempted to engage in conversation with Arif, we assess that Arif's interaction currently is very fragmented and that his most obvious struggle is maintaining any kind of genuine intersubjective connection beyond a few moments (whether verbal or nonverbal). As soon as any connection is made, he shifts away, and it becomes apparent that for now, his conversational topics serve to divert away from connection rather than to develop any meaning.

Arif is an enthusiastic, playful, and physical boy, and we decide to begin with pure Theraplay, concentrating on patterned, rhythmic games, building up experiences of delight and mutual pleasure for him and his mom. We anticipate correctly that quieter nurture and touch will be much more difficult, but over a few sessions of active and high-spirited Theraplay, Arif begins to enjoy closer contact with his mom. We become better at anticipating what kinds of activity and relational intensity Arif can manage. As the intimacy demand or excitement increases in any activity, Arif can become quite dysregulated, which can shift into aggression, so we practice going up and down in excitement and find ways to increase intimacy in ways he can manage.

In these early Theraplay-based sessions, we have learned that allowing Arif to watch activities demonstrated with mom first makes a very significant difference to what he can then engage in. He feels safer, relaxes, his natural enthusiasm for young play emerges, and he is increasingly going to mom for soothing and touch. In this quite structured, predictable, and physical play context, he can sustain more extended periods of connected interaction and intensity, and he is becoming less chaotic. This new learning has also generalized to the home setting; for instance, in the way mom wakes him up. He frequently used to hit mom when she woke him (his instant response on waking was to punch). Mom now understands his trauma and nonverbal responses in more detail and walks up and down outside his room calling him until he has roused slightly before touching him, ensuring that he can see her hand as she moves toward him. These quite specific adjustments have reduced the level of violence and anxiety in the household. Now that we are feeling more confident that we have means to both engage and help Arif remain regulated with more intense intersubjective experience, we begin to move toward more DDP.

The sessions still retain the basic Theraplay structure, with a playful entrance, a check in activity, and a few familiar relational games focused principally on regulation before moving toward conversations. We then move into DDP and end the session with some more Theraplay if it feels appropriate. This has become the new structure of sessions, and the Theraplay serves to frame the DDP. Examples of the types of Theraplay activity Arif finds helpful would include physical activity that allows deep pressure to the joints and effort, such as coming in as a wheelbarrow, tug of war (with the adult becoming a deadweight), and slippy slip (where the adult holds the child's arms near the elbows and gradually slips off). He also enjoys high-excitement games that connect him with his mom, such as mom and Arif having a balloon between their tummies, arms around each other and moving around the room while the practitioner chases them trying to push the balloon out from between them. The start and stop of this kind of activity engages and regulates him. He now knows that we know how to help him, and this allows him to remain calm enough to engage in difficult exploration of issues in the DDP.

In one session, we have been playing a pulling row the boat game, and he moves to sit on mom but hurts her in the process, sitting heavily on her chest. This level of physicality, typical of a much younger child, leads to frequent hurting of mom. We use this incident to move into the DDP. "My goodness mom, that looked as if it hurt, are you okay?" Mom says she's fine, but Arif is looking anxious. "Oh Arif, it's so hard when you want to be with mom and something goes wrong" (Arif curls up near mom looking very young), and I decide to "talk about" how Arif might be feeling, as at this point we know he will be unable to speak. Over the next few minutes, mom and I cocreate a narrative based on the mainly nonverbal responses from Arif and our shared knowledge of his history, done in a sing-song melodic voice.

> THERAPIST: You know, mom, I think Arif is upset that he hurt you and all he really wanted to do was to cuddle you [mom agrees], it's hard to get a cuddle when you're as tall as Arif [Arif starts making baby noises], and I wonder whether Arif wishes that he could just be small again and get those cuddles that he missed out on, and if he was small again he

wouldn't have hurt you, mom, and that would feel better [Arif gently clambers onto mom's lap and snuggles up doing a silly "ga-ga noise," and mom smiles and cuddles him].

This playacting of a baby seems to be Arif's way of communicating that we are on track, but he quickly finds the intimacy too hard and climbs over the back of the sofa. I then speak:

> THERAPIST: Oh this is really hard, mom. Arif wishes so much he had a mommy who could love him, and when he tries to have a cuddle it somehow goes wrong, and now he's on his own again behind the sofa, and I wonder if he's feeling lonely over there.

Mom and I both know that trying to fetch or join Arif would lead to him becoming agitated, so in order to remain connected and help him feel that we are joining him, we pass him some blankets and cushions so he can make a comfy den or nest, and as we do so we talk about his early life, mom expressing genuine sadness about the things he missed out on. Arif is quiet and appears to be listening. Mom is talking and I am stroking Arif's back. I weave in the current theme of how upset he is when things go wrong and he hurts mom.

> THERAPIST: And Arif knows what it's like to be hurt, doesn't he mom, and then when he hurts you, like he did before, I think it makes him feel scared.
> MOM: [Responding immediately] And sometimes I think he thinks I'm not going to love him anymore when he hurts me.
> THERAPIST: [With animation] He does? He worries that maybe you'll stop loving him? Oh, mom, that is a very scary thought.

We proceed to explore this fear. Arif is clearly listening very intently but remains silent.

> MOM: It makes me feel so sad to think of Arif crying and no one came."
> THERAPIST: And he was so very little, mom, wasn't he, just a small boy and no one came, that is so sad, and I know Arif tried to be brave and look after himself, mom, but he was so small and he needed his mommy to come and help him.

Arif moves and pops his head up from his den looking directly at his mom. As we continue creating the story, Arif begins to touch his mom's face, gazing at her and exploring the contours of her face. The atmosphere is intense, very calm and loving, and Arif spends an extended period of time gently touching mom's face as we continue talking about sadness for the past loss and mom's narrative about what she would have given to him had she been there. The story moves toward a natural pause after an extended period of closeness, and we move back toward some familiar nurturing Theraplay activities, singing and sharing a snack. At the end of the session, I summarize the big things we talked about.

As the sessions progressed with Arif, they became increasingly DDP focused, and the Theraplay provided a holding framework. Thinking about combining Theraplay and DDP in this particular context, it appears that the Theraplay helped provide the groundwork for the DDP work and that having both approaches created confidence for us all that we could move forward into some very difficult trauma themes in a manageable way. For Arif in particular, practicing shifts in state through play helped him develop greater capacity to manage emotional shifts in state when exploring trauma themes later. Once Arif had some experience that moving toward these themes was possible, he began spontaneously communicating with his mom about fears and relevant issues occurring in his day-to-day life.

CONCLUSION

Within this chapter, we have continued our exploration of the flexibility of DDP. We have considered adaptations and variations for children depending on their age, developmental challenges, past experiences, and current ways in which they are displaying their distress and difficulties, as well as combining DDP with another treatment modality. Length of the chapter means the authors had to be selective with respect to what issues and interventions were considered but hope the examples chosen illustrate some of the ways that DDP can be adapted and that this will encourage future innovation.

CHAPTER 10

Interventions in Specific Situations

Children who have experienced developmental trauma can experience a variety of living situations. Developmental trauma often leads to planned moves into foster care, adoption, or residential care, all of which involve a variable number of moves, each of which is disruptive of relationships. At times, children and young people who have experienced developmental trauma remain in their at-risk families, requiring a number of services in an effort to increase the safety for the children. When children and young people do not reside with a caregiver who is able to provide safety for the child during the therapy session, then individual therapy with dyadic developmental psychotherapy (DDP) may be indicated. The attachment focus of DDP is also of value for children and young people without developmental trauma but living in families with relational difficulties. Finally, DDP is a model for supervision through playfulness, acceptance, curiosity, and empathy (PACE) and provision of safety within the intersubjective manner of relating between the supervisor and supervisee. In all of these quite differing situations, the principles and interventions of DDP provide the opportunity to develop a coherent narrative and safe relationships.

FOSTER CARE

Children and young people come into care for a range of reasons; central to these are disrupted relationships. These children will have experienced separation and loss of birth family and various degrees of contact during their time in care. There is further separation and loss when the children move back to their birth family or on to a permanent family via adoption, special guardianship, or kinship care. Sadly, the challenges the children present, often compounded by too little support for the families, means further disruption as children experience breakdowns and unplanned moves.

These broken relationships extend beyond parents, family members, and pets. Placement moves often mean a change of school and leisure activities, leading to loss of significant adults and peers in the children's lives. Changes of social workers are also common. These children need interventions that take this context into account. Models that have a relational focus and a particular sensitivity to the blocked trust and fragmented sense of self that can develop from disrupted relationships will guide these interventions. DDP is both a practice and a therapy relational model that can take the unique context of children growing up in foster care into account. The focus on parental and network support alongside therapy for the child is a combination that is essential to help children rebuild trust and gain emotional well-being.

Foster care is an alternative for children who cannot live with their birth family and is used either as a long-term option or in the short term while assessments are carried out and a permanent care solution is sought. This may be a return to the birth family because sufficient changes have been made or a move to an adoptive, kinship, or special guardian family. Countries differ in their use of foster care (short and long term) and alternative family permanence, and various degrees of stability are achieved.

Foster carers are selected as biologically unrelated parents for the children. Increasingly, however, extended biological family members are assessed for this role as kinship carers. Foster care can be court ordered or established on a voluntary basis with the consent of the birth family. Parental responsibility for the children varies in these differing options.

The majority of children who live in foster care have experienced pre-care social adversity, including traumatic abuse and emotional deprivation (Tarren-Sweeney & Vetere, 2014). These authors estimate that a million children in the Western world are in care or adopted from care at any given time.

Foster care is also used for children who have been adopted but can no longer live with their adoptive family. Within the United Kingdom, between 2% and 9% of adoptions from care disrupt after the children have been legally adopted, with an overall rate of 3.2%. Teenagers are

10 times more likely to disrupt than children under 4 years (Selwyn, Wijedasa, & Meakings, 2014). This report also highlighted the high levels of violence of teens toward parents, which is a contributory factor to such disruptions. Foster care is viewed as a safer option that can allow the children to remain connected to their adopted family while reducing the level of violence being displayed. Planned use of foster care can also prevent an escalation to the point of family breakdown with no or a very difficult road back.

Emotional and mental health needs are high in this population of children and young people: about 45% have diagnosable mental health problems. This is a group of children and young people with a high level of need for therapeutic care (Rahilly & Hendry, 2014). These difficulties continue to be evident as the young people enter adulthood: Studies demonstrate that nearly half of care-leavers in the United Kingdom have mental and physical health difficulties, and these problems become worse over time. European studies have also cataloged continuing difficulties into middle and late adulthood (Wade, 2014).

State involvement in the care of children living in foster care is high. This has led to the notion of corporate parenting in the United Kingdom, with the professional network around the child being responsible for parenting in partnership with the selected parent figure, whether this is a non-related foster carer or a kinship carer. Corporate parenting is generally led by the social worker.

Dyadic developmental psychotherapy will only be effective if the context of the care system is taken into account. The DDP practitioner will build relationships with the professional network and the child and family. Complexity increases for the practitioner when the child is receiving parenting from more than one set of parents. For example, the study of Selwyn and colleagues (2014) reported that after disruption, many of the adoptive parents continued to parent and support their children in foster care, albeit from a distance. Foster care is seen as a way of helping the children to remain connected to their adoptive family when irretrievable breakdown would otherwise be likely.

The dyadic developmental practice model pays attention to all the layers around the child and family and to facilitating good working relationships within the professional network.

Damian moved into long-term foster care with his younger sister when he was 6 years old, having moved into care when he was 3 years old. An initial short-term placement was extended when an adoptive family could not be found. This was largely because of Damian's very challenging behaviors and his sister's level of learning difficulty. The children had experienced high levels of neglect and physical abuse in their birth family.

A DDP practitioner supported the long-term foster placement in the following ways:

- Regular network support, which consisted of network meetings every 2 to 3 months with carers, social workers, and school staff. The DDP practitioner allowed everyone's concerns to be spoken, facilitating shared understanding and collaborative problem-solving. For example, when Damian was experiencing a difficult school experience that was quite shaming, non-judgmental exploration allowed school staff to conclude that they were not a suitable educational provision, given the child's level of emotional need. The network joined with school staff to explore different options for him.
- The mental health child psychiatrist joined this network when Damian was 9 years old and was included by the DDP practitioner in the network meetings. This allowed the child psychiatrist to make a decision about diagnosis and treatment, including medication, on the basis of a full understanding of Damian from within the network and his assessment with Damian.
- Support for the social worker and his manager to explore their differing beliefs about what the child needed; for example, exploring a disagreement about levels of birth family contact. This allowed them to come to joint decisions about these issues.
- Parenting support, which helped the foster carers to develop a DDP-informed therapeutic parenting style, including exploration of their attachment history to understand when this style was hard to maintain.
- Dyadic developmental psychotherapy for Damian supported by his foster mother. This allowed Damian to express his fears and beliefs about not being good enough and being "kicked out" of the placement, to receive empathy for this, and to engage in some life story exploration that made sense of these fears and beliefs.

Damian remained a challenging child to care for with ups and downs in placement as the foster carers went through periods of blocked care. However, apart from one period of residential care because of concerns for the safety of Damian and family members, he was able to remain with them until he left care when he was 19 years old. The future remains uncertain for Damian, who continues to require high levels of support, not always available to him. There is concern that he could drift into antisocial behavior. However, the foster carers continue to have a role in his life, and while he does not always contact them, he does have a secure base that he can return to.

As this example illustrates, DDP interventions include work with the foster family and network support. As is good practice with any DDP intervention, this needs to begin with support for and preparation with the foster carers. As explored in Chapter 7, carers need to be helped to become DDP-informed therapeutic parents, able to hold and return to the attitude of PACE. This requires being mindful of the child's internal world alongside his external behavior and maintaining their own emotional regulation so that they can remain available to the child. Foster carers need to be able to use support to help them with these when needed. In addition, they will need to be prepared to work with the therapist if and when the child is brought into therapy.

The DDP practitioner can support the foster carer to be an active member of the network around the child. Foster carers can feel disempowered within a largely professional network, and the value of their contributions can be overlooked. Foster carers have a wealth of understanding about their foster children through their experience of parenting them. It is important that their perceptions, experiences, and unique knowledge about a child are valued. The DDP practitioner is well placed to ensure that this happens. Foster carers are also in the front line of experiencing the challenges that the children can present. This can lead to actions that are not ideal. They need support to reflect on this and to work with the network to find a way forward that is helpful for everyone at these difficult times.

For example, a social worker has newly been assigned to 17-year-old Natali and is concerned to learn about some mistakes the foster carer has recently made with this young girl. In particular, she is very worried that the foster carer locked Natali out of the home when Natali returned to placement very late and drunk. Clearly this compromised Natali's safety, and she is considering moving Natali to a different placement. The DDP practitioner helps the social worker to reflect on the attachment that Natali has with the carer and the consequence to this of a move; this is balanced with the seriousness of the incident. She then facilitates a meeting with the foster carer and the social worker. The DDP practitioner creates an open and engaged atmosphere allowing all of them to reflect on what happened. The foster carer acknowledges the mistakes she made while also talking about the good progress made with Natali. She reflects on what Natali needs going forward. The foster carer considers how she can repair her relationship with Natali. She also recognizes her need for help from the DDP practitioner to think about how Natali is triggering in her a defensive response at times, as illustrated by this incident. The social worker recognizes her own fears about letting down the child and how this perhaps led her to hasty conclusions about what should happen. They all agree on a plan for a way forward with Natali remaining in placement and further meetings to continue to reflect together.

The DDP practitioner needs to keep in mind a range of things when supporting placements. Generally, this means being in touch with the complexity of foster care:

Foster carers are performing an important parenting role for the children in their care. They are also part of the professional network around the child, attending the children's reviews, keeping records for the social workers, and sometimes supporting the child to have contact with birth families. Foster carers will also be supervisees needing emotional support as well as the more practical aspects of supervision. This in itself can be complex, as the foster carer will also be evaluated within this supervision. It can be hard to speak freely about challenges being experienced when you also know that your performance as a foster carer is being monitored.

It can be a confusing relationship between the practitioner providing DDP support and preparation and the foster carer. Both must hold the multiple roles of the foster carer in mind. It can be bewildering to know whether the foster carer is client or colleague at times as he or she juggles these roles. For example, the shifts from contributing to a review meeting, to informing the network, to a DDP session exploring feelings of anger toward the child when reminded of a tricky relationship with a birth father can be difficult to make. Talking about these difficulties will be necessary.

An important part of the parent preparation is the exploration of the foster carer's attachment history. This may be something that the foster carer had not anticipated as part of his or her fostering role. Practitioners can feel intrusive and be concerned that they have not gotten permission for this exploration. It will be important that this is talked through with the foster carer before beginning the preparation and to ensure that any worries or concerns are heard and understood by the practitioner.

Many foster carers are motivated to become foster carers following their own difficult relationship experience. This past can give them resilience, but it is important to be aware that unresolved traumas and losses can be present. Sufficient time is needed to fully explore these before commencing with therapy for the child.

Fostering is a parenting task that is under constant scrutiny. The foster carer has guidelines that must be followed, which can mean parenting in a way that is not typical when parenting birth children. How to be with a foster child in the bedroom or bathroom, for example, should be thought about and agreed to with the social worker. Foster carers will also have annual reviews, and their foster carer status has to be renewed. This can cause anxiety and will potentially make the foster carer more reserved about sharing thoughts and feelings he or she has about the foster child. An important part of DDP support to foster carers is reflecting upon the impact the child is having. The DDP practitioner needs to be sensitive to the discomfort that this may bring. Again, it is important to talk about this and acknowledge the difficulties that may be brought by being a foster carer caring for someone else's child on behalf of the state.

The foster carer and DDP practitioner will also make decisions about what needs to be shared with the rest of the network. Ensuring the whole network is working together in the interests of the child is an important part of the support being offered. This means ensuring that the network understands the support and interventions being offered to the child and foster carers but balanced with respect for the foster carers' privacy.

Foster children will benefit from DDP-informed therapeutic parenting. This will help them to develop security and to lessen the blocked trust they are experiencing. Some of the children will also benefit from therapy alongside therapeutic parenting.

Decisions to proceed to therapy can be complicated by concerns that the child's placement is not stable. While it is often suggested that children should be safe before therapy can start, this assumption is questioned by the DDP model. It is important that children who are in a home environment that is abusive are helped to reach a position of safety before therapy can commence, but this is not the same as children who are in nonabusive although not permanent homes. The dyadic developmental practice model can help to create a safe context for the child within which DDP as a therapy can be provided. This therapy can, for example, help the children to handle conflicts with their foster carers, accept comfort from them, engage in repair when things go wrong, and experience support to identify and communicate their experiences. All of these will increase the likelihood that the children will achieve stability in placement. This exploration will be of value when a permanent family home is found for them. Whether therapy actively addresses past abuse needs to be considered carefully. Sometimes it is helpful to wait for increased stability before addressing this, but there is no hard and fast answer. It can be of value in helping the child to feel safe, and this can lead to a lower risk of disruption especially if the past trauma is affecting current behaviors. Careful planning and ongoing reflection is needed to ensure that therapy is helpful, but much can be achieved when the context is carefully planned. For example, the therapist might involve a social worker who has a long-standing relationship with the child or a good respite carer who is able to remain constant through changes of placement.

There is also much that the DDP therapist can do to support the professional network and the foster carers. This can make it more likely that stability is reached for the child. It is possible to offer children focused pieces of therapeutic work to help them experience more stability; for example, life story exploration, support to manage a school transition, and support to manage contact with birth families. This therapeutic support can be informed by the DDP principles, helping the child to feel understood and providing sensitive support with this specific focus.

Dyadic developmental psychotherapy can also be a helpful model to support children with planned placement transitions; for example, a move from a short-term placement back to birth family or on to adoption. The DDP principles can help to slow down these transitions in a way that allows the children's concerns and anxieties to be fully understood, helping them to trust the adults who are transitioning them. A DDP approach reminds the adults to acknowledge the anxieties and upsets that these transitions can bring, not reassuring the child in the hope that these uncomfortable feelings will go away. The child feels understood and supported with this emotional experience. Short-term foster carers can have complex feelings about moving a child on. This can include hope and excitement for the child alongside concern that the decisions being made are the right ones. Foster carers' own feelings of loss and grief can be forgotten with this focus on the child. The DDP practitioner is well placed to hold all this emotional experience in mind, providing understanding and support to the foster carers.

Some short-term foster carers may transition to long-term carers; similarly, long-term carers might apply and be granted special guardianship for their foster children. These represent complex decisions on behalf of the foster carers that affect them, the child in care, as well as the foster carers' birth children and other family members. Having a DDP practitioner who can help them to reflect on these decisions can lead to good decisions that everyone will benefit from.

Finally, in this brief exploration of how DDP can support foster carers, it is important to acknowledge the extra complexity that can be present when family members become foster carers, kinship carers, or special guardians. Decisions to care for a relative's child can rise out of complex motivations, including feelings of guilt or shame that members of their extended family are suffering and are not able to care for their children very well. In becoming a kinship parent to these children, the parent is giving up another role in the child's life. Sacrificing the role of grandparent, aunt, or uncle in order to parent a child can lead to complex feelings of grief and loss. This is further complicated by the knowledge that a close family member is responsible for the abusive experience the child has been exposed to. Grandparents can be troubled knowing they brought up the parent involved. This has the potential to lead to highly sensitive, shame-based family dynamics, which the DDP practitioner needs to remain mindful of. All this complex emotional experience needs to be fully acknowledged and explored. The PACE attitude can enable working relationships to develop that are mindful of these vulnerabilities.

The DDP practitioner is uniquely placed to support foster carers in the range of roles that fostering can include. Slowing down processes, fully exploring emotional experience, and allowing the unsaid to become said can be an important part of ensuring a successful fostering experience. As much of the network is task focused, it is helpful if a member of that network, informed by the DDP principles, can hold onto reflection about the emotional experience of all those involved. This provides a helpful balance in a complex world where internal experience is often overlooked in the desire to move quickly toward a successful outcome. Sometimes slower is better, and time for reflection can ensure a resilient network working together allowing emotional health to grow and flourish for the children and their fostering families.

ADOPTION

Adoptive parents are unlikely to know many children with developmental traumas before a child who has experienced neglect or abuse joins their family. Adoption preparation courses provide excellent training in highlighting how things might be, as do the assessment processes of prospective adopters. It is, however, hard to grasp how things will be until a child lives with you. There is little time to understand a child well enough to respond effectively to confusing and challenging behavior. A child's behavior may well be misunderstood with a resulting escalation in anxiety-driven behaviors.

If your much-wanted son, in addition to being delightful, funny, and kind, never wants you to cuddle him, never asks for help, and never even seems to need it, family life can become different from the one anticipated. If he also constantly defies you, seems to enjoy power struggles, and tries to control you all the time, you may well become demoralized, blame yourself for being a hopeless, incompetent parent, or blame social services for never telling you just how difficult your son is to care for.

Taking the child's perspective, he moves from his much-loved foster family to your family, one his social worker told him she has carefully chosen, where he will get to know a new mommy and daddy, and that he will live with you until he is grown up. She also told him to say good-bye to his birth mom and nan, who up until this time he has been seeing regularly. He can't work out why he can't just stay with his foster family. He likes it there. He soon discovers things he wasn't told about his new family. His new mommy and daddy expect him to eat carrots, they shout at him, take away his game player, and his new mommy cries a lot. He wonders if he will ever see his mom and nan again. He misses his foster mom and foster dad, especially at bedtimes.

Steele and colleagues highlight the likelihood that children's often disorganized attachment behavior will be elicited at high intensity during the early days of a new placement, when "almost any experience would either be sensed or expected as a threat, without necessarily being based in the reality of the new situation" (2003, p. 202).

Dyadic developmental practice provides a comprehensive model for the provision of adoption support, one that enables children to recover from developmental traumas and supports adoptive parents to minimize the possibility they will develop blocked care (Hughes & Baylin, 2012). DDP-informed adoption support models can also reduce the risk that adopted children will have a future move from their adoptive family, a process referred to as adoption disruption. Hudson (2006) describes an adoption support model with no adoption disruptions for families receiving the full model over an 8-year period (see Chapter 11). This is a significant positive outcome when compared to studies such as that of Rushton (2004), which found adoption disruption rates of about 25%. This study also found increased mental health risks were indicated in the adoption of older children and children who have experienced multiple placements.

Following are the key principles of the adoption support model referred to above:

- Normalization: a context of adoption support where "having some difficulties" is anticipated and seen as normal.
- Intervention from a trauma-informed and attachment-focused perspective as early as possible; from the time of matching onward. This enables good transitional planning involving foster carers and the child's social work team in the move.
- Detailed analysis of psychologically relevant historical and current information around the time of matching focusing on the child and the adoptive parents.
- Regular multiagency network consultation on key themes from matching onward.
- Regular parental consultation, with an adoption support worker present, if agreed to as helpful.
- Interventions that enable adoptive parents to put into practice DDP-informed parenting (Golding, 2014a, 2017).
- Inclusion of adoptive parents in relevant multiagency training.
- Adoption-specific training or group work, starting with prospective adopter courses.
- Dyadic developmental psychotherapy available when assessed as required, including intermittently at key developmental stages or transitions, such as moving to secondary school.
- Routine proactive, long-term follow-up through face-to-face

parental consultations every 6 months by a known professional until the adopted child is an adult, rather than taking a "wait and see" approach to future difficulties.

What follows are examples of how network and parental consultations put these principles into practice in the time frame of a child joining a family.

The Matching Process

The principles that guide the matching process are not always easy to define. Key aims include assessment of the level of a child's developmental, emotional, and educational needs, linking these to potential needs in relation to the adoptive parents' circumstances (such as their styles of coping, stress management, and attachment). The DDP practitioner meets these aims as described below.

Detailed Analysis of Psychologically Relevant Historical and Current Information

Such analysis provides evidence for making a case of psychological need from the perspectives of both the children and the adopting adults. If potential difficulties are hypothesized before matching, the matching process is not primarily to select prospective adopters in or out. It is to recognize need, plan for short- and long-term resources required, agree how they will be financed, and suggest who will provide the interventions should the placement go ahead.

Assessment of the Needs of the Child (Individual and Relationship Based)

One example of how assessment at this point can be relevant from a child-focused perspective is assessment of the impact of sibling dynamics on both placement and matching considerations. This can include assessment of the following:

- The extent and impact of conflict, physical aggression, sexualized behavior, and inappropriate caregiving responsibilities among all sibling relationship combinations.
- The potential risks and benefits of separating siblings or keeping them together.

- The impact of adopting two or more children with differing attachment styles. This includes the potential early exhaustion of the main carer when adopting two children, one with an ambivalent attachment style, and one with an avoidant attachment style.

Consolidation of Recent Experiences and Consideration of Past History of the Adoptive Parents

It can be helpful to talk with the parents about their understanding of the adoption preparation training they attended, thinking specifically about the child they are matched with. Discussions focus on understanding the impact of neglect, trauma, and loss on their child. Many prospective adoptive parents have experienced multiple losses themselves, such as babies lost through miscarriage or many attempts at in vitro fertilization. These times will have been explored in depth during their adoption assessment. It can be helpful at this point to sensitively wonder about how having this child live with them may trigger previous losses. Who will they feel comfortable in turning to should these feelings arise to the extent that their grief affects their developing attachment to their adoptive child?

It is helpful to talk with parents about how to manage stress as individuals and, if in a couple, how their relationship works under stress. This is also the time to introduce the principles for DDP-informed parenting.

A further key factor to consider is the impact of any childhood or adulthood loss or abusive experiences, particularly if these have not been acknowledged in the past. If these include, for example, physical violence or emotional intimidation as an adult or childhood physical or sexual abuse or neglect, it can be important to sensitively wonder whether past trauma-induced feelings, beliefs, and adaptive strategies may be evoked through parenting their child. This might be the case if the child they are matched with demonstrates aggression or violent behavior, regardless of the age of the child.

Integrating Child and Adult Factors as Children Move In

A great deal is required from adoptive parents in contributing to the recovery of a child who has experienced developmental traumas. Feedback from adopters indicates that the early process of hypothesizing potentially emotionally challenging events, combined with rehearsal of responses as a parental dyad, is extremely helpful (Hudson, 2006). If hypothetical situations then occur in reality, these early discussions give a meaning to the evoked adult response. It gives a context in which to understand and explore emotions and a rehearsed response. This decreases the chance that the parent, when faced with the reality of challenging behavior, feels overwhelming shame, helplessness or failure as a parent and takes things personally. This reduces a tendency to keep silent about theperception of what is happening; feeling reluctant to seek help.

If help is not sought or provided, the consequence of such perceptions, should they become entrenched, can create an atmosphere within the home of adult shame, noncommunication about feelings and helplessness, and defensiveness when others raise concerns. These factors can immobilize a new adoptive parent's capacity to develop the type of family atmosphere and parenting attitude required to care effectively for children living with the impact of past developmental traumas.

Getting to Know Each Other in the First Few Months after Moving In

A wide range of factors contribute to the desire for adoptive parents to show they have been able to form a family that is perceived as "normal" to extended family and neighborhood networks, particularly if close relatives and friends are not supportive of the choice to adopt. Key aims of parental consultation at this point are to provide psychological input into the first impressions, explore differences between hopes and dreams and reality, and introduce DDP-informed parenting as described in Chapter 7.

Consideration is given to how the child is responding and seems to make sense of her situation through a detailed analysis of behavioral and emotional responses to the events of the transitional period. This includes the way the child is appearing to feel comfortable with the adults, whether the child is showing signs of grief regarding past or recent losses, and the extent to which the child has returned to previous adaptive strategies. The DDP practitioner may anticipate certain interactions on the basis of knowledge of the child and the parents, preparing parents for the hardest of responses. An example is asking parents:

THERAPIST: I wonder what it would be like for you if your daughter said she hated you and wanted to go back to her foster mother? How hard this would be for you and for her? This may be something you never thought could happen when you first imagined being a parent. Can we make sense of these feelings from her, also how you might hold yourself together at the time? Perhaps we could practice the kind of response you might say to her. This will be so hard as you will probably be falling apart inside.

Considerations for how the adoptive parents are managing include the extent of "click" felt by the adults at the first and subsequent meetings, and the impact of exhaustion combined with anxiety and excitement and how the parents are managing these combined stresses. An adult's previous ability to use reflective thinking may be significantly reduced when under such stress. It is helpful at this point to recall how the parents were before the child moved in.

Getting to Know Each Other 6 Months to 2 Years after Moving In

Adoptive parents can become perplexed and confused when, 6 months to 2 years or so into their newly formed family, their child's initial confusing and challenging behavior has not decreased or they witness a return of concerning behaviors after thinking things had finally settled.

For example, consider an ambivalently attached child's way of surviving anxieties about his adoptive mother not keeping him in mind. Behaviors indicate an inner world characterized by feelings and thoughts such as, "You must never leave me alone. You must always be there for me. If you leave me alone for a minute, I will become scared that you will never come back or that someone might hurt me or that you will forget about me, and I will never forgive you for making me feel like that again." The child communicates this by never leaving his mother's side, which is initially seen by his parents as loving and enjoyable. After 6 months, the same behavior becomes a source of extreme irritation and total exhaustion that few friends and extended family members understand.

Hodges and colleagues (2003) compared themes from story stem assessments of children adopted in the first year of life with those from older, previously maltreated children placed for adoption. Changes were tracked in their attachment representations over the first year of placement in their new families. This study suggests that ongoing work is likely to be required with the families of some later-adopted children. At the 1-year assessment, although positive attachment representations increased, such as of adults helping and setting limits, negative attachment representations did not decrease, such as seeing adults as aggressive or rejecting.

It is essential that regular network and parental consultations continue around this crucial time rather than reducing or stopping such consultations if all seems well after 3 months. Involvement with the child's school can be an essential part of network consultations. It is a time when both children and prospective adoptive parents can be exhausted, sleep deprived, and confused. Parental consultations emphasize the length of time it can take children to begin to trust and the persistent nature of the core beliefs a child brings with him into an adoptive family.

Development of a Shared Coherent Narrative

As explored throughout this book, DDP is about cocreating stories. The first year together for an adoptive family includes this important process, weaving in past and new narratives. Many children prefer to keep past experiences hidden. The DDP practitioner helps parents to accept the child's lack of response to talking about his past while showing interest and tentative curiosity about all the child's experiences and empathy for just how hard starting again is.

Malachi is reluctant to be part of thinking around helping his daughter integrate her memories and experiences of her past into their future as an adoptive family. He tells Fran, the DDP practitioner, in a parental consultation that it is best to leave things alone. As Fran responds with PACE and is interested in hearing his concerns, Malachi explains that if he helps his daughter recall a past that she appears reluctant to remember, he will be responsible for causing her emotional pain. His daughter will blame him and lose any trust he has established that he will keep her safe and never hurt her. She will end up hating and resenting him for upsetting her. He is not prepared to explore the subject further. The risk of directly causing pain to his daughter is simply too great to take.

Exploring the meaning of this with acceptance, Fran hears about Malachi's deeper anxieties relating to his own past experiences of his mother dying in a car accident when he was a child. He was with her at the time. Malachi knows he had put these feelings into a place where he can manage his life well. Through Fran's acceptance, genuine interest in his feelings, and empathy for how hard it must be to look after a little girl who has also lost her mother,

Malachi suddenly recognizes his terror that he will be overwhelmed by his own feelings of grief if he allows himself to fully empathize with his daughter's grief at losing her mother. When they next meet, this time with Thomas, his partner, Malachi tells Fran he now knows where his reluctance had come from. Can she return to the conversation of the past consultation so he can reconsider, this time with Thomas next to him? With both parents present, Fran wonders if they worry that their daughter might show anger about having two dads; that she really wanted a mother. They both agree and said they were anxious about raising this. Fran helps them with words to say, using PACE, if this ever happens. Thomas writes these down, just in case he needs them.

Soon after this, Fran started DDP with Malachi, Thomas, and their daughter.

Chapter 8 includes an example of how this adoptive support model works in practice when therapy is included.

As described in Chapter 8, summaries of network consultations written by the DDP practitioner involve everyone in co-constructing narratives for the child, the parents, and the network using PACE. Following is an extract from one such summary addressed to prospective adoptive parents of two siblings, who moved in 6 months ago, which was copied to those who attended and other key professionals and managers.

Thinking about how best to respond to your children when they tell you important things about their past.

These situations can provide opportunities of going deeper behind the meaning of what your children are telling you. Experiences of abuse and neglect during their early years may have led your children to feel bad about themselves, as well as feel fear, sadness, and anger about their experiences. When they tell you things, it may be helpful for you to explore using PACE the feelings that might have been around for them at the time of the incident itself. It might be helpful to make responses like: "It sounds like you have known some pretty scary people in the past" or "That must have been painful—to be so little and to have a broken arm."

We talked through how the following can increase the opportunities for your children to develop emotional safety with you:

- Sharing their strong feelings associated with past traumatic events.
- Feeling accepted by you for whatever responses they may have had then and now.

- Your warm interest and tentative curiosity about what life may have been like for them and experiencing your empathy and sadness for them.

At some point, it may feel possible to make comments like: "It sounds like it must have been hard to have a mom and dad who loved you but weren't able to look after you in the way that little children need to be looked after or keep you safe or make sure that other people didn't scare you or hurt you."

Getting to know both your children in the present, at the same time as having to integrate information about the pain and hurt they have felt in the past, may make you feel both sad and angry for them. If they continue to tell you things about their past, this can be emotionally draining. It may also make you want to "make it up to them" and feel tempted to relax the structure, routine, and limits you have worked so hard to put in place since they moved to live with you. It is important that both continue in parallel and that the emotional energy that this can require, alongside the practical organization of home life, is acknowledged by us all.

Through to Adulthood: Consultation and Intermittent Therapy when Needed as a Long-Term Intervention

Consultation combined with therapy can occur at any time, including when progress is slow, when parents begin to realize the long-term nature of difficulties, or when fears increase about whether the child will be able to stay living with the family. In this section, the example of working with the increased stress at adolescence will be used.

One long-term aim of this model is a reduction in adoption breakdown. Middle adolescence appears to be a time of particular risk, including violence to parents (Selwyn, 2014). To assist this outcome, the model includes routine parental consultations once every 6 months or at key developmental stages, such as the transition to secondary school.

Adolescence is a time when earlier challenging behavior can recur (such as violence), triggered by fears and rejections experienced as friendships deepen or a girlfriend lets one down. The effectiveness of social media in finding birth family members means real choices may need to be made with respect to telling adoptive parents about this, which risks upsetting the parents or the child choosing to run off in secret to visit birth family members. When the first signs of seeking members of the birth family are seen in a child, such as glimpses of social media pages, it is helpful to proactively address this with the child. Leaving this until the child is older, a common response, may result in behaviors that escalate into family disruption. Adoptive parents will need much support during this process, as this goes deep into the roots of fears around losing a much-loved child to his or her birth family.

To give an example, a late-adopted 14-year-old boy expresses a very strong wish to see his birth parents. Therapy sessions take place to talk through this. He doesn't want to live with them; he just wants to see them. The DDP practitioner contacts the initial social work team; one of the original social workers was still employed, and he gains permission to meet with and assess the birth family. He is allowed to be part of a carefully managed meeting, taking the birth parents. The DDP practitioner takes the adoptive parents and the 14-year-old to this meeting in a town with no emotional connections for anyone. Two further meetings take place a few months apart with the adoptive parents emotionally supporting their son to find new safe connections with his biological family. They in turn are supported by their DDP practitioner, who holds the hope that however this risky process works out, their relationship with their son is strong enough to survive.

This is one example of how, in this model, creative interventions can take place. These serve to keep parent–child connections going through difficult times that, without the model, may have resulted in disruption.

Adolescence can also be a time for a young person to check out if he will also get addicted to drugs like his mother or try to find out what is so wonderful about taking drugs that his mother chose drugs over him. These are just two examples of the challenges of adolescence for an adopted child and his parents. Such challenges are more likely to be effectively explored and managed if parents have easily accessed, nonjudgmental support in place from a service that knows them. They don't have to explain everything, or be told it is just normal adolescence and they are doing a good job, or go through lengthy referral processes for services that may not be able to offer help. The adolescent may even agree to come for therapy if he is familiar with the therapist and knows the way she works.

During adolescence when stresses increase and relationships become tense, such as when violence increases or an adolescent engages in extreme risky behavior that compromises parental safety (e.g., parents threatened by drug dealers the adolescent uses), fears about disruption increase in the network. Sometimes due to reasons of either child or parental safety, the child needs to live elsewhere. Within this model, this is discussed and planned proactively, seeking and engaging with a supportive foster family or residential unit. The aim is to enable safe-enough emotional connections to become established, for bridges to be built between the adoptive parents, the other caregivers, and the adolescent. The narrative includes one where parents and child can't manage to live together for a while, that the adolescent will live here while we work with the parents and child to keep the relationship going within the adoptive family. If this needs to be a long-term living arrangement, the adoptive parents never stop being the main parents; it's just that the parents and adolescent don't live under the same roof.

This model can challenge existing models in which disruption thinking prevails because of anxiety and doubt about the benefits of working in this way, especially as emotions can run high. The model requires good working relationships between the DDP practitioner and the parents as well as the DDP practitioner and the network. High expressed emotion, especially anger and despair, is frequent, and sharing care for the adoptive parents, who are often rudely dismissed by the adolescent, can be difficult. The acceptance of "not knowing" if things will work out eventually is crucial. The model described works well in enabling parents and children to resume a closer relationship when the child reaches young adulthood, as any breaks in the relationship are repaired whenever possible and never become too severe to warrant an irreparable split.

This long-term parental consultation works successfully as a screening method. Alongside the indirect parental consultation model, it provides a flexible, responsive, and nonstigmatizing assessment as to which families require and will benefit from other interventions. This proactive approach enables key themes to be identified and addressed positively as they arise, before potentially unhelpful parent–child interactions become established. It also enables the timely provision of DDP when required involving, if this is possible, a DDP practitioner who knows the family well, just as they know her well.

Dyadic developmental practice provides an adoption support model where safety is provided by normalization of the need for help from the start rather than waiting until problems occur. Good beginnings are seen as a foundation for effective future work. A flexible combination of consultation, training, group work, and therapy is provided with network and parental consultations at least every 2 or 3 months in the first year or until the child is formally adopted. Containment is provided by routine long-term follow-up and ease of access when help is needed by picking up the telephone to call a known person. Routine follow-up includes consultation offered by consistent practitioners at least every 6 months or at key developmental stages, such as when starting secondary school. Adolescence is seen as a key developmental time to revisit earlier themes and consolidate. These factors increase the likelihood that children will become open to trusting their adoptive parents, develop and enjoy intersubjective relationships, and reduce the risk of their parents' developing blocked care.

RESIDENTIAL CARE

When children with developmental trauma demonstrate serious social, emotional, and behavioral problems, they often have great difficulty living within a family or attending a community school. Their parents and teachers struggle to keep them—and others—safe. Impulsive and persistent acts of aggression, destruction, self-harm, substance abuse, and indifference to hurting others make it extremely difficult to provide them with the safety that is necessary if they are to heal and proceed with their development. Often these children are placed in residential care, the aim of which is to provide an adequate level of structure, supervision, and care to ensure that they are physically safe. While residential care may be necessary to better meet their needs for physical safety, it may require extra efforts to ensure that the child's needs for psychological safety are also being met. In our society, the psychological safety of children is thought to be best met most often within a stable, permanent family, where the child is cared for by one or two adults who know the child well, are sensitive and responsive to him, and who are committed to what is in his best interests. The psychological safety is also best met when the child comes to know and trust one or two particular adults and is able to seek guidance, support, and comfort from them. The ongoing challenge of residential care is to ensure the child's physical safety while at the same time providing the child with the relationships needed to ensure his psychological safety as well.

Relationships

Dyadic developmental psychotherapy as a stand-alone psychother-apy will not meet the needs of children in residential care. It needs to be embedded in the daily milieu of the home and school, especially in the relationships. For this reason, dyadic developmental practice as described in Chapter 8 is essential to providing a more flexible com-prehensive approach. The children need to experience relationships within the home and school based on principles of attachment with qualities that provide safety, intersubjectivity, comfort, joy, and rela-tionship repair. These relationships need to be reciprocal: the child and adult each influencing the other. When individual staff members come to know a child, they will be best able to understand the meanings of the child's behaviors and to develop a unique structure with the best routines and expectations for that child.

Children who have experienced developmental trauma need an envi-ronment within which they can learn to trust in relationships so that they can develop some security of attachment. Focusing on behaviors is important, but this needs to be in the context of helping the child develop successful relationships with adults who serve as parent fig-ures. Too often the daily milieu—within both the home and school settings—begins by focusing on managing the child's behaviors so that the child begins to accept and follow the rules. Such behavioral man-agement often involves training the staff to relate with all of the chil-dren in a similar manner. The same set of behavioral expectations and incentives is applied consistently so that it is predictable and fair. With the staff trained to follow the program and apply it to all of the chil-dren, however, the value of getting to know the unique qualities of each child is diminished. At the same time, the value of developing a unique relationship with each child is often not seen. In fact, it may be dis-couraged so that no child is given unfair, special treatment by the staff, and the child will not be encouraged to develop a dependency on a par-ticular member of the staff. The goal is often to have interchangeable relationships where the child learns to be equally comfortable with all of the staff, and neither child nor staff has "favorites." Decisions about the child's system of expectations, incentives, and schedule are based entirely on his behaviors. There might be room for various children to be on different "levels" in the program but not for the individual child to have an individualized program. Concern for the meaning of behaviors tends to be less than concern given to providing consistent consequences for behaviors so that the child's good behavior is rewarded and misbehavior is not "reinforced." Too often there is concern that understanding meanings encourages the child to develop excuses for his inappropriate behaviors.

For relationships in residential care to help children to heal from developmental trauma, they need to be modeled on qualities of attachment relationships. Child–staff member dyads are established. Particular staff members are responsible for getting to know particular children especially well so that they will be able to be sensitive and responsive to each unique child. In turn, children are provided with the opportunity to spend extra time with those same staff members in order to develop greater trust and to become engaged in important shared activities that are crucial for their development. These include learning to have conversations about their thoughts, feelings, and wishes; seeking and receiving comfort along with addressing conflicts; and engaging in relationship repair. The children will learn to receive guidance and support from these staff members in order to pursue their developmental tasks and to manage the challenges of daily living with peers and other adults. All of these important socio-emotional skills develop best within close relationships with adults who are known and trusted. The child cannot be expected to address his most frightening and shameful experiences with any and all adults who are involved with his daily care.

Staff Training and Support

As has been stated throughout this book, developing relationships with children who have experienced developmental trauma is often very difficult. These children do not trust adults to meet their needs. As a result, they are often defiant, challenging, withdrawn, deceptive, and unable or unwilling to enter into reciprocal conversations and relationships. Such ways of relating are likely to activate any relationship difficulties or attachment patterns from a staff member's own history. This is true for staff in the residential home and school. When the children repeatedly reject them, the staff are likely to enter a state of blocked care. For these children to benefit from residential care, the staff have to relate with them as if it is "more than a job." When children show no interest in or responsiveness to that way of relating, then the staff understandably find it hard to continue with this level of dedication. Constant hurt from the child means that staff retreat from the relationship and their care for the child does become "only a job."

To consistently relate with these children, staff need to demonstrate good emotional and social skills, including empathy and reflective functioning, impulse control and emotional regulation. They need to understand the impact of developmental trauma, be able to utilize PACE with the children and with each other, and be committed to discovering who the children are underneath their behaviors. They also need to model for the children the ability to communicate their thoughts and feelings, resolve conflicts, initiate relationship repair, and accept guidance and support from others. They need to know why the children are likely to provoke them and how to respond in therapeutic ways.

To consistently meet the needs of these traumatized children, staff will require regular support and supervision regarding their daily interactions with them. The staff need to feel safe with their supervisors and peers if they are to create safety for the children. They need to learn from their mistakes without being shamed and to acknowledge when they need assistance. Because the work is hard, the staff need to work in a safe and nurturing environment, with recognition—both psychological and financial—of their importance in helping these children to develop well. If the staff are truly to be attachment figures for the children, they need to stay and not be replaced every few months. For them to stay, their importance needs to be recognized and supported.

Residential staff will also benefit by being made aware of the three neurobiological relationship systems that we all have (Baylin & Hughes, 2016). These systems are attachment (focusing on safety and comfort), companionship (focusing on mutual play and sharing), and social hierarchy (focusing on following the rules, respect, and cooperation). A staff member needs to relate with the traumatized child using all three systems. With attachment being central in the relationship, the staff member brings strength and guidance to the companionship system of the child as well as compassion and empathy to the social hierarchy system. In this way, the staff member is not permissive (stressing companionship) or authoritarian (stressing social hierarchy).

Discipline

Children who have experienced developmental trauma are likely to present significant behavioral problems, which are made worse when they are living with similar children. Behavioral support is needed. Rather than focusing on managing behaviors through predictable rules and consequences, a daily milieu in the residence based on DDP means that behavioral support is guided by the following principles:

- Attachment-centered relationships are central in establishing and maintaining safety. This is necessary for developing reflective, regulated functioning.
- Maintaining an open and engaged attitude that encourages a similar attitude from the child is central to avoiding defensive power-struggles and escalations.
- Understanding the meanings of the child's behavior is crucial for developing an environment that promotes cooperative behavior; the attitude of PACE is central.
- Experiences of comfort, joy, joint curiosity, and interactive repair will greatly enhance a cooperative stance.
- Behavioral expectations are based on the child's developmental age, not his chronological age. Children are not getting into trouble for being asked to do more than what they are consistently able to do.
- Anxiety and oppositional behaviors are reduced by routines and rituals that are meaningful and also meet the needs of the children for various developmental activities and interests.
- As the children develop the ability to reflect and communicate their inner lives in conversations, they are less likely to communicate with their behaviors.
- As the children are able to seek and receive comfort and support in dealing with their frustrations and challenges, they are less likely to rely on anger and defiance.
- All of the above greatly reduce the tendency to rely on many and significant consequences. At the same time, the child is not shielded from natural consequences for specific behaviors that are not safe for the child or others or which harm the common good.
- Because most discipline places stress on the relationship, it is crucial that the staff initiate relationship repair after conflicts and stress caused by limits and consequences. Repair invites the

child back into the closeness of the relationship, communicating that the staff care for and are committed to the child regardless of the conflict.

School

Safe and successful residential programs are those in which the philosophy and practice of providing care is consistent within both the home and the school. Recruitment, training, support, and mentoring for the staff need to be very similar, with differences only reflecting differences in specific responsibilities. Just as the child needs to have a special relationship with a particular staff member within the home, the same is true within the school. This person needs to get to know the child well, relate with him across many activities and with a full range of conversations, and support the relationships between the child and other staff members.

The classroom needs a small class size, often six or less, with a teacher and support person. Education staff know that teaching begins when the child is safe and developing trust. Safety among the children in the classroom is supported with clear structure and guidelines. Safety is best maintained with staff who can stay regulated themselves. Staff are aware of the need for relationship repair and their responsibility to initiate repair. Children are not given negative consequences for behaviors that are secondary to their developmental trauma.

Children are taught on the basis of their developmental level of skills rather than their chronological age. Curriculum involves activities, fun and laughter, and ongoing conversations that are light and serious, quiet and lively. While the staff take the lead in organizing the day, the child's preferences and responses have a continual influence on the implementation of the schedule. The daily schedule at school is integrated with the schedule at home, and clear communication between home and school ensures that matters needed for the child to be safe and successful happen.

Psychotherapy

While the day-to-day care provided in "PACE-ful" relationships is at the heart of the stabilization and development of traumatized children in residential care, psychotherapy is still an important intervention for them. The DDP therapist has many important roles:

- Assist the child in understanding the connection between his traumatic experiences in the past and his current psychological and behavioral difficulties in his current life.
- Assist the child in understanding the nature of the traumatic events that occurred. This reduces the terror and shame associated with those events and develops new meanings and stories about them.
- Help the child to begin to differentiate past traumatic relationships from new relationships with his attachment figures. In doing so, the child will discover qualities of himself—he is lovable, courageous, clever, persistent, competent—in these relationships that he did not experience in his previous relationships.
- Assist the child to learn how to engage more easily in synchronized, reciprocal conversations that he needs in order to develop new stories within his new relationships.
- Involve two attachment figures from the staff group in the therapy. This will strengthen these relationships in ways that are crucial for the child's development. Scheduling is arranged so that one of the two is able to attend each session. This ensures that the child is likely to have one of the two present on most days and also that the child will still have an attachment figure in the milieu if one resigns. Having two may also reduce the stress that might fall on a single staff member in meeting this child's needs. Finally, it may prevent the possibility that the attachment relationship might become an exclusive one, which would not be in the best interest of the child or staff member.
- Be a consultant to the staff to help them understand the traumatized child and develop a unique service plan to best meet this child's needs.
- Render crucial assistance to the child in making the transition back to the community. Consultations and joint sessions with the child's foster carers, adoptive parents, or biological parents prior to the child returning home will greatly assist a successful transition to a home in the community. When the child is going to live with new carers, they need to be given training and support to meet the child's needs. If an adolescent is moving toward independent living, a support worker needs to be trained and in place. For transitions

to be successful, it is crucial that the caregivers also have an attachment-focused attitude toward resolving the trauma, creating new meanings, and addressing current behaviors.

For the past 2 years, Kate has been a good residential worker—sensitive, committed, and ready to learn. She had been assigned to get to know Zoe and to try to facilitate Zoe's attachment behaviors toward her. Zoe was by far the most irritating 9-year-old girl she had ever met. No matter what Kate did, it was not good enough for Zoe, who actively avoided Kate and seemed to rather spend time with anyone else besides her. This had been going on for 4 months! Kate was beginning to wonder why she should bother. Other kids liked and responded to her in ways that made all the work worthwhile. Maybe she could get someone else assigned to Zoe.

Kate brought her plea for a change to Elaine, her supervisor. Elaine listened. She did not try to talk Kate out of her experiences of Zoe, her frustration, or her discouragement. Rather, she understood how hard it was to be rejected by Zoe over and over again. Elaine asked Kate what was the hardest thing about her time with Zoe. Kate thought for a while before replying that the hardest was how actively Zoe went out of her way to avoid her. Zoe had no interest in spending time with her! Zoe made it clear that Kate did not matter to her at all! Kate said that Zoe's avoidance reminded her somewhat of her father. He seemed to be too busy to find time for her when she was a child. Elaine responded with empathy over that experience. She knew that when there is little or no reciprocity in a relationship, it is very hard to stay open and engaged with the other person, regardless of that person's age. After a bit more silence, Elaine wondered if it were possible that Zoe was afraid of Kate. Was there any fear under her avoidance? Kate wondered why Zoe would be afraid of her. Elaine suggested that they both wonder about it and talk about it some more the next week.

And Kate did wonder. The next day while she was playing a game with some of the other kids, she noticed Zoe help an unpopular 7-year-old boy to find his toy. He thanked her and she seemed embarrassed, even vulnerable, and glanced away, momentarily getting eye contact with Kate, who was then smiling at her. Immediately Zoe showed terror in her face and ran out of the room. Kate suddenly knew that Zoe was afraid of Kate liking her, seeing her as special, wanting a relationship with her. Zoe was afraid of Kate's desire to be with and get to know her. She was afraid of Kate seeing something special about her. Kate realized that she had almost stopped seeing anything special about her. She had almost been convinced that she did not matter to Zoe. The next time that she saw Elaine, she told her that she now realized that they did matter to each other—a lot.

FAMILIES WHERE THERE IS RISK

Keeping risk factors in mind is a necessary aspect of working with families and networks where a child has experienced developmental trauma. The DDP practitioner needs to be both prepared for and comfortable with the complex context of providing interventions, therapy, or consultation when there is past or current risk. This means walking the line where PACE and intersubjective communications are used to deepen experiences and knowing that at any time, considerations of child protection may arise. The DDP practitioner also provides behavioral support around specific behaviors that are a source of risk to another child or adult. Examples include working with a child who is violent to her adoptive parents or a child who finds it hard to inhibit her problematic sexual behavior when around her school friends.

Consideration of how to achieve and maintain safety is central to all DDP interventions. This might be relational safety, emotional safety, physical safety, or physiologic safety. With its foundations in attachment theory, intersubjectivity, and interpersonal neurobiology, DDP is well placed to intervene when safety is compromised.

The principles of this work are outlined through the following example involving a DDP practitioner's decision making and interventions.

Kerry is the mother of Chloe, age 13, and Harry, age 7. Harry's father was violent to both Kerry and Chloe. He left the family about 4 years ago. Kerry is a single parent. Harry comes into school most days saying he is hungry. His clothes are too small, and he rarely has enough food for lunch. Kerry is perceived as intimidating by Harry's teacher. Harry is assessed as a child in need, and a family support worker visits regularly. Harry comes into school saying Chloe, his 13-year-old sister, hit him. On the same day, Chloe takes herself to social services demanding to be placed in foster care. She has been placed voluntarily in foster care for short periods previously after fights between Chloe and her mom. Chloe is a delight to care for in her foster home. They like her, and she fits into their family well.

James, a DDP practitioner, receives a referral from Craig, Chloe's social worker, to work with Chloe and Kerry with the aim of improving their relationship, seeking to get Chloe back home as soon as possible. Craig sees the strength in their mother–daughter relationship. He wants James to help Kerry learn how to parent with PACE in the same way that her foster carers do.

In the subsections that follow, this case example is elaborated to observe the factors a DDP practitioner needs to keep in mind when providing therapy or consultation where risks are being considered.

Referral Decisions

Questions James considers on receiving this new referral include the following:

- Who is at risk in both these families?
- What is the risk?
- Who they are at risk from?
- Is this referral appropriate?
- Am I the right person to be involved?
- What will my intervention aim to do?
    Is it about collecting information?
    Is it about facilitating closer relationships?
    Is it about finding things out?
- Do I know any of the professionals involved?

James phones Craig. He has worked with him once before. Craig is clear that he would find James convening a network consultation extremely helpful, especially if James chairs it and takes the minutes. Craig knows he is feeling both stressed and stretched by his caseload. He has just felt obliged to take on four new families at the allocation meeting that morning. He wants Chloe and her mom to find a way to live together, and he knows he does not have the time to do the work.

James asks him about how he's doing and seems to have time to chat. Craig tells James about the allocation meeting and his hopes for Kerry and Chloe. When James asks about Harry, Craig feels relief. This has been bothering him too, and the family support worker is looking at this. Craig begins to look forward to the network consultation, to someone else working alongside him so he doesn't feel everything rests with him. He knows how these work now. He is slightly worried that Harry's teacher will be angry with him again for not removing Harry into foster care. He knows James will manage this, as James somehow manages to make everyone feel involved even if some disagree. Craig notices he feels a bit less stressed when he puts the telephone down.

Building relationships between key professionals using PACE is a core principle in dyadic developmental practice as explored in Chapter 8. PACE is not a technique to be achieved; it is a context within which all interactions occur. James did not deliberately ask Craig about his day, empathize about how hard his job was, or be curious about his hopes for Chloe; rather, it is how he communicates. He knows that good relationships are central to effective practice across all parts of the network.

This aspect of dyadic developmental practice is included here because it is never more important than when working with active or potential child-protection risks, especially when there are disagreements within a network as to the safest action to take. It is also the most invisible part of the approach. In a comprehensive briefing commissioned by the National Society for the Prevention of Cruelty to Children (NSPCC) about the "Signs of Safety" approach in England, Bunn (2013) writes that the best outcomes for vulnerable children arise when constructive relationships exist between professionals and between families and professionals.

Combining Confidentiality, Safety, and Trust in Network Consultations and Therapy

Clear and regular discussion around confidentially increases safety. It is helpful to distinguish trust from confidentiality. Trust can be developed when confidentiality cannot be guaranteed. Developing trust when working with risk requires openness, being transparent, stating clear expectations and limits, and giving feedback as to how things are affecting you; similar to characteristics of developing intersubjective conversations.

Providing therapy while managing informed consent and confidentiality and protecting the welfare of the child presents dilemmas for DDP practitioners. Therapeutic goals can be different from legal or investigative roles. Ways of reconciling these different roles need to be considered when undertaking therapeutic work in which there are issues of current risk. The start of a therapeutic relationship is an opportunity to discuss limits of confidentiality and the responsibilities of the therapist to share suspected abusive interactions and behaviors with child protection agencies.

Children and adults need to be clear about confidentiality limits so they can knowingly choose whether to withhold potentially reportable information. Returning to these discussions as therapy continues is an active collaborative process between the child, the adults, the social worker, the school, and the therapist. This increases the likelihood that any developing trust may continue if the need to share concerns with child protection agencies arises.

James talks with his team, and James takes the referral. The team decides that the work requires a context that all information may be shared. No confidentiality will be offered. James convenes the first network consultation. James trusts Craig's judgment that Kerry and Chloe may well be able to live together safely if they are helped to do so. Craig continued to feel this even though Chloe had recently told her foster father that she often gets so frustrated with her mother that she hits her mother. When asked about this, Kerry agrees and says Chloe has hit her about once or twice a week. She has felt too bad about this to tell anyone.

James asks Harry's teacher about her concerns. James sees Crag stiffen a little. She starts by saying how angry she is about social services doing nothing despite her repeated requests. James shows genuine interest in her perspective. He says how hard it is to work things out when she is so clear that Harry needs foster care while at the same time Craig is doing his best to keep the family together. As James listens, his initial concerns for Harry grow. James puts together the violence of Harry's father toward his mother that Harry as an infant witnessed, the fact that his mother is preoccupied now with her relationship with Chloe, and that Chloe has recently punched Harry.

James discusses his concerns about the work with Chloe, Kerry, and Chloe's foster parents, focusing on Chloe returning home when her return increases risks for Harry of being hit by her. Chloe's return will also mean Harry loses the newly experienced extra time he has with his mother. James says he will work with Kerry on her own first. He knows the family support worker is focusing on Kerry's parenting and also spends time individually with Harry. He offers to provide consultation to Kerry around DDP-informed parenting.

James and Craig meet with Kerry twice. Craig explains he wants James to see Kerry and Chloe together while she is in foster care because this makes it safer for them both. He will agree to Chloe coming home for a few hours then working up to overnights if James feels it is safe enough to do so. Craig says he wants Kerry to feel able to call the police if Chloe becomes violent when she is there. James talks with Kerry about how tricky it is to manage the balance between people being worried about her care of Harry while they are also worried about Kerry being hurt by Chloe.

James and Craig talk about the possible impact of them both being men when Kerry has had violent relationships with men. They raise this with Kerry, who says smiling that she would have preferred at least one of them to be a woman. But then again, her daughter is a young woman and beats her up, so it just must be something about her that makes people want to hit her. James plans to ask her more about this when they next meet.

Timing of Starting Therapy

James meets with Kerry for six meetings. He is clear when they start that anything Kerry says may be shared with Craig. James talks in the next network meeting that the time isn't right yet for Chloe to join them. Craig is impatient for James to start work with Chloe. He feels things are drifting. Chloe, who remains in foster care, is seeing her mom often after school. Chloe tells her foster carers that she doesn't want to go back home. Harry's teacher says she is much less concerned about him.

James says he needs more time with Kerry first to ensure that when Chloe joins them, Kerry can use PACE or will trust James enough to take the lead if necessary. Doing therapy with the child who has hit a parent when considerations of neglect are also being assessed will not be easy. It may work if Kerry can be helped to relate with Chloe in different ways. He will also have to get to know Chloe while being clear that hitting her mom is not okay. At the same time, he hopes to help Kerry acknowledge the impact on Chloe and Harry of Harry's dad's violent behavior and apologize for not being able to protect them at the time. This is what he is focusing on with Kerry in sessions now, and he is hopeful he will be able to start therapy soon.

PACE

PACE is a helpful set of guiding principles when working with families at risk. It helps talk about difficult subjects in ways that can take adults and children by surprise. The storytelling tone, the acceptance given toward perceptions and feelings, and the empathy toward how hard things might be create an atmosphere of sharing experiences rather than assessing and managing risk. Setting clear limits and consequences for behavior that is inappropriate or harmful accompanies PACE. This further increases safety, and adults and children may share more than they intend. This might include how they have harmed others as well as times when they were harmed. A DDP practitioner is responsible to recognize the effect of PACE on the other person. It can be important to remind adults and children about confidentiality limits so they can choose whether to share information that may implicate them. This is another difficult ethical line to walk that is important to share with the network when working with current risk.

James has two more meetings with Kerry. He then starts therapy with Chloe and her mom. James and Craig meet with them both first. James is clear that the aim of these meetings is not to get them back living together as soon as possible. He says that nothing will be confidential. He tells Chloe that he knows she does not want to go home. His aim is to help them get along so they can spend longer times together without violence. Chloe says she'll come.

This is how the first therapy session goes:

JAMES: Yes, I see you both sitting here with your drinks. Mom's got raspberry. Chloe, you have apple. I know you both met up after school today. Did you stop off to get those on the way here?

CHLOE: No way. She'd never have any money on her. I always had to buy stuff. My foster carer bought it for me.

James remembers his agreed aim for today was to focus on their relationship. He knows it is a possibility he might never get Kerry and Chloe to come again.

JAMES: So you like raspberry and you like apple. Is that the same with fruit as well as with drinks?

CHLOE: You think she ever gave me fruit? Burgers and chips, that was the limit, if I was lucky.

James sighs a little and hopes Chloe hasn't seen him. Chloe clearly wants to make sure he hears about the ways her mother does not provide good-enough care. He tries again. Before he can say anything, Kerry comes back at Chloe.

KERRY: That is because burgers and chips are all you will eat, young lady. And that's been the same since you were 2. Don't you go to pretending to James that you love fruit and I'm just too mean to buy you any. That's what you usually do when you meet social workers. Make me out to be a rubbish mom.

James thinks quickly on his feet: There are a couple of themes here that might lead into wondering about their relationship. "Rubbish mom" is a bit too strong too quickly. He's only just met Chloe. He has had four meetings with Kerry. Kerry had been open about her own difficult childhood, herself being in care with many foster homes and two children's homes. Kerry was also surprisingly open about how hard she has found being a mom to Chloe. He had agreed to see Chloe with Kerry for those reasons. He feels warm toward Kerry and how vulnerable she made herself with him. He does wonder if this has anything to do with him being a man, and he has discussed this in supervision. Maybe making herself vulnerable was the safest way of her being with him. He decides to go with the theme of Chloe being 2 years old.

> **JAMES TO CHLOE:** So, you knew what you liked and didn't like since being 2?

Chloe nods and smiles.

> **KERRY:** She did. You know I never had the terrible twos with her. People told me to expect it. It just didn't happen. She was just such a good little girl.

James goes with the moment using the same words Kerry uses.

> **JAMES:** Chloe, did you hear that? Your mom's telling me that at 2 you were such a good little girl.

Chloe shrugs.

> **JAMES:** [Leaning forward to Kerry] Can you tell me how she was at 2?
> **KERRY:** [Giving James longer eye contact for the first time] She was always so independent. She walked at 8 months. She hardly ever cried. She was such a tiny baby.
> **JAMES TO CHLOE:** Chloe, I have only just met you and I am learning about you from your mom. That might feel a bit weird. She remembers you being a tiny baby, that you hardly ever cried. I'm wondering what it's like you just having met me and to hear your mom telling me things about how you were as a tiny baby.

CHLOE: I don't mind.

JAMES: You don't mind. Is it okay then if I ask your mom a bit more about you being a little girl?

CHLOE: If you want.

James asks Kerry about her memories. Kerry has quite a few, and Chloe joins in with her mother's stories. They remember the day on the beach when Chloe rode a donkey and they had ice cream. James noticed they were looking into each other's eyes and smiling. He wanted to comment on what he saw but was worried that if he let them know about the nonverbal communication he'd noticed, this would instantly stop the conversation. Chloe would return to the dismissiveness of her mother that he knew she had a good reason to hold. James takes a risk.

JAMES: Kerry, when we met last week, you told me how sometimes when Chloe was living with you she just wanted to keep you near her. [He slows down, his voice lowers.] You wanted her to be off with her friends. She's 13 now. She shouldn't need your attention as much as she does.

James notices Chloe is looking at him intently, and he continues.

JAMES: Kerry, when we met last week, you also let me know that you find it hard when Chloe wants you to give her a cuddle.

KERRY: I go into panic with cuddles. I'm not a happy person with cuddles. When I'm in my chair she can give me a cuddle.

JAMES: So if you are not in your chair and Chloe wants a cuddle?

KERRY: She knows not to do that. She knows I can't cuddle her and she knows why. I told her. She's a good girl really.

James sees Chloe losing interest.

JAMES: When we met last week, another thing you told me about your daughter is that she is too grown-up for her own good. So sometimes she wants cuddles and doesn't want to leave you and sometimes she's so grown-up. And you just told me about when she was the little girl and she hardly ever cried when she was a tiny baby and then she learned to walk so early, just at the age of 8 months old.

KERRY: [Looking at Chloe] Yes, she was my little girl. She still is my little girl. She will always be my little girl. No matter what.

James notices Kerry moving her body slightly toward Chloe and Chloe moving her body slightly toward her mom.

> **JAMES TO KERRY:** I know this isn't your chair, but maybe you could just lean into your daughter?

Kerry does, and Chloe also leans into her, and mom strokes her hair.

> **KERRY:** [Looking into Chloe's eyes] You will always be my little girl.

Chloe puts her arms around her mother's waist, and her mom puts her arms around Chloe's shoulders. They rock. James finds himself rocking too. He doesn't know how long this moment will last. He is watching closely and feels he needs to be the one to stop it, as he thinks Kerry will be the one who stops this first. Just for now he says nothing. He notices his eyes welling up slightly as are Kerry's. After a minute he says, slowly, in a low voice, "talking about" and "talking for" them both:

> **JAMES:** One minute we were talking about apple drinks and the next minute something happens and Chloe, your mom has tears in her eyes and I am noticing tears in my eyes too. Maybe among all the rowing that happens in your house, all the times Kerry you can't cuddle your daughter because you panic, all the times your mom hasn't bought food, all the times your mom forgets to clean the house, maybe, just maybe that special thing between the two, between you Kerry as a mom and you Chloe as a daughter, comes through. Maybe it feels just a little bit like it was once before when Chloe was a little baby being cuddled by her mom. Maybe even though things got so hard and you both had such big fights, maybe you have just missed each other.

James knows he needs to find a way to keep this safe. Neither of them had probably anticipated this when they walked in. He gets creative:

> **JAMES:** I have this song on my phone. I'm just going to play it while you two sit there.

Kerry and her daughter continue to rock for 30 seconds. Kerry sits up.

> **KERRY:** This is such an old man song. I can't believe you have that on your phone. Find another one.

They spend time talking about songs. Chloe and Kerry keep talking for 5 minutes. Chloe doesn't say anything to James about how trashy her mom Kerry is. James feels this is enough emotional connection for today. They chat about things for the rest of the session including Harry. James is tempted to introduce a theme about hitting and hurting but doesn't. He thinks they will both come back for a second meeting.

Before providing therapy to Kerry and Chloe, Craig had convened a meeting using "Signs of Safety" (Turnell & Edwards, 1999). Kerry and Chloe were there. James wasn't able to go but was able to go to the next one. James trusts Craig to put a plan in place to enable Kerry to be a more effective parent to Chloe. James knows DDP is part of a comprehensive plan. He feels from his therapy session that the "two hands" of DDP will be possible. He is also confident that, as long as Kerry keeps coming to her meetings with him, he can help her say sorry to Chloe for the times in the past when she wasn't able to protect her. He also knows from his past work with families that a child's violence to a parent often decreases once a child seeks comfort from a parent and the parent can accept the wish and respond to it.

He also starts to look ahead to a time when Chloe's foster parents might join a session, thinking about how all three adults can care for Chloe. His main motivation is not to get Chloe home but to enable her to have enough care from adults including her mother for her to learn not to hit when she feels overwhelmed. Chloe's return home will be in the back of his mind for the future.

The primary function of attachment is to generate safety. DDP, a trauma-informed, attachment-focused intervention, can be central in helping children to begin to heal and trust their caregivers. When DDP is undertaken with birth parents who are the source of the hurt and pain, and these relationships can be made safer with increased attachment security and intersubjective connections developing over time, therapy can be particularly effective in resolving traumatic experiences. When child-protection concerns are present, such therapy needs to be provided as an integral part of a comprehensive plan involving all other relevant agencies.

INDIVIDUAL THERAPY

The goal of DDP is to provide the child with developmental trauma with therapy that includes the active presence of the child's attachment figure—foster carer, residential worker, adoptive parent, biological parent. The attachment figure serves to provide the child with comfort and support while exploring past traumas and to help the child to differentiate the attachment figure's care from that given by the original attachment figures who traumatized the child. However, it is necessary that the attachment figure provides safety for the child and relates with the child in a manner that will not activate shame or fear. If the child is not residing with a person who is willing and able to provide attachment security for the child, then individual therapy is necessary.

Following are situations where individual therapy could be considered:

- The child lives with a parent who is unable or unwilling to engage in DDP in a manner that is safe for the child. The therapeutic goals would involve assisting the child to differentiate the relationships that she has with her parents from those available with other adults; to develop a sense of self that includes strengths not intersubjectively seen by her parents; and to develop a sense of resilience. Individual therapy is of value to a child being raised in a challenging environment, but it is likely to be less valuable than if the therapist were able to positively affect the home environment. Such therapy is never a substitute for child-protection services when indicated.
- An older adolescent who lives alone or in a supported residence. Regular joint sessions with the young person's social worker will be considered when indicated and agreed to by the young person.
- Older adolescents in foster care who have no significant attachment to their current foster parent and who have no motivation to develop one.
- Homeless young people. Regular joint sessions with the young person's community worker will be considered when indicated and agreed to by the young person.

Within the individual therapy context, the DDP therapist still focuses on relational safety and positive intersubjective experiences. The DDP therapist still utilizes affective–reflective dialogue, coregulates affect, and cocreates new stories involving past and present events. The process of therapeutic explorations of traumatic events and current events associated with shame and fear will most likely be slower. When the child explores a trauma in DDP in the presence of her attachment figure, she is able to remember and speak of those events at home, knowing that she will receive any needed comfort and support from that same person. Without such an adult being present in therapy, memories evoked might be dysregulating for the child if further memories emerge between sessions. The DDP therapist therefore needs to approach the traumatic events of the past more slowly to have confidence that the child will not have to face too many memories when alone between sessions.

Because the child is alone with the therapist during the session, the child will not have the comforting presence of an attachment figure to touch or hold her when she is crying or experiencing intense fear or shame. Without the presence of the child's attachment figure, such physical comforting of the child by the therapist is less likely to be psychologically safe for either the child or the therapist. The therapist certainly may support with her nonverbal expressions of empathy and comfort, but these may not provide the child with the support given by being held by an attachment figure.

The DDP therapist might choose to take on more of the role of an attachment figure for the child if the child does not have another attachment figure in her life to provide safety. The DDP therapist's intersubjective experiences of the child's strengths and of the child as being enjoyable, clever, delightful, and likable may take on extra importance. The DDP therapist often acknowledges the child's birthday with a card or gift or has contact with the child outside of the therapy session (such as attending the child's performance at a school concert when the child makes the request). These acts may often be of value even when the child is being actively supported by her parents in therapy; they are especially meaningful for the child who does not live with an attachment figure who provides safety.

Of course, when the DDP therapist does communicate her positive experience of the child in these ways, the therapist needs to be clear about the boundaries that are still present in their relationship. The child must be assisted in expressing any confusion that she might have about the relationship as well as any disappointment or anger over the boundaries. The DDP therapist must also reflect on their therapeutic relationship and bring it to supervision if necessary to ensure that the therapist is not developing a relationship with the client that is taking on the traits of a relationship between friends or relatives.

When the child is being seen in individual therapy, the DDP therapist is mindful of the value of helping the child to develop relationships with someone who is able to become an attachment figure. Potential attachment figures might be seen separately to facilitate their ability to provide safety for the child. They might also be referred to another therapist. The DDP therapist would maintain the goal of having joint sessions in the future if safety is ensured. If there is no such potential attachment figure, the DDP therapist is likely to encourage the child to reflect on relationships with other adults. As the child is able to reflect on her relationship with the therapist, she might become aware that a caring adult may well want to be her mentor, teacher, or support person. As she discovers her worth and is aware that good adults would enjoy having a mentoring or supportive relationship with her, she will become more resilient.

Emily was a DDP therapist who had been providing therapy for 7 months to a 12-year-old foster girl, Christine, who had resided in a group home for the past year. Christine's angry and defiant behaviors had caused her to be asked to leave five foster homes since she was first placed in foster care when she was 8. It was a behavior-focused group home, and Emily did not want any of the staff to be part of the sessions because their program did not take an attachment perspective, and attachment relationships were not encouraged. During the course of the 7 months, Emily had discovered and expressed delight with Christine's sense of humor, amazement over her extensive knowledge of the characters of Harry Potter, as well as enjoyment over her feats of memory in recalling—and challenging her on any inconsistencies—everything that they had spoken about.

Emily gave Christine a card on her 12th birthday. It was a photo of the Sun rising over the ocean. On the inside, Emily wrote that on Wednesday, the day that they met every week, the Sun was brighter and even would shine through the clouds, "because you are you." Christine sat silently and stared at the card. Emily accepted her silence. The next week Christine told Emily that she had asked her social worker to find her a good foster home, and the next month her social worker had found one where she could live. Emily reminded her that she had said a few months before that she never wanted to live in a foster home again and she wondered what had changed. Christine replied, "I have. Because you are you."

FAMILIES WITHOUT DEVELOPMENTAL TRAUMA

Soon after DDP was developed as a model of therapy for children and young people who manifested developmental trauma, it began to be used as an intervention model that was applicable for all families where children were experiencing psychological or attachment distress. There are differences when using DDP with families generally and using it specifically to assist children and young people to resolve such trauma.

Frequently in DDP with children who have experienced developmental trauma, the source of a child's difficulties did not arise with his current caregivers but from abuse or neglect with previous caregivers. There are differences in how DDP is applied when the source of the child's psychological difficulties originates within the family itself. These may relate to the parents having their own psychological or relationship stressors due to issues related to their family of origin or to the parents' relationship with each other. Alternatively, parents may not be able to fully attend to their child's developmental needs because of external stress related to work, health, or issues arising outside the family. The child's problems can reflect patterns of communication or behavior within the family that are finding expression in the behaviors of one or more of the children. They may also relate to the child's separate challenges, such as those involving school, peers, learning difficulties, or anxiety or despair involving external pressures and failures.

It is much easier for parents to support the child with empathy and understanding, without defensiveness or shame, when the problems do not relate to the parents themselves. When the parents are aware that their own behaviors (anger, absence from family life, substance abuse, postpartum depression, intense conflicts between themselves) or their histories (past history of abuse or neglect; history of absent, critical, or disinterested parents) have contributed to their child's challenges, the parents may experience shame and associated defensiveness or anger when these issues are addressed by the DDP therapist.

When working with these issues, the therapist may need to meet with the parents alone for a number of sessions because of the shame associated with their involvement in the origins of the child's difficulties. The parents may also need to be seen regularly without the child in between joint sessions in order to assist the parents with whatever challenges that they are facing along with raising their child. DDP therapists need to engage them with PACE, helping them to experience themselves as having the courage and strength to face their own challenges, traumas, or difficult histories in order to help their child. Parents need to experience safety with the therapist. They are not being judged as being poor parents regardless of behaviors in the past and present that are not in the child's best interests.

Once the DDP therapist initiates joint sessions with the parents and child, the child's psychological safety is never overlooked. If the parents are able to be open and engaged, without defensive shame, the child will experience a sense of safety. The child is helped to share his experience of events involving his parents. The parents are helped by the therapist to focus on understanding, accepting, and experiencing empathy for the child's stressful experiences, regardless of the parents' motives or reasons for the event. The child's experience is understood and valued, even if the parents have a different experience or memory of the event. After conveying acceptance and empathy for their child's experience, the parents then explore ways to help the child with other events in the future that might be stressful. The parents are committed to work with the child in handling the situation rather than finding what the child needs to do on his own to manage it.

In using DDP with families where the child has not experienced developmental trauma, the child may have less severe problems than if she had experienced developmental trauma. In those situations, the interventions for the child are likely to be less comprehensive and intense. However, it might be more difficult for the child to speak about her anger or disappointment with regard to her current parents than if she were speaking about the behavior of other parents in the past. If parents become defensive and annoyed with the child for complaining, not letting it go, exaggerating, or feeling sorry for herself, then there will be less improvement in the parent–child relationship and in the child's overall functioning. However, interventions are likely to be helpful if the parents are not defensive but stay open and engaged and understand and apologize for their part in their child's distress. This is further helped if they change their behaviors to show that they listened and took her experience seriously.

The DDP therapist takes an active role in changing relationship patterns that undermine the child's sense of safety. She sees the parents alone first to assess their concerns about their child, to understand how they have addressed their concerns, and to tell them how the joint sessions will be structured and about PACE and other parenting interventions that the DDP therapist will be recommending. In the joint sessions, if the parents are routinely angry at the child's behavior or make comments that are likely to evoke shame, the DDP therapist interrupts what is being said and leads it back to the principles of an affective–reflective dialogue. The DDP therapist will also take the lead in the dialogue if the parents are expressing negative thoughts and feelings about the thoughts and feelings of their child. Two examples follow:

- Mom is shouting about her son habitually ignoring her rule to come home at a certain time. The DDP therapist says, matching her intensity: "I can see, Jane, how upset you are about his regularly coming home late! Your anger about it is still quite strong! Would you let me explore this with your son in order to understand what his thoughts are about this?"
- Dad is suggesting that his daughter is being selfish for not playing with her little sister more. The DDP therapist says: "I can see that this is bothering you a lot, Adam. You're making a guess about your daughter's reason for not playing with her sister, and I fear that your guess is going to make it unlikely for your daughter to feel safe enough to tell us how she sees things, what's going on for her. Would you mind if I ask her about that? Just to understand what she thinks and feels, but not to judge her reasons."

As is true in utilizing DDP with other populations, the therapist strives to make sense of the meaning of the behaviors about which the parents are concerned. Often the meanings involve fears, shame, and doubts around attachment themes. The parent and child may perceive each other as not trusting the other. The child may believe that the parent is disappointed in her, does not love her as much as her sibling, or does not care about her happiness. The parent may believe that the child does not respect him. The word *respect* often refers to beliefs that the child does not value his guidance, does not rely on him for comfort, does not feel close to him, or does not perceive him as being important in her life.

Seventeen-year-old Stan and his father, Dr. Rhines, had been engaged in ongoing conflicts for many months. Stan would complain that his father didn't trust his judgments, and his dad would respond that he was too young to make some of the decisions that he wanted to make himself. One mistake now might affect the rest of his life! Their patterns of angry or sullen defensiveness were wearing them both down. Their DDP therapist had spent a number of sessions with Dr. Rhines alone where she was able to help him to see the value of relating with PACE with his son rather than communicating with the goal of getting his son to accept his authority. He had become vulnerable when he expressed the worry that his son would disregard his advice when he left home and that they would have a distant relationship much like he had with his own father.

In the first joint session, as Dr. Rhines listened without interrupting, Stan exclaimed to the therapist that he thought that his father was disappointed in him and that no matter what he did, he never would be good enough for him. His father, with some gentle guidance from the therapist, responded with empathy—not trying to change his son's experience but rather simply understanding it with empathy for the pain that he was expressing. Within minutes, father and son were both tearful. When Dr. Rhines exclaimed—in a tone similar to how his son had expressed despair over not being good enough—that he also feared that he was not a good-enough father for his son and that someday they would seldom see each other, Stan embraced his dad and said that would never happen. They only met with the therapist for a few more sessions. They still argued somewhat about what Stan could decide for himself without consulting his dad, but their arguments were no longer attacking. Their relationship was strong enough to include their differences—which now seemed smaller—and they were both confident enough to spontaneously express their love for each other in many small ways.

DDP SUPERVISION

Supervision involves giving feedback on the moment-by-moment analysis of interactions. It is recommended that therapists video-record their work for this. The DDP supervisor models the core principles of DDP: communicates with and about using PACE and develops reciprocal interactions, staying intersubjectively connected while acknowledging mistakes followed by repair. She matches affect, shares interests, uses a storytelling tone, and cocreates narratives using cycles of affective–reflective dialogues. The DDP Rating Scale summarizing the core principles and components of DDP can be used during supervision. As with all aspects of dyadic developmental practice, the relationship between supervisor and supervisee is seen as central to enjoyable and effective supervision, and the supervisee knows her background and attachment history may be discussed during supervision.

The supervision example that follows is with Emma, a supervisee, during her DDP practitioner practicum. Emma is the clinical lead in her service and an experienced therapist. Rebecca, a DDP consultant, is her supervisor. They live 150 miles apart, and supervision uses Internet screen sharing. They have met occasionally at conferences. In this example, a few core themes are described. We join the supervision as Emma starts her second practicum review.

Supervision Theme: Initial Responses about Supervision Involving Video-Recording Therapy

Some individuals starting the DDP practicum are accustomed to having therapy sessions recorded. For others, entering the practicum will be the first time their therapy has been recorded for supervision. Some may have experienced this during their initial therapy training, possibly years ago, since then becoming experienced and confident in their own model. Starting DDP supervision where your supervisor watches your video-recorded work often evokes uncomfortable feelings of being scrutinized and evaluated.

Emma starts the supervision of her second practicum review by saying that the process takes her right back to doubts she experienced when first starting her professional training.

> EMMA: I thought I could do this. Now I feel lost. I'm floundering and I don't like feeling like this. I'm just a rubbish therapist. I'll just give up now and become a gardener. I can talk to the plants all day. They won't judge me. I read through that Rating Scale you sent me. All I got was "Starting to develop" with a few "Good skill developing." I thought DDP wasn't supposed to evaluate people.

Rebecca notices she starts to think defensively. Before starting to supervise Emma, Rebecca initiated conversations about how hard it might be—that learning new ways of working when you are already an experienced therapist is rarely easy; that learning to use PACE and focus on developing intersubjective connections may seem familiar at first. This often becomes harder as the practicum progresses. Emma said this excited her. She loved learning new things and being challenged. She was really looking forward to the practicum. She loves this model and one day hopes to be a DDP trainer.

Rebecca feels a response forming on the tip of her tongue: "Emma, we talked about this before we started. Remember how excited you felt. Nothing comes without hard work. It's good to remember what it's like to struggle." She notices the lecturing tone that accompanies the words in her head and shudders slightly. Where has this come from, this unhelpful response, not at all modeling DDP? It certainly isn't about Emma. Rebecca recognizes she has reverted to her past lack of empathy for people who expect to achieve without putting in the work. Rebecca places the unhelpful response firmly into another part of her brain. Rebecca remembers how hard it was when she started, although for reasons different from Emma's. Once she recognizes her defensive response is about her, she relaxes, and empathy returns for Emma.

> REBECCA: [With a playful, light tone, matching Emma's affect] And you've come back for more! [With empathy, slowing down with a lower voice tone.] It's hard when you know you are good at your job to start again with something new, and with something similar to what you do so well already. Thank you for being so honest about the Rating Scale. It goes right to that place of being judged. [Acceptance] I am sorry I didn't do a better job of warning you [acknowledges mistake with repair].

Emma's shoulders go down; she smiles and says she is sorry for starting with a rant. Rebecca realizes she is tempted to continue the discussion and that she needs to get started on reviewing the session.

> REBECCA: I guess we could happily talk about these dilemmas all day. Maybe a part of you is hoping I will get side tracked and chat about evaluation and DDP, putting off the time I look at your session and you get that horrible feeling coming up again.
> EMMA: [Smiling] "That would be nice."
> REBECCA: [With empathy] If I could make this easier, I would. Just keep letting me know when you feel lost. I am not sure I know you well enough yet to see this, and I expect you are really good at hiding it. I guess you must be, to do the job you do managing the service. Can I ask you something? If I think I see any signs that you feel lost and are floundering, can I check this out?

Emma agrees. Rebecca feels hope about how supervision will develop with Emma. Emma shows the openness, honesty, and genuineness that is central to DDP. Rebecca is also more than a little impressed with Emma's courage, doing this when she already has a successful job and is a respected therapist using a different approach.

Supervision Theme: Develop the Supervisee's Reflective Capacity about Her Work

- Focusing on exploring and deepening a child experience of events rather than asking for more information or focusing on a parental perception of events.

During the practicum, it is important to develop the supervisee's reflective capacity around her practice. When learning a new skill, the capacity to reflect is reduced. With repeated practice, over time, familiarity with the model increases, as does confidence. This is when supervisors notice supervisees coming in with their own comments based on their reflection as they watch themselves.

Emma e-mails Rebecca to say she is beginning to enjoy the practicum and even looks forward to their supervision sessions, something she never thought could happen when they started. She has started working with a new family, and she would like to bring clips of her work with them as the subject for supervision at her next practicum review. Emma attaches a summary of the family background and her reflections about her work.

At the start of the supervision, Rebecca asks Emma, as always, to say what she wants from supervision and asks how she is finding it to bring into her work the practice recommendations from the previous supervision.

EMMA: I want feedback on everything really. I have looked through the videotape, and as I watch myself I wonder if I am talking too much rather than exploring. I think I go too fast.

REBECCA: I wonder how I can be most helpful about this when we look through your session. I could ask you to stop the video when I noticed this happening. [Rebecca pauses] I have an idea! Rather than me say when I think this is happening, what if you stop your session when you consider you might be talking too much? We could then see if we agree. You might have your own ideas as to what you could say instead when you think you are talking too much.

Rebecca has previously asked Emma to look through the session recording she is bringing for practicum review to choose specific clips she finds most helpful to bring to supervision. Emma starts the session at the point that she has chosen beforehand. It is a clip of her work with Tina and Jenny, foster parents, and Eva, their foster daughter. They are discussing their recent holiday. In the session, Emma says that she notices just how relaxed they are talking together about times they enjoyed and times when it wasn't so good. Eva says, "It's best not to admit to anything, else you get into trouble." Tina says, with indignation, "What do you mean! I never tell you off for telling the truth." Emma then asks Tina for more information, and they all talk about details of minor holiday disagreements. Rebecca successfully resists the urge to ask Emma to stop the recording after 3 minutes. Emma stops the recording after 5 minutes.

> EMMA: [Exclaims, with surprise] I am just talking far too much. And I am just asking for more and more information. I could have stopped there, slowed things down. And I have gone straight to supporting Tina and Jenny, ignoring what Eva said.
> REBECCA: [With curiosity, also relationship focused] What's it like when you notice things yourself rather than me saying things?
> EMMA: It's great. It feels good. It means I am beginning to get what you mean when you talk about exploring the experience in the moment.
> REBECCA: It sounds like you can almost feel the difference.

Emma says she can. Rebecca and Emma talk for a while about what this feeling is like, how the brain and body feel different as skills become familiar and it becomes possible to look in on yourself, from the outside, to reflect. How creativity flows from safety.

> REBECCA: Any ideas as to what else might you have said at this point?

Emma struggles to find the words. She hesitates and stumbles. Rebecca realizes she has just put Emma right back into that place where there is no safety, where her brain shuts down. Rebecca guesses this out loud and apologizes for getting carried away, jumping in too quickly, expecting too much too soon. Rebecca connects this to Emma's work with Eva, Tina, and Jenny and PACE, therapy, and life. Rebecca asking might have been quite appropriate nine out of ten times, but here it did not quite fit where Emma was, hence, the need for interactive repair. Rebecca tentatively asks if she can make some suggestions for words for Emma to try out, where Rebecca role-plays Eva and Emma speaks to her as if she is Eva. Emma agrees, feeling relieved as her brain had suddenly frozen. Rebecca suggests these words:

> REBECCA: I just noticed, here we are all talking about how you disagreed about what to eat on holiday when just a while ago you said, Eva, that it's best to never admit to anything, else you get into trouble. Maybe that makes it tough to let Tina or Jenny know when things have been difficult for you; thinking you will just get into trouble?

Emma tries these words out using role-play. Emma says she likes them; she can imagine saying something like this. If only she could think on her feet at the time. Rebecca responds with empathy, and Emma notices that she did add in some words of her own once the flow started.

Emma continues the session recording. After another 4 minutes, Emma stops the session again.

> EMMA: I get it. I am doing this all the time. I am missing so many times when I could have gone into finding out more about Eva's experiences and showing her foster parents what I mean in practice about PACE, not just talking about it later when we meet up. It's not just about me stopping talking too much. It's about going down further into things. Going deeper; going into the experiences that Eva and Tina are having. Not being scared to stop, to pause, to slow things down, to wonder, just do that tentative meandering curiosity you talk about.

Emma now finds her own words for what she could say to Eva and Tina and tries these out in role-play. She tells Rebecca she reckons she can do this. She is excited.

Looking through therapy recordings before supervision and finding clips isn't always possible. It takes time. Emma discovers she finds this so helpful that she makes time to go through her therapy session recordings before supervision. Sometimes she makes time to look at them whether or not she's taking them to supervision. Sometimes she feels confident enough to show her colleagues at work in her peer supervision. Emma notices that when she looks at her recordings later, she often feels she had a better therapy session than the version she remembers. Emma realizes that she has a tendency to only remember the parts that didn't go well, berating herself for not being good enough. She edits out the parts of the sessions she did well.

This interests Emma, and she talks about her reflections with Rebecca. Rebecca links this to one of the principles of DDP: The therapist ensures that she validates the parent for his or her good parenting and in ways that the child can clearly hear. Rebecca mentions that developmentally traumatized children often find it hard to see and say something positive about their parents. When a therapist notices this and says it out loud, this may enable a child to pause and be a little curious about this.

Rebecca wonders if this is in any way similar to how Emma notices she only remembers her negative memories of her work and edits out the positive. Emma mentions her father who rarely praised her and was often critical. They talk together about Emma's critical father and the impact this may have on Emma. Rebecca wonders whether she seemed a bit like Emma's critical father when Emma started the practicum— how Emma felt judged in the beginning. Emma says that's a possibility and she will think about that one and let Rebecca know.

Supervision Theme: Sessions with Parents

- Asking about parents' attachment histories, backgrounds, and relationships.
- Increasing confidence to explore parents' experiences more deeply.

Rebecca suggests that Emma talk with Tina and Jenny about how they work out parenting tasks together. Jenny finds PACE much easier to put into practice than Tina does. Jenny is getting frustrated and is taking over, often undermining Tina in front of Eva rather than supporting Tina. In the DDP assessment, Tina had talked about how, after her mom died, her dad was hard on her. Tina was clear this was good for her. It helped her keep going with her education when she went a bit astray as an adolescent. She is grateful to him now. Rebecca suggests that Emma returns to this theme in their next parental consultation. Emma isn't too keen.

> **EMMA:** Tina has worked so hard. I've already asked her about her relationship with her father. I can't ask her any more. She's a foster carer and it's not really my business.

Rebecca notices a similar theme with Tina's and Emma's histories—a father being critical—and tells Emma this. Emma makes a link she hasn't made before, and certain things begin to make sense about her feelings toward Tina. Emma shares these connections with Rebecca.

Rebecca and Emma then talk about how hard it can be to provide parental consultation without crossing over a line and becoming a couple counselor or an individual therapist—how it helps to always keep in mind that all conversations have at their center how to help people parent their children and what is best for their children.

Rebecca suggests ways that Emma can take the lead in asking Tina about her father. Rebecca also suggests that Emma revisits asking Tina and Jenny about their hopes and dreams of caring for a child before they became foster parents. How did they imagine this would be? Did they visualize doing certain activities together? When did initial doubts creep in that things were not going to be as they imagined? Emma says she will take a deep breath and give this a go when she meets with Tina and Jenny later that week for a parental consultation.

What follows are Emma's reflections on her experience of her parental consultation with Tina and Jenny soon after this supervision. This piece of writing is included with the consent of the therapist who wrote it. All identifying details have been removed, and it has been adapted to be relevant to this composite supervision example.

Working with parents without the child in the room is something I find more challenging than being with the family. There is a fine line between "being a therapist," being "a psycho-educator," and actually delivering a good-enough DDP session. In my experience, I find the deepening the experience for the parents painful for them, and not really what they think they are there for. I worked, outside of DDP, primarily with the children, and my involvement with parents was in a "parent interview" where I would share information or gather information.

Deepening the relationship with the parents is something that opens the door to the process with the child, and through supervision I feel more able to do so. In my most recent supervision, I shared a video of parents of a fostered young girl, who had experienced horrific physical abuse and neglect. Her foster parent, Tina, is struggling to control her emotions as she has been through so much to become a foster parent, to have a family—she wants it to be perfect. She shows her sadness and anxiety through anger that has professionals reacting and questioning her parenting abilities. She wants to believe other people are negative toward them because they are both women, but she knows this probably isn't the case. Every time she "gets it wrong" it deepens her feeling of not being good enough, which leads her to "get it wrong again." She believes she is a useless angry woman and she should probably stop being a foster carer.

Rebecca, my supervisor, helped me to see Tina's anguish and pain and how important it is to have empathy and curiosity about how she now feels. She gave me permission to revisit themes in the session that I may not have been confident to go back to. By showing the videotapes of the session, it also gave me a chance to really see my role in this process (and have some empathy with how overwhelming my role feels at times).

Following this supervision, I met with Tina and Jenny and we spoke about the process of them becoming foster parents. I asked them again, as Rebecca suggested, about their hopes and dreams around caring for a child before they were accepted as foster parents. Jenny explained they had been through six cycles of in vitro fertilization, and every time they were told there was a good chance. It never happened. Although they had talked about how sad they were when it didn't happen, they had never sat and experienced the other's pain.

Tina sees herself as strong and believes she must not show weakness. Her mother died when she was 11, and she was raised by her dad to be tough; to never show feelings and to never talk about her mom. She then went straight to talking about the time before they decided to foster. Tina said she used to park her car near the local school on the way to work, watch mothers pushing their babies and taking their small children to school. She would then go to her office, shut the door, and cry for the babies she didn't have.

Her partner, Jenny, had no idea about this before our session. I was able to help her see the qualities Tina was bringing to their family, love, care, protection, and so much more. I also helped Tina see that what she sees as a weakness was very much strength for Jenny. I felt confident to speak for Tina, in the same way I will for a child, and somehow my recent supervision made that feel okay to do.

It was through my relationship with Rebecca, who is so reflective and allows me the space to learn, that I had the courage to revisit these themes. It was a really emotional session. The parents e-mailed me saying that they sat all evening talking about their lost babies and how lucky they are to have their foster daughter.

They have said that they will be more aware of the emotional impact for the other—this I am sure will be tested, but this is a different level of thinking for these parents. Tina is feeling less useless, and Jenny assures Tina she will stop undermining her to make herself look like the better mother. She will be more supportive.

I could go on about the benefits of supervision—the help with the language to use, recognizing and experiencing the deepening of the relationship, my role, and the importance of having my supervisor's experiences and support every time I go into a session.

Emma completed her practicum within the next 6 months. She continues to be a service lead. She ensures that she has time in her job to practice DDP, now her preferred therapeutic approach. She continues to have regular supervision with Rebecca. Occasionally, Rebecca audio-records her supervision sessions with Emma (with consent). Rebecca takes these for supervision with her own supervision group, sharing the feedback she receives with Emma.

Rebecca's supervision-group peers are impressed at Emma's courage in giving consent for this. Rebecca is too, given Emma's initial feelings about feeling scrutinized and judged using video-recorded supervision.

Dyadic developmental psychotherapy is about moment-to-moment intersubjective experiences. Effective supervision requires being able to see these directly. Describing these to a supervisor can never quite capture what happens. Just as therapists ask parents and children to respect the consent they give for therapy to be recorded, so the therapists themselves learn to trust their supervisors to supervise their work with respect, always holding an attitude of PACE.

CONCLUSION

This chapter has explored ways in which DDP interventions can be adapted to help children and families in a range of contexts. DDP focuses both on helping the child to develop trust and secure attachments while healing developmental trauma and on helping the home and school environments to provide the safety and opportunities to develop that the traumatized young person needs to thrive. Finally, through DDP-informed supervision, the practitioner is provided with the same safe relational engagement and discoveries that she is attempting to provide for the children she is trying to help.

CHAPTER 11

DDP Research, Evidence Base, and Outcomes

Our discipline is in the early stages of building a strong base of empirical and experimental research findings to support the efficacy of dyadic developmental psychotherapy (DDP) as both a therapy and a practice model. This is a complex initiative because of the nature and complexity of the DDP model and how it is applied in practice. In this chapter, the issues and challenges of developing an evidence base will be described. Current research findings will be presented, and questions and issues for future research will be discussed.

DEVELOPING AN EVIDENCE BASE FOR DDP: THE JOURNEY SO FAR

The development of an evidence base for a model is a long process. It needs to consist of the following:

1. A clearly articulated model and a range of interventions based on this model.
2. The model should be established on theoretical underpinnings that explain the interventions.
3. The expected outcomes of the interventions need to be clear and measurable.
4. A skilled workforce to deliver the interventions needs to be developed. This should consist of appropriately trained and supervised therapists and other practitioners who can deliver the interventions in a consistent manner that has fidelity to the model.

5. With the above in place, a range of quantitative and qualitative research studies can be carried out based on clearly articulated questions.

While the randomized control trial (RCT) is generally regarded as the gold standard for research methodology (e.g., see Akobeng, 2005, cited in Stock, Spielhofer, & Gieve, 2016), this does need to be supported by a range of exploratory and pilot studies that further develop the model and clarify the main research questions.

Dyadic developmental psychotherapy and practice is a complex model that has multiple applications through a range of interventions adapted to the unique needs of each child and family. Although a standard for these interventions is articulated, as described in this book, there will also be a lot of variety within this standard as the differing needs of the client group are understood, and support is offered to the children, parents, and professional networks surrounding them. This makes the gathering of RCT evidence more challenging and complex as discussed by Turner-Halliday and colleagues (2014).

The DDP community, led by Dan Hughes, has done a lot of work to move us through this process of developing an evidence base.

- We have a clearly articulated model and range of interventions. This includes therapy alongside a range of support interventions aimed at parents, school staff, and other members of the professional network that surrounds the child and family. This has been published in a range of books and papers, including in this current book (e.g., Casswell et al., 2014; Hughes, 2007, 2009, 2011; Hughes, Golding, & Hudson, 2015).
- The theoretical underpinnings for DDP are drawn from a careful study of attachment theory, developmental trauma, and neuroscience research and theory. Dan Hughes, supported by colleagues, has used this understanding to develop a theoretically based model so that interventions are grounded in this theory. (e.g., along with this book, see Baylin & Hughes, 2016; Hughes, 2017; Hughes & Baylin, 2012). In addition, the model of intervention has been informed by evidence for what works in the therapeutic relationship. For example, Dan Hughes (2014) argues that DDP is consistent with the findings of the American Psychological Association second task

force on evidence-based therapy relationships as described in Nor-cross and Wampold (2011).

- We have clarity for expected outcomes based on the theoretical understanding. For example, the development of child trust and security in the parent follow on from the mistrust and insecurity that developmental trauma brings. Operationalizing these in the form of inexpensive and easy to use measures is more difficult. Advice and guidance for researchers is provided on the DDP Network website (Gurney-Smith & Phillips, 2017).

- The Dyadic Developmental Psychotherapy Institute (DDPI) has been working hard for several years to support the development of a workforce skilled in using DDP-informed interventions. We have a training program delivered by highly skilled DDP trainers. This is skills based and includes levels 1 and 2. This is supported by a growing number of DDP consultants who can provide a supervised practicum leading to certification as a DDP therapist or practitioner. Rating scales have been developed to support the certification process. These can be seen on the website (see https://ddpnetwork. org/?s=rating+scales&post_type=library-item). Therapists and other practitioners are encouraged to engage in continuing supervision leading to recertification every 4 years. There is also a professional standards committee that is convened to deal with issues related to the practice of DDP.

- Professor Helen Minnis from the University of Glasgow has been leading the implementation of work moving toward an RCT trial. This is supported by a range of qualitative and quantitative studies of DDP-informed interventions. This research program is described more fully later in this chapter.

Clearly there is still work to do, but we have produced a strong foundation for continuing research developments in a relatively short period of time.

This has not been without its challenges. Developing an evidence base for DDP means considering a range of interventions. The DDP model began as a model for psychotherapy but has expanded into a model to inform practice in parenting, teaching, and social care support as well. Research has to grapple with this complexity. We need to know not only that all these individual components are effective, but also the efficacy of combinations. For example, is the effectiveness of therapy for the child supported by parents enhanced when the parents have engaged in a program to develop DDP-informed therapeutic parenting? What is the impact of attachment history exploration of the parents when a child is taken into therapy? Is DDP-informed therapeutic parenting more effective when the social workers supporting them are also DDP-informed? Does effectiveness increase when the child attends a DDP-informed school?

The parenting environment is another complexity. The children DDP is aimed at helping might be living with birth family, in foster or kinship care, be adopted, or living in residential care. Therapists are also exploring applications for children living in their birth families (see Chapter 10) and for children with a range of neurodevelopmental and sensory difficulties (see Chapter 9). There is no uniformity of family situation or child characteristics to make research studies tidy.

In addition, complexity is increased when we consider the standardization of the interventions. We encourage therapists and other practitioners to understand and explore a range of DDP principles (see Chapter 4). They will use these principles with the children and families they are working with but always keeping the relational focus of DDP central. They will be guided in the use of these principles by the unique needs of the child and family in front of them. Norcross and Wampold (2011) note the often-quoted need for a standardized "cookbook" approach to make it easier to establish an evidence base, but how this contradicts the need to modify the intervention based on the needs of the individual client. There is no cookbook for DDP; the therapist has to be flexible and innovative. A manual can offer guidance but is not able to list what to do in the intervention, as this will not be the same from family to family.

Finally, we also encourage therapists to be integrative in their approach to intervention. Norcross and Wampold (2011) note the need for interventions to be inclusive and flexible to help with pervasive and complex difficulties. This is very applicable to children with developmental trauma. One size does not fit all, and there is a range of interventions that can offer important help to families of these children. Often, integration of DDP with other models or techniques central in other models is necessary. This makes research more complex. DDP can provide an overarching umbrella, offering a theoretically based model of intervention, but this does not preclude other interventions. Thus, therapists are exploring the combination of DDP with Theraplay (see Chapter 9), Eye Movement Desensitization and Reprocessing (EMDR), sensory integration, nonviolent resistance, and Dialetical Behavior Therapy Dialetical Behavior Therapy (DBT) interventions as potentially increasing the efficacy of the DDP-informed intervention. Over time, all these combinations of approaches also need to be researched. Preliminary work is beginning in this area (e.g., Andrew, Williams, & Waters, 2014).

DDP: FIT FOR PURPOSE

In this section, we consider DDP as a researchable model. We are guided by the criteria laid down in the UK Department for Education commissioned report on the evaluation of interventions to support the implementation of the Adoption Support Fund (Stock et al., 2016). This is a useful guide to illustrate how DDP fits in terms of being a well-defined model that is open to research.

Roots of DDP

Dyadic developmental psychotherapy was developed in the United States by one of the authors (Dan Hughes) in the late 1990s. Since that time, Dan has continued to develop the interventions with the aid of colleagues. The psychotherapy model has developed further into a complementary practice model, principally through work in the United Kingdom where social care has found it to be an applicable model for practice (see Chapter 8 and the Appendix). In addition, DDP has informed adaptations for education staff (Bombèr & Hughes, 2013; see also the Appendix). There has additionally been work to develop DDP-informed parenting, leading to the development of group work programs (Golding, 2014a, 2017; see also Chapter 7).

The Population DDP Was Designed For

The model has been developed around the needs of children who have experienced developmental trauma. It is most frequently used with children living in out-of-home care and in adoption. More recent developments are exploring the use of the model with children living with birth family, with care leavers, and with adults with learning disability.

Training and Certification

The DDPI acts as the body to oversee training and certification; this is supported in the United Kingdom by a community interest company, DDP Connects UK. Certification is dependent on the individual having a relevant professional training and being governed by an official body. The individual also has to complete a DDP level 1 and level 2 training by a certified DDP trainer and a supervised practicum by a certified DDP consultant. There is a recommended text to support this training (Hughes, 2011).

Delivery

There is no specific assessment prior to intervention. In accordance with preparing for any mental health intervention, therapists would be expected to undertake assessment to understand the needs of the child and family and to identify any likely confounding difficulties, such as neurodevelopmental difficulties. In addition, therapists are expected to work with parents prior to bringing a child into therapy. This will include some exploration of attachment history and assessment of the presence of blocked care. Good practice dictates that parents are helped to adopt a DDP-informed therapeutic parenting approach either through group or individual support before or alongside therapy offered to the child. Therapy is likely to be long term, typically around 9 months to 2 years.

Target Group Needs

The difficulties that the children present with are those typical for children who have experienced developmental trauma. These effects are well summarized in a white paper (Cook et al., 2005) that identifies seven domains of difficulty:

1. Attachment
2. Biology

3. Affect regulation
4. Dissociation
5. Behavior control
6. Cognition
7. Self-concept

Cook and colleagues (2005) recommend best-practice interventions focusing on six categories that will address these seven domains of difficulty. These are:

1. Safety
2. Self-regulation
3. Self-reflection
4. Traumatic experience integration
5. Relational engagement
6. Positive affect enhancement

The DDP model addresses all of these areas of difficulty within its interventions.

Theories of Change

Dyadic developmental psychotherapy is a model that is informed by attachment theory and our understanding of intersubjectivity. Children will have increased emotional well-being when they can overcome their fear of relationships with attachment figures and discover safety in reciprocal relationships that offer emotional connection and attachment security. With the safety provided by the attachment figure and the therapist, the child has increased ability to regulate the emotions associated with the past traumas and to create new meanings of these events. This model is relationship and regulation based rather than behavioral. This suggests that behavioral support will work best when parents attend to the relationship and regulation needs of their children.

Research Design

We are currently supporting small-scale research, pilot work, and pre- and post-survey designs, which are allowing us to address the research design questions that Stock and colleagues (2016) suggest.

This includes identifying expected effect sizes, potential for recruiting sufficient numbers of participants, and finding suitable and reliable outcome measures. Feasibility studies have helped us to do some initial work (Boyer et al, 2014; McAleese, 2015; Turner-Halliday et al., 2014;). Small-scale studies and pilot work have helped us to identify potential outcome measures (see Gurney-Smith & Phillips, 2017).

Research Ethical Issues or Barriers

The high level of need and stress within families will affect the ethics of using control groups within research. The delay in intervention can potentially lead to placement breakdown. This means considering different research designs, including the use of comparison groups with alternative treatments or treatment as usual.

CURRENT EVIDENCE BASE

In this section, the research that has been carried out to date will be reviewed. Some of this has been published in peer-reviewed journals and some in professional newsletters or forums. Some work is still being prepared for publication at the time of writing.

We have again drawn on Stock and colleagues (2016), who helpfully provide a scale of evidence to organize this review.

Good Practice

In this subsection, anecdotal and qualitative evidence is presented that indicates participants like the DDP model and feel it has made a positive impact. This evidence suggests that DDP provides interventions that are good practice. This includes evidence about DDP as developed by Dan Hughes (2011) and the practice model as it has developed from the original model (Casswell et al., 2014). This includes DDP-informed parenting programs (Golding, 2014a, 2017).

Dyadic Developmental Psychotherapy

- Service user feedback is collected in the form of anonymized "Family Stories" that are true and verified. These can be read on the DDP Network website (see https://ddpnetwork.org/parents-carers/

family-stories/). These are stories that have been given to us spontaneously, some by the children and young people who want their stories told. These support the positive impact of DDP.

In addition, some small-scale qualitative research has explored the use of DDP as a therapy.

- A single-case research design explored the impact of DDP on the attachment relationship between the carer and child in a long-term foster placement (McGoldrick, 2016). The interviews with the foster carer revealed a developing understanding and empathy for the child and increased emotional warmth and acceptance toward the child. The child developed trust in the carer. In addition, the carer reported that the intensity and impact of the child's negative attachment behaviors decreased during the course of the therapy. This in turn appeared to positively influence the child's self-esteem, relationship, and placement stability. McGoldrick suggests that the child's increased attachment safety as reported by the carer allowed the child to begin to integrate his past trauma experience and to make sense of his lived experience. This was aided by the therapist establishing safety and attunement with both the carer and the child.
- A qualitative study explored the experience of adoptive parents who had supported their children in DDP (Wingfield, 2017; Wingfield, submitted). A semi-structured interview schedule was established in line with interpretative phenomenological analysis (IPA) guidance. Interviews were conducted with 12 adoptive parents (seven mothers and five fathers) once therapy had finished. Analysis using IPA revealed four superordinate themes and 10 subthemes. These are explored in detail in Box 11.1, which gives parental voice to the experience of participating in DDP.

Dyadic Developmental Practice: A Trauma-Informed, Attachment-Focused Model of Adoption Support

In research, adoption disruption rates vary widely and are crude indicators of how well families are doing. More complex indicators include children's well-being, quality of relationships, and factors that enable families to manage relationships effectively during difficult times. In a study of 108 late-adopted children (5–11 years of age), Rushton (2004)

BOX 11.1 Adoptive Parents' Experiences of DDP

Megan Wingfield

This study explored the experience of adoptive parents who have participated in their child's DDP. Semi-structured interviews were conducted with 12 parents and analyzed using interpretative phenomenological analysis (IPA; Smith, Flowers, & Larkin, 2009). The analysis revealed four superordinate themes, which were increased understanding, a different method of parenting, the DDP journey, and a shared kind of experience.

Increased Understanding

"It's that ability to reflect, that ability to sort of stop, that ability to not, not assume that actually Katie's just doing it to be a bit bloody-minded, that actually she can't help herself, you know, this is predetermined, this is about her own, her own early trauma and the impact that early trauma is having on her now" (Ben, 527–531). All but one parent described gaining a better understanding of his or her child and increased curiosity about the child's mind. This fresh insight provided parents with a new way of working in terms of strategies, skills, and techniques to support their child. *"You get that glimpse into his mind"* captures the way in which parents spoke about an increased sense of understanding their child, which led to more curiosity about what the children's behaviors were communicating. In many cases, the significance of their child's past was brought to light during DDP. For many parents, accepting and gaining insight into their child's history helped them to see how their child saw themselves. Exploring the child's past relationships also helped parents make sense of the child's current relationships. Many parents also gained insight into what was missed in their child's early life and the importance of trying to address this in therapy. *A new way to help* emerged as parents gained increased understanding. Parents spoke about originally using techniques that did not fit. Increased understanding appeared to allow parents to respond in a new way. This included the ability to stop, reflect, and attempt to understand behavior.

"It's a Different Method of Parenting Generally"

"Katie is better able to tackle life day-to-day, she's more open and she is um, she has a better understanding of who she is, of her own identity and how she works. And actually, she knows that in certain situations she will freeze but actually that's okay, these are the strategies she can use to be able to move on from that" (Ben, 590–594). This theme incorporates parents' descriptions of DDP as different. Every parent described getting to a place where he or she felt that *DDP fit* his or her situation. This was linked to DDP being described as unique and different to more traditional approaches. *Acceptance* was a key element of DDP that differentiated it from other approaches. This included accepting difficult emotions rather than trying to fix them as parents may have done previously. Some parents described feeling initially uncomfortable about not reassuring their children straightaway and worried that their child might be having an experience that made them feel worse.

The DDP Journey

"So it's not just the therapy happens in that room, the therapy happens, not continuously. . . I'm not that good, you know what I mean [laughs] . . . but it happens more generally through our lives" (Laura, 53–55). Most parents described undergoing a "journey," initially knowing very little about DDP and questioning its validity. When parents saw evidence of progress, they appeared to become committed, despite difficulties. All but one parent felt that after some time, progress became evident in the way his or her child started to feel about himself or herself and others and the child's improved ability to name and regulate emotions, increased empathy, openness, and sense of security. These changes led to more tangible progress such as improved sleep, less behavioral difficulties, placement stability, and better peer relationships. Progress led a handful of parents to conclude that DDP ultimately kept the family together. *Commitment to the journey* encompasses the idea that therapy was difficult but, in most cases, considered worthwhile. Difficulties included the practicalities of making time for sessions. DDP was also described as emotionally difficult for both parent and child during and after sessions. Some also described how difficult it was to acknowledge their own attachment histories and to be reappraising themselves as parents. Despite the difficulties, all but one parent stated or alluded to DDP being worthwhile. The *significance of ending* was described as important for parents who experienced fear of managing post-therapy or sadness at it being over.

"It's a Shared Kind of Experience You Go Through and Come Out Together"

"I want them to recognize they've been heard and because I've just done that and I've just articulated to Bella that I totally get what she's just been feeling and what she's described to me, but I'm not fixing it, it means she feels she's at one with me, so she is there with me" (Chloe, 875–878). Parental involvement appeared important to all, mainly because it enabled strengthening of the parent–child connection and allowed parents to support children in regulating themselves. However, the therapist was also identified as an important part of the process and relationship. *Trust and security* was described as key to improving parent–child relationships. *Emotion regulation* was described as a core part of the process and outcome of therapy. It was described as something shared between parent and child. Additionally, parents described gaining better insight into their own emotional reactions and how this affects their child. Every parent spoke about *the therapist's stance* as crucial to making the therapy effective. Parents described the therapist as creating a safe environment that was accepting of whatever the child brought. PACE was described as part of the therapist's stance. Parents also spoke about the therapist being an important support for them and that having another separate mind helped them to think.

Overall, parents in the study were positive about their experience of DDP with their children. While there were variations in the parents and in the DDP, relatively consistent experiences were described, and parents' descriptions of DDP were generally consistent with the DDP approach. All but one parent explained that DDP helped give him or her a better understanding of his or her child. Parents experienced DDP as different to approaches tried before. In particular, parents spoke about acceptance of their child's distress and not trying to "*fix it.*"

The DDP journey was described as beginning with an initial "*cry for help.*" Adoptive parents identified with feeling so overwhelmed that they were willing to try DDP despite it being unknown. Given that there is still a lack of an evidence base for DDP, it is reasonable that parents may have felt initially uncertain. Over time, all but one parent felt that DDP fit his or her situation and led to positive change. Alternatively, one parent felt that she did not see the progress she had hoped for. Parents also referred to DDP being emotionally challenging but worthwhile. Parents also spoke about having significant feelings about ending treatment. However, along with difficult feelings about ending, most parents described also experiencing a readiness to move on. Finally, parents spoke about the importance of the therapist creating safety, modeling PACE, and being a separate mind when parents became overwhelmed. The author concludes that the findings support suggestions that there is a need for different, more relational approaches for attachment difficulties.

found approximately 50% settled, 25% had difficulties, and 25% disrupted. Four factors relevant in disruptions were older age, singled out from siblings, time in care, and high level of behavior problems. Selwyn (2014) found mid-adolescence to be a critical time with increased family breakdowns.

An adoption support model informed by DDP was developed by one of the authors (Julie Hudson). This is described in more detail in Box 11.2. In 2002, a UK National Health Service child and adolescent mental health services (CAMHS) unit and a local authority jointly funded a comprehensive trauma-informed and attachment-focused adoption support service. The model was informed by DDP and was built on existing close working relationships between the National Health Service, Child and Adolescent Mental Health Service for looked after children and the local childrens' Social Services teams. Between 2002 and 2010, 125 adopted children received some level of service from this model. This proved very successful with no disruptions for families receiving the full model over an 8-year period (Hudson, 2006). Regular consultation during the first 2 years plus follow-up appointments every 6 months enabled interventions to be carefully targeted with only 18% of families requiring intensive interventions, including therapy (DDP).

Parental feedback confirmed that knowing support was available if needed increased the confidence of parents to manage when difficulties arose.

SUMMARY OF LESSONS LEARNED

Adoption disruption rates decrease when DDP-informed support services are routinely provided that normalize the need for help from the beginning of the adoption process, not waiting until problems occur. Important components included the following:

- Good beginnings are seen as the foundation for effective future work. Early consultation at the time of matching and during early months after placement informed later practice.
- Seeing all parents and children during the first year after moving in to routinely "check in." This is not problem based, but aims to be preventative.
- A flexible combination of parental and network consultation, therapy, training, and group work.
- Normalization of difficulties is crucial as opposed to "wait and see" if problems occur before offering help.
- Long-term follow-up until the adopted child reaches 18 years, plus ease of access when help is needed, such as parents knowing they can pick up the telephone to a named, and preferably known, professional anytime.
- Adolescence is viewed as a key developmental time to proactively revisit earlier themes and consolidate rather than as a time of increased anxiety.

NURTURING ATTACHMENTS GROUP

Nurturing Attachments is an 18-session group work program based around a house model of parenting developed by one of the authors (Kim Golding). This model reflects the DDP model. The PACE attitude is central to the therapeutic parenting being developed within the group participants. Nurturing Attachments developed from the original Fostering Attachments program. It was updated on the basis of the early research.

There has been a range of studies evaluating the efficacy of the DDP-informed Nurturing Attachments group with foster carers and adoptive parents (Golding, 2014a). Quantitative evaluation is described

BOX 11.2 Summary of Outcomes on a
Trauma-Informed, Attachment-Focused Model
of Adoption Support: From Matching to Late
Adolescence, 2002–2010 (first published in Hudson, 2006,
and updated to include data between 2007 and 2010)

There were no family breakdowns for the 33 children who received
the full adoption support model from matching onward. Only
18% of these children (6 out of 33) received intensive support
(DDP-informed parental and network consultation plus therapy
with child and parent).

Adoptive Parents' Perceptions of What Made a Positive Difference

- Talking about the importance of high structure and routine from the start, being given a clear idea about how
  to do this, plus planning before their child moved in.
- What it really means to "accept what was" and linking difficulties with accepting their child with
  their own personal issues as an adult.
- Having the opportunity and being encouraged to consider their
  own personal issues, such as reexperiencing as an adult the
  feelings of victimization as a child when caring for their child.
- Learning about attachment trauma–informed parenting
  strategies that help them make sense of their child's behavior as part of providing discipline and setting limits.
- Learning ways of keeping calm rather than
  feeling irritated for long periods.
- Input at a local and strategic level to education services
  about specific needs, including extra resources required
  for children with primarily emotional difficulties.

Patterns for an Adult's High Concern That Triggers a Request for More Professional Input

- Recognition of the effect of the persistent nature
  of a child's perceived need to control on parents
  and on the child's emotional development.
- An increase in verbal and physical expression of

aggression toward the parents, usually toward one more
than the other; often this is the main parent.

- New information from the child about the
  child's past, such as past sexual abuse.
- Troubles at school for children who are academically able
  but who have emotional difficulties and were not ready to
  manage the complexities of a school environment without a
  safe adult figure nearby to help them translate the world.
- Splitting parents into one good and one bad.
- Parental worries about not feeling able to like a child.

Highlighting "Best Practice" to Maximize Positive Outcomes for Adopted Children

This involves the recognition, normalization, and evaluation of key
processes involved in adult cognitive and behavioral change over
time. These include:

- Integration of loss and grief for what will never
  be, anticipation (pre-adoption), excitement, and
  fear (at matching and during introductions).
- Using known coping strategies or developing new ones to manage reality, such as parental exhaustion (first 3–9 months) and
  feelings of "it's a job, not a family" (possible blocked care).
- Acknowledgment of the process of falling in love. Making
  sense of and normalizing feelings if this does not happen.
- Being recognized as and feeling like any other parent and
  family as well as being seen as an adoptive parent and family.

below. Qualitative analysis suggests very high satisfaction with the
intervention, and a positive range of comments about participation in
the group exists (Green, 2011; Gurney-Smith et al., 2010; Laybourne,
Andersen, & Sands, 2008; McAleese, 2015; Golding & Picken, 2004;
Wassall, 2011). In addition, an in-service evaluation of the program
delivered over 10 sessions was conducted with 23 residential workers
(including 10 managers). The participants reported that the training was highly valued, helping them in developing knowledge and
skills. It helped them in their roles, increasing understanding of the

presentations of the young people, and some participants reported increased feelings of competency (Bailey, 2017).

Additionally, as part of an evaluation of the Nurturing Attachments group with adoptive parents across four geographic areas, eight of the parents were randomly selected to participate in a qualitative analysis of their experience (see Golding & Alper, 2016; Hewitt, Gurney-Smith, & Golding, 2018). The results of this study are included in Box 11.3. They highlight that the group in its delivery and facilitation was positive for all interviewed.

FOUNDATIONS FOR ATTACHMENT

The Foundations for Attachment program has been developed by one of the authors (Kim Golding) to provide a shorter program that can complement Nurturing Attachments (Golding, 2017). It is a six-session or three-day program that introduces group members to four significant challenges of parenting children who have experienced developmental trauma. Group members are then helped to explore DDP-informed therapeutic parenting that is focused on the use of PACE and the importance of self-understanding and self-care. This program can stand alone or can provide a foundation for the more intensive Nurturing Attachments program.

Pilot work has been carried out with the Foundations for Attachment program involving around 100 foster carers, adopters, and residential workers across seven sites in England. Satisfaction ratings were very high, and group members demonstrated statistically significant increases in knowledge using a short quiz. In addition, small but statistically significant positive changes were recorded for well-being, feelings of efficacy, and reflective functioning. The carer questionnaire revealed statistically significant positive changes.

When results for parents were compared to those for residential workers, differences were revealed. Parents appear to gain more benefit from the group in improving well-being and efficacy, possibly because their scores were initially lower compared to those of residential workers. Similarly, the parents demonstrated improvements in reflective functioning. The residential workers but not the parents showed a statistically significant increase in knowledge on the knowledge quiz, possibly a reflection of the residential workers lower knowledge prior to attending the group. Both parents and residential workers reported positive and statistically significant change on the Carer Questionnaire.

Promising Approach

Dyadic developmental psychotherapy has been classified as a promising approach in the Department for Education (DfE) review (Stock et al., 2016). The report notes that "there has been a recent study conducted in the UK to explore the feasibility of conducting an RCT of DDP (Turner-Halliday et al., 2014), which indicated a strong desire and willingness to produce more robust evidence of this intervention (p. 33)."

In addition, DDP was mentioned as a promising approach that should be supported by research programs in the NICE (2015) guidance on children's attachments.

Research-Based Approach

In this subsection, we will review the research studies that have explored the DDP-informed Nurturing Attachments group (Golding, 2014a). This represents a growing range of studies using pre- and post-treatment scales together with an explorative randomized trial with a waiting list comparison group. It is this body of research that led to this program being categorized as research based in the DfE review (Stock et al., 2016). Additionally, early results from an educational program will be shared (S. Phillips, 2017, personal communication).

Nurturing Attachments Group

Five in-service evaluations were carried out on Fostering Attachments. These used pre- and post-scales. Four of these studies were with small sample sizes of between five and 13 participants (Golding & Picken, 2004; Green et al., 2011; Gurney-Smith et al., 2010; Laybourne et al., 2008), and one study had a sample size of 25 (Wassall, 2011). All of these studies included foster carers, and three studies also had adopters in the groups. All the studies demonstrated positive change, but as would be expected with small sample sizes, not all change reached statistical significance. Thus, carers reported increased understanding, confidence, and an improved relationship with the child on the Carer Questionnaire. Parenting stress changed variably from statistically significant reductions in two studies and no change in a third. Two studies explored mind-mindedness, finding no change or a statistically significant increase in mind-mindedness at the point of rupture in the relationship with the child. While participants reported changes in the child's behavior, this was not always supported by the Strengths & Difficulties Questionnaire (SDQ) scores. Sense of competence demonstrated a statistically significant improvement in the one study that used this measure. Two studies included some follow-up. Gurney-Smith and colleagues (2010) found sustained improvements at 3-month follow-up. Wassall (2011) found sustained improvement in sense of competence at 8-month follow-up and a latent statistically significant improvement in feelings of efficacy at the follow-up point. Two studies included some comparison. The original pilot study compared the SDQ scores with a nonrandomized group of children receiving service as usual. The statistically significant change in SDQ was only observed in the treatment group. Wassall (2011) included a waiting list comparison group. Improvements in the treatment group were not found in the comparison group during the waiting list period.

This research informed the further development of the Fostering Attachments group, leading to publication of the Nurturing Attachments program. This followed the same model and format but with increased focus on encouraging reflection and greater attention to the modeling and discussion of the parenting attitude of PACE. To date, two studies have evaluated Nurturing Attachments. The first was a feasibility study with foster carers conducted in Northern Ireland (McAleese, 2015). This explored recruitment and retention; acceptability; initial outcomes; and fidelity to the manual. The author concluded that the intervention is feasible and positively affected many levels of the care system.

Most recently, a quantitative and qualitative study was conducted by Adoptionplus involving 29 adoptive parents as described in Box 11.3 (Golding & Alper, 2016). This demonstrated the efficacy of the program for increasing support to adoptive parents. Participants reported benefits, and significant changes were demonstrated. While a control or comparison group is needed to confirm that changes are a result of the intervention, participants were highly positive and reported that attending the group helped them to meet their goals selected at the start of the program.

BOX 11.3 A Quantitative and Qualitative Evaluation of the Nurturing Attachments Group Work Program across Four Geographic Sites (Golding & Alper, 2016)

An evaluation of the Nurturing Attachments group work program run for adoptive parents was led by Adoptionplus and supported with DfE funding. The evaluation comprises two parts: a quantitative evaluation led by Prof. Julie Selwyn, The Hadley Centre for Adoption and Foster Care Studies, University of Bristol; and a qualitative study led by Dr. Ben Gurney-Smith and supported by Dr. Olivia Hewitt, The Oxford Institute of Clinical Psychology Training.

Quantitative Evaluation

Forty-eight parents (41 families) completed the groupwork program over the four geographic sites. Of these, 34 families consented to be part of the research study, and 29 of these families completed both pre- and post-questionnaires. Thus, 71% of families who completed the program contributed to the completion of the questionnaires.

Pre-measures and post-measures were collected and analyzed by Prof. Julie Selwyn. Parents reported that the group environment was helpful, supportive, and nonjudgmental. Session-by-session ratings of goals revealed that these were met during the course of the groupwork program. There was some indication that parents were feeling less overwhelmed and more confident by the end of the program, with improved well-being for some but not all. This is despite the challenges presented by the children remaining high. This led to statistically significant increases in feelings of self-efficacy and improved reflective functioning. Ratings of the SDQ revealed increased emotional distress and peer difficulties but lower conduct problems. It is speculated that parents were more aware of the emotional needs underlying their children's behavior after attending the group, hence emotional distress ratings were higher. A follow-up was conducted 7 to 8 months later with 18 (62%) of the parents completing the measures at this third time point. There was a tendency for families with most difficulty preintervention to have returned questionnaires, and those with least difficulty preintervention not to have returned questionnaires. Overall, the follow-up suggests that the majority of families (12) continue to benefit from the group parenting intervention 7 to 8 months after the intervention ended, with progress being maintained or continuing to improve. No reported improvements reached statistical significance between the end of the intervention and the follow-up, but this is not surprising given the small numbers and the presence of a subgroup of six families where benefits were not sustained. This follow-up highlighted that the intervention was valued and helpful for the majority of parents, but for some parents experiencing substantial difficulties, the group parenting intervention was not sufficient. These families may need intensive individual support or therapy. It may be that the group parenting intervention will be a useful starting point for this, but research is needed to confirm this suggestion.

Additionally, eight parents were randomly selected to participate in a qualitative analysis of their experience. This involved participating in a telephone interview about their experience of attending the group with a researcher independent of the group intervention. These interviews were transcribed and then independently analyzed using IPA methodology by Dr. Olivia Hewitt.

Five superordinate themes were identified:

- "A supportive group." Support was reported from increased understanding and confidence in the strategies linked to this knowledge. Participants appreciated a safe place to come, which normalized experience and reduced their isolation. Facilitators were viewed very positively as skilled and knowledgeable.
- "A shift in perspective." Participants reported that they noticed changes in their ability to reflect, and that this changed their relationships with their children and others. They expressed hope that these changes would continue to develop.
- "Turning trauma into secure attachment." Participants described feeling more attuned to their children. This helped with self-regulation and also helped the children to regulate.
- "Am I doing it right?" Adoptive parents expressed anxieties linked to the need for support. Group support was needed to reduce distress and avert placement breakdown. The timing of this support was seen as important, especially during preparation and early in the participants' adoption journeys. Support to reduce isolation was noted as important.

- "Continuing the adoption journey." Participants felt that they had new tools and skills to help them going forward; this brought hope for the future.

Overall, participants reported that attending the group had been a positive experience of a safe and supportive environment offering peer and practitioner support. This helped them to normalize their experiences. By the end of the group program, feelings of hope had increased, and parents felt less overwhelmed. Participants recognized having new understanding that had led to new parenting approaches, which they anticipated would continue to grow and develop beyond the lifetime of the group. The children continued to present them with challenges, but they were now better able to reflect on underlying emotional experience, and this was helping them to remain regulated and therefore helped their children to regulate. There was little negative evaluation of the group to the independent interviewer, although some participants would have liked the support earlier. Seeking support was problematic because of fears of being judged as failing as a parent. For some parents, attending the group was reported to have been a life-changing experience.

An Educational Program Informed by Attachment Principles and the Establishment of Safety

Dr. Sian Phillips (2017, personal communication) has supported the development of an educational program, "Belong," for children who have experienced abuse and neglect and are struggling in their schools. The program aims to meet the children's needs and increase academic and social success. The staff are trained to use aspects of DDP, especially PACE, as a means of creating safety and constructing healthier relationships.

Analysis of questionnaires used when children come into the program, at the end of 1 year, at the end of their time in Belong, and then 6 months into their return to their home school consistently shows exciting evidence of what appears to be better neuronal organization. At the end of 1 year, as measured by school staff, there is a statistically significant change in both behavioral regulation and executive function as measured by the Behavior Rating Inventory of Executive Function (BRIEF) as well as statistically significant improvements in the Intrapersonal Strength and Affective Strength subscales of the Behavior and Emotion Rating Scale (BERS). Also evident is a statistically significant decrease in absenteeism for students who attend the program. There has been a dramatic improvement in school attendance, especially for the two students who were missing up to 2 months of school prior to attending the Belong program. Anecdotally, parents are commenting that their children like school for the first time and that students protest the arrival of weekends and holidays.

An increase in literacy measures has been observed. Improvement in comprehension has been targeted, and this is meeting with success. These data are currently being analyzed.

Research is under way to integrate parent ratings of behavior and to compare this sample to a control group of same-aged children who attend a classroom that is organized around behavioral principles. It is hypothesized that there will be bigger effects and longer-lasting changes in the group of students where emotional safety and relationships are considered the primary agents of change.

Evidence-Based Approach

For an intervention to be considered evidence based, rigorous evaluation is needed to demonstrate consistent benefits. Large-scale cohort studies and RCTs are considered the gold standard in research design. A research program is under way to provide this evaluation, and some pilot and feasibility work has been carried out (Turner-Halliday et al., 2014). We are hopeful that a future bid for funding will be successful in order to progress toward an RCT of dyadic developmental psychotherapy. Potential sites have been identified, and outcome measures are being developed to support this research. A control group is being considered, but finding a comparison intervention of similar length is problematic, and therefore treatment as usual will probably be the best option.

FUTURE DEVELOPMENTS

Diverse service and project developments that are based on the DDP model are occurring across the world . A summary of these can be seen in the Appendix. These are at various stages of evaluation, and we look forward to the continuing evaluation and research, which will contribute to the development of the evidence base for DDP.

CONCLUSION

Developing an evidence base for DDP is an exciting and challenging venture. DDP is not a single intervention but rather comprises a therapy and a practice model, each of which is adapted to the unique needs and circumstances of individual children and their families. In addition, DDP has applications in supporting education staff in schools and the professional social care and health networks surrounding the families. Developing an evidence base for the efficacy of dyadic developmental psychotherapy, practice, and parenting will require a wide range of evidence using a range of research designs. This will include single-case studies, practice- and research-based evidence, as well as anecdotal and qualitative evidence. DDP has established face validity grounded as it is in research from attachment theory, trauma, child development, and neuroscience. Robust processes are in place for the training, certification, and supervision of therapists and practitioners guided by the sister organizations Dyadic Developmental Psychotherapy Institute (DDPI) and "DDP Connects UK," and there is published work and a website (https://ddpnetwork.org) to guide the practice of DDP. It is encouraging that early qualitative and quantitative research focused on DDP as therapy, applied in an educational setting and informing parenting, has been positive, and this is beginning to establish the efficacy of the DDP model. We look forward to the future as this developing evidence base is increased.

Examples of
Dyadic Developmental Practice

There are many exciting developments in the use of dyadic developmental psychotherapy (DDP) as part of projects and in service-led developments. These are beginning to be evaluated, and we anticipate that over time these evaluations will contribute to the further development of DDP. In this Appendix, some of these developments will be briefly summarized.

EXAMPLES OF DYADIC DEVELOPMENTAL PRACTICE IN SCHOOLS

In 2013, Dr. Sian Phillips, a Canadian trainer, consultant, and DDP practitioner, proposed an educational program, "Belong," designed to meet the children's needs and increase academic and social success. This program, informed by attachment principles, has at its core the establishment of safety. School staff learn that emotional and physical safety is essential to help children calm their nervous systems; that an increase in oxytocin production will result through the establishment of safe relationships; and that the production of dopamine will allow the experience of pleasure and reward from relationships and learning. They learn that it is through safe relationships that the children begin to be open to learning. The staff are trained to use DDP principles, especially PACE, as a means of creating safety and constructing healthier relationships.

Outcome measures consistently show exciting evidence of what is believed to be better neuronal organization. Further information about the developing outcomes are included in Chapter 11. Given the success of the Belong program, the Limestone District School Board in Kingston, Ontario, Canada, has established an initiative to train all staff at three elementary schools that serve students and families with complex needs. Components include all staff attending 2 days of training of how to use playfulness, acceptance, curiosity, and empathy (PACE) as an alternative means of classroom management. In addition, regular consultation for staff is available throughout the school year to ensure support and encouragement for this change of philosophy.

Anecdotally, teachers have expressed success in using PACE to help students develop better relationships and to de-escalate behavior. Both teachers and administration staff report better appreciation of how trauma affects brain development and how that helps them to remember that students require their help to regulate rather than being punished for not being able to self-regulate.

A second example is a recent intervention in a school in Nottingham, England, with Mikenda Plant, consultant and practitioner in DDP, and a colleague, Sarah Stockley. Mikenda is also trained in Theraplay. The project, "Bonding and Building Brains Project: Kick Starting Connections to Be Ready for Learning," will be running as a pilot project beginning in October 2017 for the children of families supported by a local adoption agency, with consideration to be given to extending to other schools. This project supports adopted children who struggle to settle in school and build trusting relationships. It helps school support staff in practical ways that are drawn from DDP, sensory integration theory, and Theraplay-informed practice. It is based on the principle that when teaching staff are supported to connect confidently with adopted children, this connection enables and enhances learning. The project also involves parents of the children involved, reinforcing in their parenting at home the approach and methods the school staff are learning. This aims to enhance the home–school relationship. Eight sessions offered over a 10-week period include theory and practice for teaching staff, plus the children joining their teaching assistant for a group-based activity session alongside other children. All teaching staff involved are offered follow-up group supervision.

EXAMPLES OF DYADIC DEVELOPMENTAL PRACTICE AS THE CORE SERVICE PROVISION MODEL FOR AN ORGANIZATION

South of England Local Authority

One local authority enables clinical psychologists, children in CARE, social workers, and fostering support social workers to jointly provide relationship-based interventions with foster carers and their foster child. The importance of consultation with a DDP practitioner combined with regular team meetings is recognized. Structured weekly team meetings focused on implementing DDP principles into work with children and families is seen as crucial to implementing the model.

Examples of themes discussed during team meetings and consultations include the following:

- How to intervene safety when there is a high risk of violence.
- Forming relationships using PACE with parents who manage their fear through doing their best to intimidate social workers.
- Where to set thresholds for threatened aggression to workers, and how to do this while maintaining some level of engagement.
- Helping parents to care for children and set limits when the parents feel intimidated by their children.
- Managing complex couple dynamics where a social worker providing parental consultation to two parents increases safety for the mother, who has her own history of abuse to the extent that she talks about her early history, which in turn evokes fears about dependency on the social worker. At the same time, the partner is asking the social worker to stop talking with his partner about her childhood, as this is making his life hell.

Adoptionplus

Adoptionplus, an adoption agency based in Milton Keynes, England, has set up a social work service in London using the DDP model funded by a government grant.

Joanne Alper, Director of Services at Adoptionplus, writes about this innovative service for this book:

At Adoptionplus we believe DDP offers the potential to improve the contribution social workers make to supporting families caring for children who have experienced developmental and relational trauma. We consider an early intervention and prevention approach essential and believe the social work role has the potential to be pivotal to this in the United Kingdom. Often the first port of call, social workers with the right training and support have the potential to make a significant difference to families caring for children with a trauma history. Social workers are the largest and most expensive resource in the majority of UK local authority children services, and as such it is clearly sensible to ensure that they are utilized as effectively as possible. We believed DDP could assist with this, so when new government innovation funding became available, we made an application to fund the establishment of a new pioneering DDP social work service in London.

In establishing this new service, we used PACE to assist in our social worker selection and are now supporting all of our social workers to become DDP certified. The service provides DDP-informed family work, life-story work, parenting support, and therapeutic groups for adopted teenagers. Alongside this, we are working with colleagues at the University of East Anglia, who are evaluating the effectiveness of a DDP social work approach and are keen to share our findings.

Play Kenya: An Example of Dyadic Developmental Practice in Africa

Anne-Marie Tipper, a DDP practitioner in the United Kingdom, developed Play Kenya (see https://playkenya.com), a registered charity that initially established safe homes near Nairobi in Kenya for girls who have been sexually abused. Play Kenya is still growing and now provides a model of community-based, trauma-informed, and attachment-focused practice. One recent development enables boys of all ages living on the streets in Nairobi to have a permanent home as an alternative to life on the streets. Many boys now feel accepted enough and safe enough to choose to live in these local homes with other boys and with adults to care for them. Play Kenya is best described here using Anne-Marie's words, written for this book:

The whole concept of bringing DDP to Kenya was mind-blowing. It felt like it had to be "all or nothing," and I was aware that the staff we employed had possibly had many similar experiences to the children they were parenting. Over time and with supervision, it became easier to slowly introduce components of the model with outstanding successes.

Using therapeutic parenting was, and still is, outside of Play Kenya, an alien concept in Kenya. Culturally, children are not acknowledged; physical chastisement is the norm, and until recently corporal punishment was still allowed in schools. Children are often beaten, and rarely is their voice given space. All our staff had experienced violence in their own childhoods and believed it to be the acceptable norm. By using therapeutic parenting, teaching PACE to our staff of 44, and giving them an in-depth knowledge of trauma and attachment, we have witnessed the most traumatized children, who often resorted to intense violence and abuse as their "go-to" coping strategy, develop the ability to pause and reflect and use empathy in situations that would have exploded before.

The 67 children who live in our four houses do not have access to individual DDP sessions, as our staff are still developing the model, but most of the conversations and interactions with the children are DDP motivated. The experience for the child to be heard, acknowledged, and understood has had effects in more ways than we could have imagined. Our children are developing empathy for each other and the staff: When you remember that our boys survived the vicious life of living on the streets, where sometimes the most violent attacks came from the police, you may picture why figures of authority evoked fear and violence. These same boys, because of therapeutic parenting, are now able to truly stand in the shoes of another and imagine how that person feels.

Life is still intense, but watching our staff repair with the children when things go wrong, and then seeing the children do the same with each other gives immense hope that these damaged, beautiful children will be the partners, parents, and adults they deserve to be, truly breaking the cycle of abuse that they have lived through.

Our houses parent 67 primarily calm and reflective children and teenagers who are able to debate and discuss in a way that many adults cannot do. These children have used and experienced violence that many of their peers didn't live through, and their physical scars are often the only reminders of where they used to be. DDP is helping them to heal from the inside out.

Play Kenya is a working example of how the principles of DDP including PACE can be applied to the provision of safe homes for the most vulnerable of children. There is flexible shifting given the multiple roles of caregivers between the dyadic social systems of attachment and caregiver; the social hierarchy system involving cooperation, rule following, and respect; and the companionship system involving mutual play—all focused on staying in connection (Hughes & Baylin, personal communication).

AN EXAMPLE OF ORGANIZATIONAL CERTIFICATION

In 2017, "Children Always First" became the first DDP-certified organization in the United Kingdom. Children Always First is a fostering agency set up by Julie Elliott and Jan Blazak and operates in Worcestershire, England. Children Always First has a strong commitment to making a real and lasting difference to children living in foster care and a focus on ensuring that the children are parented therapeutically. From the beginning, a DDP model was adopted by the agency. Julie, Jan, and the team work to ensure that the DDP model informs every process and procedure in the setup and running of the agency. This applies from registration with the Office for Standards in Education, Children's Services and Skills (Ofsted) to policies, development of the website, recruitment of staff and foster carers, and development of the foster carer training program and the support network for children and carers. They describe a "DDP golden thread" to inform the ongoing development of the organization and training of staff and foster carers.

REFERENCES

Akobeng, A.K. (2005) Understanding randomised controlled trials, *Archives of Disease in Childhood*, *90*, 840–844.

Andrew, E., Williams, J., & Waters, C. (2014). Dialectical behavior therapy and attachment: Vehicles for the development of resilience in young people leaving the care system. *Clinical Child Psychology and Psychiatry*, *19*(4), 503–515.

Bailey, E. K. (2017). Attachment focused caregiving training in residential children's homes: A pilot study. *Clinical Psychology Forum*, *292*, 47–51

Baumrind, D. (1978). Parental disciplinary patterns and social competence in children. *Youth and Society, 9*, 238–276.

Baylin, J., & Hughes, D. A. (2016). *The neurobiology of attachment-focused therapy: Enhancing connection & trust in the treatment of children & adolescents* (Norton Series on Interpersonal Neurobiology). New York, NY: Norton.

Bohlin, G., Eninger, L., Brocki, K. C., & Thorell, L. B. (2012). Disorganized attachment and inhibitory capacity: Predicting externalizing problem behaviors. *Journal of Abnormal Child Psychology, 40*, 449–458.

Bombèr, L. M. (2007). *Inside I'm hurting. Practical strategies for supporting children with attachment difficulties in schools.* London, UK: Worth Publishing.

Bombèr, L. M. (2010). *What about me? Inclusive strategies to support pupils with attachment difficulties make it through the school day.* London, UK: Worth Publishing.

Bombèr, L. M., & Hughes, D. A. (2013). *Settling to learn. Settling troubled pupils to learn: Why relationships matter in school.* London, UK: Worth Publishing.

Booth, P. B., & Jernberg, A. M. (2009). *Theraplay. Helping parents and children build better relationships through attachment-based play* (3rd ed.). Hoboken, NJ: Jossey-Bass.

Boyer, N. R. S., Boyd, K. A., Turner-Halliday, F., Watson, N., & Minnis, H. (2014). Examining the feasibility of an economic analysis of dyadic developmental psychotherapy for children with maltreatment associated psychiatric problems in the United Kingdom. *BMC Psychiatry*, *14*, 346.

Bunn, A. (2013). *Signs of safety in England* (NSPCC commissioned report on the Signs of Safety model in child protection). London, UK: NSPCC.

Cassidy, J. (2016). The nature of the child's ties. In J. Cassidy & P. R. Shaver (Eds.), *Handbook of attachment* (3rd ed., pp. 3–24). New York, NY: Guilford.

Cassidy, J., & Shaver, P. R. (2016). *Handbook of attachment* (3rd ed.). New York, NY: Guilford.

Casswell, G., Golding, K. S., Grant, E., Hudson, J., & Tower, P. (2014). Dyadic developmental practice (DDP): A framework for therapeutic intervention and parenting. *Child & Family Clinical Psychology Review, (2),* (Summer) 19–27.

Coan, J. A. (2016). Toward a neuroscience of attachment. In J. Cassidy & P. R. Shaver (Eds.), *Handbook of attachment* (3rd ed., pp. 242–269). New York, NY: Guilford.

Cook, A., Spinazzola, J., Ford, J., Lanktree, C., Blaustein, M., Cloitre, M., . . . van der Kolk, B. (2005). Complex trauma in children and adolescents. *Psychiatric Annals, 35*(5), 390–398.

Cottis, T. (2009). *Intellectual disability, trauma and psychotherapy.* New York, NY: Routledge.

Cozolino, L. (2017). *The neuroscience of psychotherapy: Healing the social brain* (3rd. ed.). New York, NY: Norton.

Davis, E. P., & Sandman, C. A. (2010). The timing of prenatal exposure to maternal cortisol and psychosocial stress is associated with human infant cognitive development. *Child Development, 81*(1), 131–148.

DeKlyen, M., & Greenberg, M. T. (2016). Attachment and psychopathology in childhood. In J. Cassidy & P. R. Shaver (Eds.), *Handbook of attachment* (3rd ed., pp. 639–666). New York, NY: Guilford.

Dozier, M. (2003). Attachment-based treatment for vulnerable children. *Attachment and Human Development, 5*(3), 253–257.

Dozier, M., & Rutter, M. (2008). Challenges to the development of attachment relationships faced by young children in foster and adoptive care. In J. Cassidy & P. R. Shaver (Eds.), *Handbook of attachment: Theory, research and clinical applications* (2nd ed., pp. 698–717). New York, NY: Guilford.

Fonagy, P., Gergely, G., Jurist, E. L., & Target, M. (2002). *Affect regulation, mentalization, and the development of the self.* New York, NY: Other Press.

Fonagy, P., Luyten, P., Allison, E., & Campbell, C. (2016). Reconciling psychoanalytic ideas with attachment theory. In J. Cassidy & P. R. Shaver (Eds.), *Handbook of attachment* (3rd ed., pp. 780–804). New York, NY: Guilford.

Golding, K. S. (2014a). *Nurturing attachments training resource. Running groups for adoptive parents and carers of children who have experienced early trauma and attachment difficulties.* London, UK: Jessica Kingsley Publishers.

Golding, K. S. (2014b). *Using stories to build bridges with traumatized children. Creative ideas for therapy, life story work, direct work and parenting.* London, UK: Jessica Kingsley Publishers.

Golding K. S. (2017). *Foundations for Attachment training resource. The six-session programme for parents of traumatized children.* London, UK: Jessica Kingsley Publishers.

Golding, K. S., & Alper, J. (2016). *A quantitative and qualitative evaluation of the Nurturing Attachments group work programme across four geographical sites* (Summary report). Retrieved from http://tiny.cc/mywafy

Golding, K. S., & Hughes, D. A. (2012). *Creating loving attachments to nurture confidence and security in the troubled child.* London, UK: Jessica Kingsley Publishers.

Golding, K., & Picken, W. (2004). Group work for foster carers caring for children with complex problems. *Adoption & Fostering, 28*(1), 25–37.

Green, H. (2011). *Fostering Attachments: Improving placement stability in a local authority.* Retrieved from http://www.c4eo.org.uk/themes/general/vlp-details.aspx?lpeid=393

Green, J., Stanley, C., & Peters, S. (2007). Disorganized attachment representation and atypical parenting in young school age children with externalizing disorder. *Attachment and Human Development, 9*, 207-222.

Gurney-Smith, B., & Phillips, S. (2017). *Measurement in DDP. Guidance for practitioners and services.* Retrieved from https://ddpnetwork.org/library/measurement-in-ddp/

Gurney-Smith, B., Granger, C., Randle, A, & Fletcher, J. (2010). In time and in tune. The Fostering Attachments group. Capturing sustained change in both caregiver and child. *Adoption & Fostering, 34*(4), 50–60.

Haughton, C. (2014). *Oh No, George!* London, UK: Walker Books.

Hewitt, O., Gurney-Smith, B. & Golding, K. S. (2018) A qualitative exploration of the experiences of adoptive parents attending 'Nurturing Attachments', a Dyadic Developmental Psychotherapy informed group. *Clinical Child Psychology & Psychiatry, 23*(3), 471–482 (first published January 22, 2018, https://doi.org/10.1177/1359104517753511).

Hodges, J., Steele, M., Hillman, S., Henderson, K., & Kanuik, J. (2003). Changes in attachment representations over the first year of adoptive placement: Narratives of maltreated children. *Clinical Child Psychology and Psychiatry, 8*(3), 347–363.

Hudson, J. (2006). Being adopted. Psychological services for adopting families. In K. S. Golding, H. R. Dent, R. Nissim, & E. Stott (Eds.), *Thinking psychologically about children who are looked after and adopted. Space for reflection* (pp. 222–254). Chichester, UK: John Wiley & Sons.

Hughes, D. A. (2007). *Attachment-focused family therapy.* New York, NY: Norton.

Hughes, D. A. (2009). *Attachment-focused parenting.* New York, NY: Norton.

Hughes, D. A. (2011). *Attachment-focused family therapy: The workbook.* New York, NY: Norton.

Hughes, D. (2014). Dyadic developmental psychotherapy. Toward a comprehensive, trauma-informed treatment for developmental trauma disorder. *The Child & Family Review, DCP, British Psychological Society, 2*(Summer), 13–18.

Hughes, D. A. (2017). *Building the bonds of attachment, awakening love in deeply troubled children* (3rd. ed.). Lanham, MD: Jason Aronson.

Hughes, D., & Baylin, J. (2012). *Brain-based parenting: The neuroscience of caregiving for healthy attachment.* New York, NY: Norton.

Hughes, D., Golding, K. S., & Hudson, J. (2015). Dyadic developmental psychotherapy (DDP): The development of the theory, practice and research base. *Adoption & Fostering, 39,* 356–365.

Kabat-Zinn, J. (2004). *Wherever you go, there you are: Mindfulness meditation for everyday life. London:* Piatkus.

Laybourne, G., Andersen, J., & Sands, J. (2008). Fostering attachments in looked after children. Further insight into the group-based programme for foster carers. *Adoption & Fostering, 32*(4), 64–76.

Malloch, S., & Trevarthen, C. (2009). Musicality: Communicating the vitality and interests of life. In S. Malloch & C. Trevarthen (Eds.), *Communicative musicality.* New York, NY: Oxford University Press.

McAleese, A. (2015). *Nurturing attachments in looked after children: A feasibility study of a group-based programme for carers.* Belfast, UK: Queen's University Belfast.

McGoldrick, S. (2016). *The impact of using dyadic developmental psychotherapy to encourage the growth of the attachment relationship between a foster child and their foster carer in a long-term foster placement, and integration of the child's past trauma* (MA in Social Work dissertation). University of Central Lancashire, Preston, UK.

Meins, E., Ferneyhough, C., Wainwright, R., Das Gupta, M., Fradley, E., & Tuckey, M. (2002). Maternal mind-mindedness and attachment security as predictors of theory of mind understanding. *Child Development, 73*(6), 1715–1726.

NICE (2015). Children's attachment: Attachment in children and young people who are adopted from care, in care or at high risk of going into care (Guideline NG26).

Norcross, J. C., & Wampold, B. E. (2011). Evidence-based therapy relationships: Research conclusions and clinical practices. *Psychotherapy, 48,* 98–102.

Perry, B. D., & Szalavitz, M. (2006). *The boy who was raised as a dog and other stories from a child psychiatrist's notebook. What traumatized children can teach us about loss, love and healing.* New York, NY: Basic Books.

Porges, S. W. (2011). *The polyvagal theory: Neurophysiological foundations of emotions, attachment, communication, and self-regulation.* New York, NY: Norton.

Porges, S. W. (2017). *The pocket guide to the polyvagal theory: The transformative power of feeling safe.* New York, NY: Norton.

Rahilly, T., & Hendry, E. (2014). Introduction. In T. Rahilly & E. Hendry (Eds.), *Promoting the wellbeing of children in care. Messages from research.* London, UK: NSPCC, pp. 11–22

Ross, E. J., Graham, D. L., Money, K. M., & Stanwood, G. D. (2015). Developmental consequences of fetal alcohol exposure to drugs. What we know and what we still must learn. *Neuropsychopharmacology, 40*(1), 61–87.

Rushton, A. (2004). A scoping and scanning review of research on the adoption of children placed from public care. *Clinical Child Psychology and Psychiatry, 9*(1), 89–106.

Schore, A. N. (2012). *The science and art of psychotherapy.* New York, NY: Norton.

Schore, J. R., & Schore, A. N. (2014). Regulation theory and affect regulation psychotherapy: A clinical primer. *Smith College Studies in Social Work, 84*(2–3), 178–195.

Selwyn, J., Wijedasa, D., & Meakings, S. (2014). *Beyond the adoption order. Challenges, interventions and adoption disruption* (Research brief). London, UK: Department for Education.

Siegel, D. J. (2010). *The mindful therapist. A Clinician's guide to mindsight and neural integration.* New York, NY: Norton.

Siegel, D. (2012). *The developing mind* (2nd ed.). New York, NY: Norton.

Smith, J.A., Flowers, P. & Larkin, M. (2009). Interpretative phenomenological analysis: Theory, research, practice. London: Sage.

Solomon, M., & Siegel, D. J. (Eds.). (2017). *How people change: Relationships and neuroplasticity in psychotherapy.* New York, NY: Norton.

Sroufe, L. A. (2016). The place of attachment in development. In J. Cassidy & P. R. Shaver (Eds.), *Handbook of attachment* (3rd ed., pp. 997–1011). New York, NY: Guilford.

Steele, M., Hodges, J., Kanuik, J., Hillman, S., & Henderson, K. (2003). Attachment representations and adoption: Associations between maternal states of mind and emotion narratives in previously maltreated children. *Journal of Child Psychotherapy, 29*(2), 187–205.

Stern, D. (2000). *The interpersonal world of the infant.* New York, NY: Basic Books.

Stock, L., Spielhofer, T., & Gieve, M. (2016). *Independent evidence review of post-adoption support interventions* (Research report). London, UK: Department for Education.

Tarren-Sweeney, M., & Vetere, A. (2014). Establishing the need for mental health services for children and young people in care, and those who are subsequently adopted. In M. Tarren-Sweeney & A. Vetere (Eds.), *Mental health services for vulnerable children and young people. Supporting children who are, or have been, in foster care* (pp. 3–20). New York, NY: Routledge.

Thompson, R. A. (2016). Early attachment and later development: Reframing the questions. In J. Cassidy & P. R. Shaver (Eds.), *Handbook of attachment* (3rd ed., pp. 330–348). New York, NY: Guilford.

Thorell, L. B., Rydell, A., & Bohlin, G. (2012). Parent-child attachment and executive functioning in relation to ADHD symptoms in middle childhood. *Attachment and Human Development, 14*(5), 517–532.

Trevarthen, C. (2016). From the intrinsic motive pulse of infant activity to the life time of cultural meanings. In B. Molder, V. Aristila, & P. Ohrstrom (Eds.), *Philosophy and psychology of time* Switzerland: Springer International Publishing (pp. 225–266).

Troy, M., & Sroufe, L. A. (1987). Victimization among preschoolers: The role of attachment relationship history. *Journal of the American Academy of Child and Adolescent Psychiatry, 26*, 166–172.

Turnell, A., & Edwards, S. (1999). *Signs of safety: A safety and solution orientated approach to child protection casework.* New York, NY: Norton.

Turner-Halliday, F., Watson, N., Boyer, N. R. S., Boyd, K. A., & Minnis, H. (2014). The feasibility of a randomised controlled trial of dyadic developmental psychotherapy. *BMC Psychiatry, 14*, 347.

Wade, J. (2014). The mental health and wellbeing of young people leaving care. In T. Rahilly & E. Hendry (Eds.), *Promoting the wellbeing of children in care. Messages from research.* London, UK: NSPCC. 241 - 259Wassall, S. (2011). *Evaluation of an attachment theory based parenting programme for adoptive parents and foster carers* (Clin.Psy.D. thesis). University of Birmingham, Edgbaston, UK.

Wingfield, M. (Submitted). Adoptive parents' experiences of dyadic developmental psychotherapy. *Clinical Child Psychology and Psychiatry.*

Wingfield, M. (2017). Adoptive families: working with parent and child (PhD thesis). University of Oxford.

INDEX

Note: Italicized page locators refer to illustrations.